THE ULTIMATE GUIDE TO
DOG CARE

Tammy Gagne

lumina
MEDIA

The Ultimate Guide to Dog Care

Project Team
Editor: Amy Deputato
Copy Editor: Joann Woy
Design: Mary Ann Kahn
Index: Elizabeth Walker

LUMINA MEDIA™
Chairman: David Fry
Chief Executive Officer: Keith Walter
Chief Financial Officer: David Katzoff
Chief Digital Officer: Jennifer Black-Glover
Vice President Content: Joyce Bautista-Ferrari
Vice President Marketing & PR: Cameron Triebwasser
Managing Director, Books: Christopher Reggio
Art Director, Books: Mary Ann Kahn
Senior Editor, Books: Amy Deputato
Production Director: Laurie Panaggio
Production Manager: Jessica Jaensch

Library of Congress Cataloging-in-Publication Data
Names: Gagne, Tammy, author.
Title: The ultimate guide to dog care : everything you need to know to
  keep your dog happy and healthy / Tammy Gagne.
Description: Irvine, CA : Lumina Media, 2016. | Includes index.
Identifiers: LCCN 2016025653 (print) | LCCN 2016034754 (ebook) | ISBN
  9781621871507 (hardcover) | ISBN 9781621871514 ()
Subjects: LCSH: Dogs.
Classification: LCC SF427 .G249 2016 (print) | LCC SF427 (ebook) | DDC 636.7--dc23
LC record available at https://lccn.loc.gov/2016025653

This book has been published with the intent to provide accurate and authoritative information in regard to the subject matter within. While every precaution has been taken in the preparation of this book, the author and publisher expressly disclaim any responsibility for any errors, omissions, or adverse effects arising from the use or application of the information contained herein. The techniques and suggestions are used at the reader's discretion and are not to be considered a substitute for veterinary care. If you suspect a medical problem, consult your veterinarian.

2030 Main Street, Suite 1400
Irvine, CA 92614
www.facebook.com/luminamediabooks
www.luminamedia.com

Printed and bound in China
16 17 18   1 3 5 7 9 8 6 4 2

Introduction 5

PART I

YOUR NEW DOG

1: Selecting Your New Dog 8
2: Preparing for Your New Dog 30
3: Your Dog Comes Home 52
4: Socializing Your Dog 68

PART II

EVERYDAY CARE

5: Feeding Your Dog 80
6: Grooming Your Dog 98
7: Exercise and Activities 110
8: Keeping Your Dog Out of Danger 126
9: Your Daily Routine 138
10: Traveling with Your Dog 146
11: Caring for the Senior Dog 154

PART III

TRAINING AND BEHAVIOR

12: Housetraining Your Dog 166
13: Communicating with Your Dog 172
14: Training Your Dog 182
15: Behavior Problems and Solutions 194

PART IV

HEALTHCARE

16: Visiting the Vet 208
17: Parasites 212
18: Illnesses and Injuries 220
Index 232
Photo Credits 239
About the Author 240

DEDICATION

To Jemma, who has taught me that some of the best things in life aren't planned.

INTRODUCTION

The bond between people and dogs represents one the strongest interspecies relationships in the history of the world. To many humans, no other animal is quite as endearing as the canine companion. Our dogs greet us after hard days of work, they join us for relaxing days of play, and they ease our suffering when we are sad or sick. Just by being there, dogs often make our daily lives brighter.

I have always considered people who share their homes with dogs to be among the luckiest individuals. To know a dog's friendship is to understand unconditional love, compassion, and appreciation for the simplest yet best things in life. Few things are as exciting or rewarding as becoming a dog owner. Whether you have had dogs since childhood or you are adding a dog to your household for the first time, you will never find a truer friend than this cold-nosed, four-legged, furry companion.

PART I

YOUR
NEW DOG

CHAPTER 1

SELECTING YOUR NEW DOG

Canine Considerations

Deciding that you are ready to become a dog owner is just the first step in the process of adding a canine companion to your life. You must also consider the age, sex, and, of course, breed or type of dog that will be the best match for your household.

Puppy or Adult?

Young dogs offer many advantages, not the least of which is an overwhelming amount of cuteness. From their puppy breath to the adorable way puppies run—as if their back ends haven't quite mastered moving at the same pace as their front legs—young dogs quickly steal our hearts with their juvenile ways. Their youthful charm is only part of their appeal, however. Buying or adopting a puppy also comes with the potential of a clean slate and a long lifetime. In many ways, a puppy becomes the adult dog that his owner helps him to become. And, with a dog's typical life span being more than a decade, puppy owners get to enjoy the fruits of their training efforts for many years to come.

An adult dog may already be housetrained or know some obedience commands.

Old Friends Make Good Friends

Dogs who have entered the final third of their lives, typically around eight to ten years of age, are considered seniors. Senior dogs can make excellent pets for the right people. Many owners find this out by buying puppies or adopting adult dogs and then caring for them all the way into their senior years. Other owners find out what gems senior pets can be by adopting one.

Senior dogs offer a wealth of benefits as pets. Unlike excitable pups, older dogs have calm natures. Most have become masters at housetraining, and they are well past problem behaviors such as inappropriate chewing or counter surfing. Senior dogs still need exercise, but instead of long walks or runs, they are satisfied with shorter strolls. They are also more than happy to curl up at their owners' feet at the end of the day.

For any prospective owner, the most important step in adopting a dog is finding the right match. Because of their lower activity levels, senior dogs often make ideal pets for human senior citizens or disabled people. Numerous studies have revealed the physical and mental health benefits that canine companions offer senior owners. From easing loneliness to lowering blood pressure, a dog can make a person's senior years much better. A person can likewise improve—and often even save—the life of an older animal. Many of the dogs who go unadopted in shelters are seniors. Sadly, a great number of these homeless pets end up being euthanized. All that many of these animals need are loving owners to find and rescue them.

Of course, puppy ownership also comes with its share of challenges. Young dogs need an extensive amount of training. From teaching your new pet where to relieve himself to dealing with the inappropriate chewing that often accompanies the teething process, puppyhood can be a mighty stressful time for everyone in the household. Puppies also have an incredible amount of energy. Keeping a pup exercised and occupied can be draining at times, even for the most active owners. An adult dog may seem much cuter in the middle of the night when he is sleeping instead of stirring or needing to make another trip to his potty spot like a puppy would.

Adult dogs have established temperaments. Owners can stack the odds in their favor by selecting a puppy of a particular breed or with a specific personality type, but neither of these things guarantees that a pup will retain his most desirable traits into adulthood. Spending time with an adult dog who is available for adoption offers more insight into the kind of pet he will be. As his new owner, you may have missed the puppy stages, but you get to open your heart and home to an animal who needs it. And many adult dogs still have years of love and companionship left to offer their new owners.

Spay or Neuter Your Dog

Nearly 4 million dogs in the United States find themselves in shelters each year. Many of these animals lose their homes when their owners get divorced, become ill, or move to rental properties that don't allow pets. Other shelter dogs began their lives homeless, born to strays or mother dogs who have been surrendered themselves. Each year, more than 1 million dogs lose even more than their homes—they end up being euthanized after being deemed unadoptable.

Spaying and neutering pets can drastically reduce the number of animals in shelters.

Sterilization also keeps dogs healthy. Owners of female dogs greatly reduce their dogs' chances of getting mammary, or breast, cancer by spaying them before their first heat. And spaying completely eliminates the risk of both ovarian and uterine cancer. Owners of male dogs can likewise eliminate their pets' risk of testicular cancer by having their pets neutered.

At one time, veterinarians recommended waiting until a dog was at least one year old before spaying or neutering, but today many vets insist that there are several advantages to performing the surgery much earlier. Vets can spay or neuter puppies as young as eight weeks old, although some veterinarians prefer to wait until a pup is four to six months of age. While sterilization is highly safe in general, younger dogs typically tolerate surgery and anesthesia even better than young adult dogs do. The procedure is also less expensive for owners when it is performed earlier.

Many myths surround sterilization. For example, some owners believe that a female dog's maternal instinct runs deep and that she will be happier if she has at least one litter of puppies before getting spayed. Similarly, old wives' tales circulate about male dogs becoming less masculine, and consequently less fulfilled, if they are neutered. Both beliefs are completely false. Sterilized animals are as happy as unaltered animals—often even happier because they live longer and healthier lives.

Male or Female?

Ask a dozen people whether male or female dogs make better pets, and you are bound to get half a dozen votes for each. Males and females are definitely different in some substantial ways, but which gender you prefer is likely a personal matter. Many people base their preference on positive experiences they have had in the past. If you have always owned female dogs and have enjoyed them, you may understandably want another female pet.

Female dogs typically mature more quickly than males. This trait often makes them easier to train when they are younger. Some people mistake this fast track to maturity for a higher intelligence level, but it truly isn't a matter of brainpower. Males catch up eventually. They just might have a few more housetraining mishaps in the meantime.

A female dog's anatomy creates some added challenges. Unless she is spayed, a female dog will go into heat about twice a year. The bloody discharge that goes along with the estrus cycle can stain carpets and furniture, although owners can place canine diapers on their pets to protect their belongings. Heat usually lasts about two to three weeks,

In most pure breeds, the female (right) is at least slightly, if not noticeably, smaller than the male (left).

and it can also trigger unwanted attention from male dogs in your area. Owners must keep female dogs separate from these suitors or risk an unwanted pregnancy.

Male dogs also offer their share of both advantages and challenges. Many pet owners insist that male dogs are more affectionate than females. At the same time, males are known for displaying more problem behaviors, such as mounting and marking. Owners can help prevent many of these issues, however, by having their dogs neutered. In addition to preventing unwanted pregnancies and lowering risks for several types of cancer, sterilization is thought to improve the temperaments of both male and female dogs.

Temperament

Whether you prefer a purebred dog or a mixed breed, the most important factor to consider when selecting a pet is his temperament. No other trait even comes close to this one. Perhaps you plan to show off your dog's impeccable looks in conformation events, or maybe you will utilize his scenting abilities for hunting or search-and-rescue work. Even in these scenarios, his temperament is still his most important quality.

A dog with a sound temperament has the best potential to grow into a loving companion, a star show dog, or anything else you want him to be. Friendly animals are welcome in many circles. Dogs with good temperaments only help expand the list of places where owners can take their pets. But what exactly denotes a good temperament? Generally speaking, a dog's temperament is his unique combination of personality and behavior. While some owners may prefer a more outgoing dog, others might like a dog who doesn't gravitate to just anyone.

Smile! A friendly, even-tempered dog makes a wonderful family companion.

Many aspects of a dog's temperament are obvious. Running to greet guests with a wagging tail is an excellent sign of sociability, for example. Still, it is smart to consider how the animal behaves in a variety of scenarios to get a better idea of his temperament. How does the dog react to having his ears, paws, or tail touched?

To get the best sense of a dog's temperament, pay attention to how he acts with other animals as well. A puppy's role in his litter reveals much about his temperament and potential for handling and training. For example, how does he play with others? A pup who tries to boss around his brothers and sisters may try to do the same thing with you or other pets in your home. Likewise, a pup who initiates play is likely to continue that behavior. Neither a gregarious nor shy pup is necessarily better than the others, but you should know where your dog falls on this scale before deciding that he is the one for you.

Activity Level

Dogs vary greatly in terms of their activity levels. For example, Australian Shepherds and Vizslas typically have a lot of energy to burn each day. Active breeds like these cannot get by

A dog who rolls over for belly rubs feels at ease around you.

Do you want an active companion who's ready to explore with you?

with mere walks around the block. They must run. If you choose a high-energy breed, you must be willing to put some time and effort into exercising your dog. This doesn't mean that you have to sign up for the next 5K run in your community—although it might be fun—but you will need to provide your pet with outlets for his energy. A large fenced yard and a ball can help tire out a restless dog without requiring you to match his vigor.

If you are an active outdoor person, a dog with similar abilities and interests will be the best match for you and your lifestyle. Dogs are happiest when they are spending time with their favorite people. Likewise, taking your pet along on outings will make them even more enjoyable for you. Many dogs delight in accompanying their owners on hikes, swims, and even bike rides. On the other hand, if your idea of fun is ordering pizza and streaming movies, a more laid-back dog is your ideal companion.

Whether you want a small dog or a large one, you should seek the best match for your own activity level. Pugs and Mastiffs, for example, are very different in most ways, but both are known to be low-energy breeds. Don't mistake a lower activity level for a lack of one, though. All dogs need a certain amount of exercise to stay healthy. For less active breeds, owners can simply meet this need with short daily walks or an invigorating play session in the backyard.

Size

Some people are drawn to big breeds while others prefer little dogs. Although size is mostly a matter of personal preference, there are a few factors that make a larger or smaller dog a better

Large-breed puppies become large adults, something for which owners must be prepared.

choice for certain people. You may like the idea of a Saint Bernard, but you might not relish the cost of feeding one. The amount of food that a larger breed eats is just one of the things that make owning a bigger dog more expensive. Larger pets also need larger bowls, beds, and toys. Even medications can be pricier for bigger animals.

Larger dogs obviously need more space, but don't overvalue this consideration. Many people mistakenly think that big dogs and apartment living don't mix. The truth is that many large breeds can live comfortably in small spaces or without large fenced-in yards, providing they get enough exercise each day.

Necessary space is actually just one of the many misconceptions about big dogs. Some people also stereotype bigger pets as more aggressive by nature or as poor matches for homes with children. Some of the largest breeds actually have the best temperaments with and tolerance for kids. The Newfoundland, for example, is often called the "nanny dog" because of the breed's fondness for children.

It is important for all dog owners to train their pets, but this is especially vital for those who own larger dogs. Regardless of how friendly a big dog is, he can injure someone without meaning to just with simple exuberance without proper manners. Owners, too, can get hurt if they don't train their larger pets. Imagine trying to walk an Old English Sheepdog who hasn't been taught proper leash etiquette when you wish to go one way and he wants to head in the opposite direction.

Little dogs also suffer from their share of undeserved labels. Many people assume that smaller dogs are less, well, doglike. Don't tell the Miniature Pinscher or Parson Russell Terrier that, though. These dynamic breeds have energy to spare and can do nearly everything that bigger pets do. They enjoy playing, going for walks, and even participating in organized activities. Havanese, Papillons, and Rat Terriers are just a few of the smaller breeds that have competed in the American Kennel Club's National Agility Championship.

Popular City Breeds

If you live in a city, you have probably noticed that some breeds are more popular in urban settings than others. These include:

Boston Terrier	Miniature Pinscher
Cavalier King Charles Spaniel	Norfolk Terrier
Dachshund	Pug
French Bulldog	Shih Tzu
Labrador Retriever	Yorkshire Terrier

A dog must have a specific combination of traits to be an ideal city dweller. For one thing, he should be relatively quiet. A hound who bays at all times of day in the country, where the nearest neighbor is a mile away, usually won't cause his owner any problems, but a neighbor on the other side of the wall is likely to complain about the noise.

If you live above the first floor, you should also consider how often you will be taking your dog outdoors. An elevator can make trips outside for potty breaks and walks considerably easier, but if you will be taking the stairs with your pet, he must be up to the task. Many people carry smaller breeds on stairways, but even the fittest owner may find it inconvenient to lug a French Bulldog up and down the stairs several times a day.

If you own a larger breed, indoor housetraining might never occur to you, but it is a common choice of small-dog owners living in cities. Many pet-supply companies now make odor-absorbing pads and faux-grass patches for this purpose. Some owners find that litter boxes sold for cats also work well for toy dog breeds. Pet-supply stores even sell litter made specifically for dogs; it is typically larger and more absorbent than varieties made for felines.

Like their larger counterparts, small dogs also have a few drawbacks. Many owners insist that smaller breeds are more difficult to housetrain than bigger pets, although I have found this to be based more on the individual animal. Their smaller size also makes many toy breeds more vulnerable to several medical conditions, such as dental problems (due to tooth crowding), patellar luxation (loose kneecaps), and pancreatitis.

Coat and Grooming

Another important consideration is how much care your new dog's coat will need. While some breeds require virtually no coat care other than an occasional brushing or bathing, others need both frequent and intensive grooming. Longhaired breeds like the Afghan Hound, Poodle, and Yorkshire Terrier require daily brushing to keep their hair from tangling. A dog doesn't have to have a long coat to be high maintenance, however. Bulldogs and Chinese Shar-Pei need their wrinkles cleaned as often as other dogs may need to be brushed. The Chinese Crested's skin is prone to acne, making skin care a top priority for owners of this breed.

After owning Cocker Spaniels for more than two decades, I adopted a mixed-breed dog. Jemma's short brindle coat was one of the first things that drew me to her. In addition to her coat's stunning appearance, it doesn't grow like the more profuse coats of our Cockers—a fact that I hoped would make life a bit easier. I soon realized that while grooming Jem is definitely easier, I now had to deal with an immense amount of shedding. She is totally worth the inconvenience, but this point illustrates that even shorthaired dogs can require coat care. In our case, it comes in the form of regular brushing, extra vacuuming, and a lint brush by the

More than Looks

No matter how much you may appreciate the look of a particular breed, it is paramount that you don't base your choice of dog on appearance alone. Some of the most beautiful breeds can also be the most challenging pets, especially for a person new to dog ownership. One example is the Australian Shepherd. With the breed's mix of dark patches and light markings, Australian Shepherds are stunning animals. They are also impressively intelligent and active, which means that without proper training and leadership, this breed can develop numerous behavior problems.

Rottweilers also need early and consistent training, as well as frequent and vigorous exercise. The Bichon Frise is among the breeds that need meticulous grooming. If you aren't prepared to meet a particular breed's needs, that breed clearly isn't the one for you.

Even after you have settled on a specific breed, it is important to select the best possible pup for you. Sure, the dog with the best markings may be fun to look at, but the

one with the best temperament will make the most pleasant companion. Intelligence and trainability are traits to look for in a potential pup, especially if you plan to compete in any organized activities, such as obedience trials. Don't worry, though. The canine species is filled with dogs who possess both beauty and brains.

The joy of canine companionship is well worth the effort of caring for your pet.

door. Some shorthaired purebred dogs known for shedding include the Cardigan Welsh Corgi, Dalmatian, and Labrador Retriever.

Space Considerations

It is a myth that a home needs large amounts of space for a dog. Even the largest breeds don't take up as much room as you might expect. An Irish Wolfhound won't care whether you live in a spacious ten-room colonial in the suburbs or a rent-controlled two-bedroom apartment in the city as long as he has enough space to eat, sleep, and move around a bit. Even in situations where you feel cramped, your dog will likely still have all the space he needs.

Still, it is important to consider how much space you are willing or able to devote to your new pet. An Irish Wolfhound's bed or crate will take up a lot more room than one for a Cavalier King Charles Spaniel. If your dog will spend most of his time—and get much of his exercise—indoors, make room for a toy bin of some sort as well as an open floor area where you can play with your pet.

It's a bit of a myth that owners of active dogs need large, fenced yards. While it is certainly easier to have an expansive play area at your disposal, what matters is that your dog gets enough exercise. A Boxer who runs on leash with his owner each morning will stay just as fit as one who chases a ball in the backyard every afternoon.

Daily Schedule

I often joke about how wonderful it would be to live a dog's life. Having someone prepare all my meals, never having to clean up after myself, and playing whenever the urge strikes me definitely hold a certain appeal. Napping several times a day would be rather splendid, too.

Although it is easy to assume that a dog's life is an easy one, it important to understand that dogs need routines just like people do. Eating at specific times is important for your pet's health. It also helps you predict when he will need to head to his potty spot. Dogs also need regular activity and time to de-stress. If you think there is nothing stressful about being a dog, try staying cooped up at home each day while you wait for everyone else in your household to return home from work.

Choosing a dog who fits into your existing household schedule well is smart, but do expect that you may need to make some changes when you become a pet owner. Adjustments might be as simple as getting up 20 minutes earlier to walk your dog before breakfast and going for another walk at the end of the day when you don't always feel like doing it. You can allow

Members of the Family

With approximately 200 AKC breeds and a virtually unlimited number of mixed breeds to choose from, finding a dog who matches your family's needs shouldn't be too difficult as long as everyone is in agreement about the endeavor. Before you add a pet to your family, discuss the idea with each member of your household. Everyone must be prepared and willing to deal with all that owning a new dog entails. This doesn't mean that each family member must take on an equal share of caring for the animal, but everyone should be in agreement about this life-changing decision.

Your significant other may love dogs as much as you do but might worry that you don't have enough time or other resources for a pet right now. If you both work full-time jobs, you must consider who will perform vital tasks like feeding, walking, and housetraining before you get the pet. Don't try to delegate tasks as you go along; discuss them beforehand. A little planning goes a long way in making sure that you are ready for a pet.

If anyone in the household has an issue with getting a dog, take his or her concerns seriously. Perhaps one family member is comfortable with a smaller pet but not a larger one. Likewise, even a dog's age can make the difference in the decision to welcome a specific animal. Puppies can be demanding creatures. Adopting an older dog is often a better choice for families with busy schedules, but they must have enough time to devote to a new pet, regardless of his age.

Dealing with Allergies

If one family member is allergic to dogs, the family must address this problem before getting a pet. Some breeds, like the Labradoodle and Miniature Schnauzer, are classified as hypoallergenic, meaning that they are unlikely to cause allergic reactions in people. In many cases, choosing the right dog can make all the difference, but it is still essential for the allergy sufferer to spend time with a particular animal before assuming that the problem has been averted; some allergic dog lovers can experience symptoms even with so-called hypoallergenic breeds. If this is the case for you or one of your family members, see a doctor. In many cases medication can help, but postpone making any decisions until you know if this is the case in your situation.

yourself a little flexibility within the schedule, but what matters most is that you establish and stick to a healthy routine for everyone in the household, including the four-legged members.

Tag-team caregiving often works well in a home with multiple people and schedules. The earliest riser is often the best person to perform the first walk of the day. The next person up may be the one to feed the dog and take him out before everyone heads to work or school. Older kids returning home from school in the afternoon can also help out. Children often make the best playmates for energetic pups, providing they are old enough to be respectful. A busy household can offer plenty of room for a dog, as long as everyone is willing to play a role in fulfilling his needs.

Finding Your Dog

Once you've carefully thought about all of the foregoing considerations, it's time to decide on the type of dog you want and where you might find him. You might have narrowed it down to a particular breed, or you may have your heart set on a mixed breed. Either way, you will have many choices.

Is a Purebred Right for You?

Members of a particular breed share a general appearance as well as many temperamental traits. Personalities will vary from one individual to another, of course, but many of these characteristics are also linked to a dog's breed. Golden Retrievers are known as friendly and affectionate pets, whereas Akitas are more independent or aloof. None of these traits is good or bad, per se. Prospective owners must simply decide which combination of traits creates the best match for their lifestyles.

The American Kennel Club (AKC) divides its recognized dog breeds into seven different groups:

- Herding Group
- Hound Group
- Non-sporting Group
- Sporting Group
- Terrier Group
- Toy Group
- Working Group

The members of each group typically have several traits in common, most often related to the breeds' original functions. Members of the Working Group were first bred to serve laborious purposes such as guarding property, pulling sleds, or rescuing people from drowning. Likewise, Herding Group members helped farmers by herding cattle or other livestock. Hounds, sporting dogs, and terriers all hunted, but in different ways. Toy dogs had the easiest job—to serve as loving companions. The non-sporting dogs make up the most diverse of the seven groups, as what these dogs have in common is that they don't fit into any of the other categories.

If you don't yet know exactly which breed is best for you, you might have more luck narrowing your choices down to one of these groups. If you are a hunter looking for a canine

Whether it's herding sheep or catching Frisbees, the bright, active Border Collie needs a job to do.

Certain aspects of purebreds are predictable. For example, you can be reasonably certain that your Golden Retriever will enjoy romping and splashing at the beach.

assistant, a hound or sporting breed is likely your best match. People who want to participate in organized activities, such as agility or rally, often find that herding dogs make excellent athletes; Australian Cattle Dogs and Border Collies in particular are highly intelligent and trainable as well.

If you are seeking a smaller yet playful pet, consider a toy breed such as the Italian Greyhound or Maltese. With proper training, working breeds like the Anatolian Shepherd and Doberman Pinscher often make capable guard dogs as well as loving pets.

One of the biggest benefits of adopting or buying a purebred dog is that you'll know much of what you are signing up for beforehand. You won't be shocked when your Dogue de Bordeaux puppy tips the scale at 120 pounds (54 kg). Likewise, you will expect your Pekingese pup's coat to grow long over time. You can keep it shorter if you prefer, of course, but those grooming bills won't catch you off guard.

Different qualities attract people to certain breeds. Perhaps you love the looks of more exotic breeds, such as the corded Komondor or the hairless Xoloitzcuintli. Maybe you prefer the Golden Retriever due to its steadfast reputation as the quintessential family dog. You might not even be able to articulate your reasons for fancying a specific breed. No matter what draws

Questions to Ask a Breeder

Before visiting a breeder, make a list of questions to ask during your visit. These may pertain to a specific litter, the breeder's policies, or general care information. If the breeder has a website or social media account, look for answers there first. Doing so will free up more time during your visit to gather information that you can't find online. Following are some common questions:

HOW AND WHEN DID YOU START BREEDING DOGS?

While there is no right answer to this question, experience is always a plus. Since everyone must start somewhere, though, ask a less experienced breeder about mentors and other resources he or she has found helpful. This follow-up question should offer insight into whether the breeder is a responsible one. The best breeders want to learn as much as they can from responsible breeders who have experience.

WHAT TYPE OF HEALTH TESTS DO YOU PERFORM ON YOUR DOGS?

Nearly all breeds are prone to at least one or two health problems. Responsible breeders test their animals for these conditions before breeding them. You should ask to see the health clearances for both parents of any puppy you're considering. Don't worry about offending the breeder. A knowledgeable, caring breeder will expect no less.

DO YOU OFFER A HEALTH GUARANTEE?

While no one can truly guarantee the health of an animal, the best breeders stand behind the health of their puppies. The most common guarantee, or warranty, typically states that the breeder will allow you to return the animal with a refund if a major health problem arises within a certain time period.

you to one breed or another, just make sure that all of its qualities—and needs—suit your lifestyle before making your final decision.

How to Find a Breeder or Breed Rescue

The first place many of us go to find information these days is the Internet, and for good reason. Nearly all businesses and organizations have websites or a social media presence these days. Dog breeders are no exception. These electronic resources offer potential dog owners efficient ways of researching and gathering valuable details. A breeder's website will probably list whether he or she has or is expecting a litter of pups, and the breeder may also share breed-specific advice on general care, grooming, and training. It is important to remember, though, that not everything is always as it seems online.

WHAT ARE MY RESPONSIBILITIES?

Good breeders want the best possible homes for their dogs. Some even ask owners to sign contracts. Common stipulations include agreeing to keep the dog on a leash whenever he ventures outdoors, to spay or neuter the animal by a certain age, and to contact the breeder if the owner is ever unable to keep the dog. Many breeders have working relationships with rescue organizations and prefer to participate in rehoming their former pups if it becomes necessary.

WHEN ARE YOUR PUPPIES READY TO GO HOME?

The age at which breeders can sell puppies varies slightly by state, but no pup should leave his mother before he is seven weeks old. Eight weeks is ideal and, for some smaller breeds, older is even better. As much as you may want to bring your new puppy home as soon as possible, a breeder who errs on the side of caution is putting the pups' best interests first.

DO YOU OFFER ANY FOLLOW-UP SERVICES?

A breeder has no formal obligation to help new owners raise their puppies. You will be your puppy's primary caregiver, after all. It isn't uncommon, though, for breeders to want to be consulted if a new owner is having a problem. Often, the breeder can offer the best advice in these situations, and the best breeders will be more than happy to do it. A breeder friend of mine once told me that the saddest part about breeding is the owners she never hears from again. So if the breeder asks you to stay in touch, consider reaching out every so often, even if just to share that things are going well. A recent photo is often appreciated as well.

Dog breeders are different from most other businesses in that their job is raising live animals. A responsible dog breeder's job is to produce pups who will grow into healthy adult animals with sound temperaments. The best breeders also strive to adhere to their breed standard, which is an official description of a breed's desired physical and temperamental traits. A dog does not have to match his standard perfectly to make a good pet, but the best breeders want their puppies to match the standard as closely as possible. This goal takes a great deal of time, patience, and planning to accomplish. Breeders who merely produce dogs as quickly as possible to meet demand are much less likely to be putting health and temperament at the top of their priority list.

The best dog breeders are hobby breeders. These are people who breed first and foremost because of their love for a particular breed. Few people can afford to breed dogs for free, of

A good breeder stands behind every puppy that he or she produces.

course. Breeders need to make money just like everyone else, but after doing some research, you will likely be able to discern a responsible hobby breeder from a commercial breeder who is mainly interested in profit.

Breed rescues are another great resource for finding a purebred dog. These nonprofit organizations work to rehome dogs who have been displaced for various reasons. Rescue organizations help by placing these dogs in volunteer foster homes until they find new homes for them. Many dogs in rescue are surprisingly young, but older dogs can also make excellent new pets for the right people.

Online searches and links provided by the breed's "parent club" (national breed club) are the quickest ways to find breed rescues in your area. Your local humane society may also recommend nearby rescue organizations. Many breed rescues are devoted to a single breed or AKC group, but some work with a variety of dogs. I found my dog Jemma, a mixed breed, through Maine Lab Rescue. The night Jemma joined my family, the director shared with me that the rescue group had actually been started with the rescue of a cat!

What to Expect When Visiting a Breeder

Once you have identified a breeder within driving distance of your home, call or email to arrange a visit. If you can't find a breeder within a reasonable distance, some breeders are willing to ship puppies by plane. In rare cases, this might be necessary, but finding a breeder you can meet face to face is ideal. If you cannot visit the breeder's facilities, you won't know for certain if you are buying a dog from a responsible breeder or a puppy mill.

Schedule your visit in advance, and do not be offended if the breeder wants to wait until the pups are a few weeks old. Breeders often limit visitors when their pups are most vulnerable to catching serious illnesses, such as parvovirus. Well-intended dog lovers can carry this disease in on the bottoms of their shoes without even realizing it. While parvo usually doesn't cause serious illness in most dogs, it can be deadly to a mother dog and her young puppies.

Look for a friendly, alert dog who seems happy to meet you.

The breeder's facilities should be clean, but expect to see toys and other items strewn here and there. Caring for a litter of newborn puppies is much like caring for human infants. What matters most is that the pups get what they need. Cleanliness is a sign of a responsible breeder; neatness is optional.

Being able to meet the dam—and the sire, if he is owned by the same person—can be especially helpful when choosing a puppy. A pup's parents are the best indicator of what kind of adult dog he will become. Training and nurturing certainly play a role in the development of a dog's personality, but both physical and temperamental traits are often inherited. The friendliest dogs usually produce the best tempered puppies.

Puppies should stay together, and with their dam, for at least eight weeks, like this German Shorthaired Pointer litter.

Adopting from a Shelter or Rescue

Adopting a dog may require just as much planning and research as buying one from a breeder. First, you will need to decide what kind of dog you wish to adopt. The answer might be as simple as wanting an active dog who enjoys the outdoors or as detailed as wanting a specific

Racing Greyhounds make loving pets once their days on the track are over. Because so many of these dogs needs homes, there are numerous rescues across the country.

breed within a certain age range. Whatever qualities you seek in your future pet, knowing what you want before you start your search will be helpful in finding an animal that meets this criteria.

Sometimes, people do not have a specific breed or type of dog in mind, and this is fine, too. Perhaps you are confident that you will know the right dog when you meet him; sometimes a person and a dog just "click." This can work out well, too, as long as you try to get as much information about the dog as possible before making your final decision.

Animal shelters offer a clear advantage when it comes to assessing one's rapport with a potential pet. Although you can certainly scroll through all of the online photos and write-ups of the dogs available for adoption, you can also meet them all in a single day at the shelter. Breed rescues, on the other hand, typically keep their animals in foster homes. Some rescues regularly hold adoption or meet-and-greet events at pet-supply stores and other public places, but you may need to schedule an appointment or wait for a certain day to meet a particular animal.

Once you have found the dog you want to adopt, the next step will be filling out an application. This process may sound a bit intimidating, but it is an important step in matching each dog with his ideal owner. Bear in mind that dogs in shelters and rescues have already lost their homes. Some have never had real homes at all. The people who run rescue organizations simply want to do everything they can to ensure that a dog's next home will be his last.

Applications ask for general information about you and your family, along with your past experience as a pet owner. A shelter or rescue may also ask for details that will help the volunteers determine how well you can fulfill a particular dog's needs. Some dogs may do best in homes without cats or other dogs. Other dogs might lack the temperament to tolerate young children.

A rescue or shelter will also ask you if you own or rent your home. Renting will not keep you from adopting, but the rescue volunteer will want to contact your landlord to make sure that you are allowed to keep a pet on the property. Additionally, many rescues require a home visit prior to approving a prospective owner's application regardless of whether that person owns or rents. This step may seem a bit intrusive at first, but it is usually a quick and simple process that confirms the information you provide on your application. Everyone who lives in the household should be present for the visit.

What to Look for in Any Puppy or Dog

Whether you prefer a puppy, a young adult dog, or an older pet, you should look for a healthy animal with a good temperament. But how will you know if the dog you choose fits this description?

The healthiest dogs have bright, clear eyes and cool, wet noses. A dog's nose will not always feel cold, but an extremely warm nose can sometimes be a sign of an issue. Red or cloudy eyes or discharge from the eyes or the nostrils often signals a health problem. Ears should be clean and free of odors. Head-shaking and tenderness around the ears are both red flags as well because they can indicate an infection or ear mites.

The dog's coat should be clean and free of mats, and his skin should show no signs of irritation. Excessive dryness, sores, or scratches are symptoms of numerous health problems—from external parasites to a thyroid imbalance. Even if no skin abnormalities are visible, persistent itching is often a sign that something is awry.

When you meet the dog, run your hands gently over his body. Doing so can offer insight in

Plenty of friendly dogs wait in animal shelters for their forever homes.

Beware of Puppy Mills!

Breeders, rescue organizations, and animal shelters—not necessarily in this order—are the best places to look for the dog of your dreams. You should never buy a dog from a puppy mill. Few people would intentionally support these deplorable businesses that make money by overbreeding animals for profit, but many well-intentioned owners simply do not realize when they are dealing with a puppy mill. A likely sign is a single breeder who offers multiple breeds. A reputable breeder may breed two different breeds, but three or more is usually a cause for concern. Sometimes it can be hard to tell how many breeds a breeder has because many commercial breeders use different ads for each breed they sell. You can double check, though, by running a search with the phone number, which is often the same in each ad.

Some animal lovers misguidedly think they are rescuing puppy-mill dogs by buying them. The harsh reality is that while these young animals are born into horrible conditions, they are actually the luckier ones. As soon as pups are old enough to be sold, commercial breeders ship them to whoever is willing to pay the price. Some dogs may be sold to pet stores; others may be sold directly to the public. The parents, however, pay the highest price. The dams in particular spend the majority of their lives in cramped, filthy cages with little interaction with people aside from the most basic care. They are forced to deliver litter after litter, as long as their bodies will cooperate. Every time a person buys a puppy-mill dog, he or she is helping support these abusive and greedy businesses.

more ways than one. First, a dog shouldn't have a negative reaction to being touched. Second, this step allows you to check his body for anything unusual. A swollen abdomen might mean that the dog has worms or an umbilical hernia. Both problems can be fixed—the former more easily and inexpensively than the latter—but it is better to know about any problems beforehand and make your decision with this information in mind.

Watch the dog as he moves around. Does he show any signs of discomfort when walking or running? Does he get up from lying down with ease or show signs of lameness or weakness? Neither issue is

A healthy dog is able to run and play with ease.

necessarily a deal-breaker, but it can indicate an orthopedic issue. Arthritis is common in older dogs, and although it can be a chronic problem, it can usually be managed. More acute problems, such as patellar luxation or hip dysplasia, may require surgery.

A well-adjusted puppy will play nicely with his siblings and welcome attention from people, but there are many nuances to canine personalities. While you can certainly help shape what kind of adult dog a puppy becomes, many early temperamental traits will intensify with age. If a pup is the most assertive member of his litter, chances are good that he will try to take the lead role with other pets in your household as well. Likewise, a more timid pup might come out of his shell some over time, but he probably won't grow into an especially confident or outgoing adult. Both of these theoretical puppies can make good pets for the right people; just bear in mind that a dog who already possesses specific qualities is more likely to retain these traits than another dog is to develop them.

Look for clear eyes, a cool nose, and clean ears.

CHAPTER 2

PREPARING FOR YOUR NEW DOG

Whether you are a seasoned dog owner or you are completely new to canine companionship, taking your dog home for the first time is an exciting event. New dog owners may feel a bit overwhelmed by homecoming day, though. What if you forget an important item that your pet needs? What should you do if he gets sick or injured? What if your new dog slips out the door and gets away from you?

Fortunately, a little planning goes a long way when it comes to pet ownership. Perhaps you have picked out a puppy and are waiting for him to be old enough to come home with you, or maybe you are adopting a dog from a rescue group and need to pick him up in a few days from his foster home. In either case, you can use this waiting period to make sure that both you and your home are ready for your new arrival.

Equipment, Supplies, and Accessories

The sheer number of items that a dog needs is a big part of why pet ownership can seem overwhelming at first, but you will need to buy many of these things only once. Think of your dog's crate, bowls, and grooming equipment as investments rather than expenses; they should last for many years. Certainly, consumable items like your dog's food and shampoo will need replenishing periodically, but he probably won't run out of everything at once.

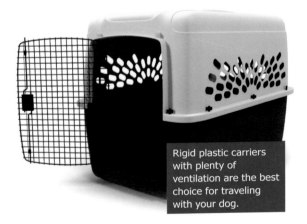

Rigid plastic carriers with plenty of ventilation are the best choice for traveling with your dog.

Crate

You can help your dog feel right at home by having his crate all set up before he walks through the door for the first time. A crate—or kennel, as it is often called—is the perfect place for your pet to eat meals, take naps, and enjoy special

A crate with soft bedding makes a comfortable den for your puppy or adult dog.

treats. Using a crate can also help with housetraining because dogs are known for not wanting to soil the areas in which they rest.

Pet-supply retailers sell several different types of kennels. You can choose between hard plastic models, wire crates, soft-sided kennels, and even decorative pet enclosures that double as end tables. The exact type of kennel you need depends on certain factors. First, you must consider all the purposes that this item will serve. Do you plan to take your dog on trips with you? Airlines require rigid-sided pet carriers for safety purposes. These more resilient kennels are also a smart option for traveling by automobile. If your dog's crate will remain in a fixed location, you might opt for a wire model. A wire crate offers a dog a special place of his own while simultaneously making it easy for him to see all of what's going on around him. The more social your dog is, the more he may prefer a wire crate. You can always place a blanket or towel over the crate for privacy when needed. Another important consideration is your dog's age. A puppy is much more likely than an adult dog to chew a crate made of plastic or one with cloth (usually canvas) or mesh sides.

Place your dog's kennel in a location that will allow him to rest without feeling too far away from the action of the household. A corner of the kitchen or living room is ideal. Remote locations of your home are usually a bad idea because they typically isolate your pet from the rest of the family. You don't want your dog to view spending time in his crate as a social-deprivation experiment.

Once you set up the kennel, leave the door open so your dog can go inside as soon as he likes. Place a toy or other treat in the crate to encourage him to investigate the enclosure. Don't forget to add a crate pad or other type of bedding for comfort. If your dog is still a puppy, you may want

SIZING THINGS UP

Choosing the right size crate for your dog is essential. The ideal kennel offers your pet enough space to stand up and turn around comfortably. While it might seem like an indulgence to buy your dog a crate that is far more spacious than he needs, doing so is a bad idea. If you are planning to implement crate training as part of the housetraining process, a crate that is too big will likely negate its housetraining perks. A resourceful dog is likely to create his own "bathroom" at one end of a too-large enclosure and still have plenty of space to lie down. If your dog is still a puppy, look for a crate that will accommodate his adult size, but block off part of the crate in the beginning. A piece of cardboard can serve this purpose, although some crate models come with their own divider panels.

If you have an adult dog, it is important to measure him as well as the crate you choose for him. After measuring your dog's height and length, add about 4 to 6 inches (10 to 15 centimeters) to each measurement. These two totals should equal the respective height and length of the crate you select for your pet.

The chart on the opposite page offers an overview of the most popular crate sizes, as well as examples of the breeds and sizes that these crates most commonly serve. If you have a mixed-breed dog, select a crate based on what you know about his background. A Beagle-Pug crossbreed, for example, typically grows to be closer to the size of a Beagle than to that of a Pug.

to use an old blanket until he becomes reliably housetrained. Some pups will chew on crate pads, so waiting a while to purchase one could save you from having to buy several. I still use a blanket with my two-year-old dog, Jemma, because she has "de-stuffed" three crate pads to date.

Leashes

The only safe way to take your new dog home is on a leash. Your pet will also need to be on leash when going for walks and any other time you take him out in public. In addition to keeping dogs safe, leashes are required by law in many municipalities. A leash will also come in handy when training your new pet.

At one time, leashes occupied only a small part of an aisle in most pet-supply stores. Today, however, leashes can take up an entire aisle all by themselves. The materials, functions, and prices of these items can vary dramatically. Owners can choose from a wide range of leash colors and patterns in a variety of options, including conventional fixed-length leashes, extendable leashes with ergonomic plastic handles, and leashes with attachments that hold small rolls of cleanup bags.

CRATE MEASUREMENTS (APPROXIMATE)	DOG SIZE (BY WEIGHT)	BREEDS THIS CRATE ACCOMMODATES
Extra-Small (XS) 22 in. (56 cm) long / 16 in. (41 cm) high	Up to 10 lb. (5 kg)	Chihuahua / Pug / Yorkshire Terrier
Small (S) 24 in. (61 cm) long / 20 in. (51 cm) high	11 to 25 lb. (5 to 11 kg)	Dachshund / French Bulldog / Miniature Schnauzer
Medium (M) 30 in. (76 cm) long / 24 in. (61 cm) high	26 to 40 lb. (12 to 18 kg)	Bulldog / Beagle / Cocker Spaniel
Large (L) 36 in. (91 cm) long / 27 in. (69 cm) high	41 to 70 lb. (19 to 32 kg)	Dalmatian / Golden Retriever / Labrador Retriever
Extra-Large (XL) 42 in. (107 cm) long / 31 in. (79 cm) high	71 to 100 lb. (32 to 45 kg)	Alaskan Malamute / Collie / German Shepherd Dog
Giant (XXL) 48 in. (122 cm) long / 33 in. (84 cm) high	Over 100 lb. (45 kg)	Great Dane / Mastiff / Newfoundland

The best first leash for an average-sized dog is a simple 6-foot leash made from a sturdy material. For larger dogs, you'll need a wider leash, but smaller pets fare better with narrower leads, which tend to weigh less. Likewise, a small dog or one with a delicate neck, such as a Greyhound, should never be walked on a heavy leash made of chain.

Leather leads often hold up better than those made from cloth, but they are typically more expensive. Cloth leads come in many choices, though, such as nylon and hemp. The latter is a highly renewable resource, so it's environmentally friendly as well as economical.

Some brands are marketed as "chew-proof" or "indestructible," and choosing one of these leads may be wise if your dog is still a puppy. If your pup chews on his leash when you walk him, you can teach him to discontinue this behavior, but until he has reliably stopped chewing, going with a chew-proof brand is a smart move.

You may choose to invest in more than one leash for your pet. Perhaps you want a longer lead for walking your pet in large, open areas. Most trainers discourage owners from using an extendable (retractable) leash because it is more difficult to control a dog's behavior with this device. A retractable lead must be inspected regularly to make sure the cord has not frayed. Still, many owners enjoy using this type of leash, which allows them to walk their dogs at a 4-foot length, a 26-foot length, or anywhere in between. If you go this route, just make sure that the leash you select can safely accommodate your dog's size. And use added caution if you wear shorts, skirts, or other warm-weather clothing, because this type of lead can inflict nasty burns or cuts if it wraps around a bare leg.

Collars and Harnesses

Like leashes, collars come in a wide variety of materials, colors, and patterns. Some even offer special technology that makes them safer for your pet. Once again, leather is usually the most durable—albeit costliest—option. A less expensive cloth collar may be the better choice if your

dog is still a pup, as he will almost certainly outgrow his collar before reaching his adult size. A large-dog owner may have to buy several sizes during the dog's first year or two, while the owner of a smaller dog may be able to get by with a single collar that adjusts to accommodate the animal's moderate size increases. To measure your dog for a collar, place a tape measure around his neck and adjust it to the point where you can slip two fingers underneath.

A smart safety feature to look for when shopping for conventional

A sturdy leather leash should give you years of use.

collars is breakaway technology. Because collars can become caught on household objects, many owners choose to remove the collars from their dogs when they are inside their homes. The downside to this is that it leaves the animal without identification tags in the event he slips out the door. A breakaway collar, however, keeps a pet safe indoors by breaking apart if it becomes caught on anything, effectively preventing the collar from strangling the animal. When walking a dog on this type of collar, you must make sure to hook the leash onto both of the loops. With just one loop attached to the leash, even a slight amount of pulling will cause the collar to release.

A retractable lead is housed inside a plastic handle, and the leash extends or retracts with the push of a button.

If your dog has a special talent for slipping out of his collar—or if he is one of those breeds with a delicate neck—a harness may be a better option. Instead of circling your dog's neck, a harness wraps around your pet's chest and midsection. To measure your dog for a harness, place the tape measure around his chest, just behind his front legs. Use the same two-finger rule as when measuring for a collar. Many owners find that harnesses also work better for dogs who pull on their leashes.

Food

While it may seem elementary, food is one of the most important items to have on hand before your new dog's arrival. In all the excitement and commotion of preparing for a new pet's homecoming, many owners do not even realize that they've overlooked this essential provision until dinnertime. If you've had to travel a long distance to pick up your dog and bring him home, he will surely be hungry soon after his arrival—and a young puppy must eat more frequently than an adult dog.

Check with your breeder or foster family to see what kind of food your dog is currently eating. If it is a healthy food and your dog is thriving on it, consider keeping him on it. Even if you plan to switch your pet to a different brand or formula, you will need some of the food he is presently eating. Sudden dietary changes can cause stomach upset in dogs, so veterinarians recommend gradual transitions. For the first day, give your dog only the food he is used to. The stress of moving to a new home can be enough to cause tummy troubles, so wait at least twenty-four hours before starting the changeover.

Begin by replacing a quarter of your dog's current food with the new type. Keep in mind that dogs typically adjust more quickly to a new food when the protein source is the same. For

Consider a Halter or Harness

A great option for walking an overly enthusiastic dog is a head halter. This specially designed harness helps prevent a dog from pulling without tightening around his neck. Two simple straps wrap around your pet's muzzle and neck, placing the ring for attaching his leash just below your dog's chin. If he pulls while walking on his leash, this collar will pull his head downward and toward you, interrupting his motion. A head halter can help solve a pulling problem quickly without causing your dog any pain.

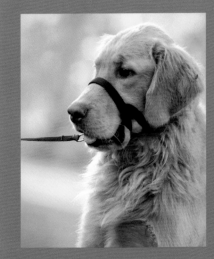

Head halter

HEAD HALTER

For a correct fit, the halter's nose strap should sit just underneath your dog's eyes, and the strap around his neck should sit as high up as possible—just behind your dog's ears. Like a conventional collar, a head halter should fit your pet snugly yet comfortably. Unlike a regular collar, though, you should be able to fit only a single finger between a head halter and your dog's neck. A proper fit ensures that your dog won't slip out of the collar.

HARNESS

A harness is another option. With a front-clip harness, the ring for the leash is located at the center of the chest strap. If your dog pulls while wearing this type of harness, it pulls him around toward you. This interruption to his movement will discourage him from pulling further. While a head halter does not tighten around your dog's neck, he can still give himself a hard jerk if he runs to the end of his leash too quickly while wearing one; using a harness usually prevents this from happening.

Most dogs adjust to wearing halters or harnesses fairly quickly, but if your pet resists, put it on him for short periods of time indoors to help him acclimate to it. Both head halters and harnesses are designed for on-leash walking, however, and should always be removed once you return home from a walk.

Harness

example, a dog will have an easier time swapping from a chicken-based formula to another brand made with chicken. Continue feeding one-quarter of the new food with three-quarters of the original diet for about a week. The following week, increase the ratio to a 50/50 mix. You can then swap to feeding three-quarters of the new food with just a quarter of the old brand. After four weeks, your dog should be eating full portions of his new formula.

This adorable hound sports a standard buckle collar and ID tag.

No Choke Collars!

Choke chains are marketed toward people who own larger dog breeds, with a pervading message that using these items is the only way to control bigger pets. However, a choke chain won't teach your dog how to walk properly on a lead—that can result only from proper training—and can injure your dog. A choke chain works by applying pressure to the animal's windpipe when he pulls. For smaller dogs, those with delicate necks, or animals who pull despite the use of a choke chain, this item can be dangerous. No matter how large or unruly your dog may be, you should never under any circumstance use a prong collar, which isn't safe for any dog.

If you must use a restrictive collar on your pet until he learns to walk nicely on a leash, I recommend using a martingale collar. This type of collar is flat and made of cloth instead of chain. It is more humane than a choke collar because it limits the amount of pressure applied. Fans of martingales often say that these collars apply just enough pressure to get the dog's attention. If you buy a martingale for leash training, you can use it as a conventional collar once your dog has mastered proper leash etiquette. Simply hook both loops to the lead when you no longer need the collar to counteract pulling.

You should not use any type of restrictive collar, even a martingale, on brachycephalic dogs. These flat-faced breeds, such as the Boxer and Pug, have shorter breathing passages and can suffer from respiratory distress if their breathing is compromised in any way.

Stainless steel bowls are safe for your dog and easy to clean.

Bowls

Your dog will need at least two bowls: one for his food and one for his water. I recommend investing in two sets of dishes if you can, because doing so will ensure that you always have a clean set when one is being washed. If you plan to use the dishwasher, make sure that the bowls you choose are dishwasher-safe. The easiest way to make sure that your pet's dishes are dishwasher-safe is to buy stainless steel bowls. Stainless steel is the safest, most durable material for dog dishes. Ceramic bowls can contain lead. Plastic dishes are vulnerable to chewing and can also cause a condition called plastic dish nasal dermatitis, which can remove the pigment from his nose and lips.

Choose bowls that will be big enough for your pet when he reaches adulthood, providing that he can eat and drink from them comfortably now. If your dog is going to grow considerably, it may be wise to purchase one smaller set of dishes for the time being. Shallow bowls with raised centers, made specifically for puppies, are perfect for this situation, as these dishes prevent the food from moving away from the edges. Once your dog gains some size, you will then be able to invest in a set or two of larger bowls.

Grooming Equipment and Supplies

Your list of grooming equipment and supplies will vary depending on the kind of dog you choose. Longhaired breeds typically require far more coiffing than those with shorter coats, but even shorthaired dogs need to be brushed and bathed at least occasionally. Many smooth-coated breeds are among the heaviest shedders. Longer, fuller coats require slicker brushes whereas shorter, finer hair needs a soft-bristled brush. A metal flea comb is a smart investment

Did You Know?

Even if you do utilize a groomer's services, you will need a set of nail clippers. Your groomer can certainly trim your dog's toenails during a groom, but this important task must be performed more often than shampoos or haircuts.

A fine-toothed comb can help detangle delicate facial furnishings.

no matter the coat type. If you do opt for a dog with a profuse coat that grows rather than sheds, you will also need a set of clippers for trimming his hair unless you plan to use a professional groomer for this task.

Consumable items that your dog will need include shampoo, a toothbrush, canine toothpaste, and ear cleaner. Do not use your own shampoo or toothpaste on your pet! Shampoos formulated for people are too acidic for canines and will strip the natural oils from your dog's coat and skin. Likewise, your toothpaste isn't meant for dogs; using it on your pet's teeth will likely upset his stomach. You may discover other tools and products that help with grooming once you get into a routine with your pet, but the aforementioned items are the essentials for every dog owner's grooming kit.

Toys

Dogs are incredibly intelligent animals. As such, they need ways to stimulate their minds and occupy their time. Dogs also need to exercise regularly in order to stay healthy physically. Many breeds also have instinctive urges to hunt, chase, or herd. Toys help fulfill all of these important needs. Playing with your dog is a great way to bond with him, train him, and have a whole lot of fun in the process yourself.

Dogs often enjoy interactive toys that encourage their owners to join the fun.

There is no magic number when it comes to buying toys for your dog, but it is wise to provide your pet with enough variety to keep him from becoming bored. Many dogs single out a few favorite playthings that they turn to over and over, but having something new to play with can brighten a pet's day as much as it would a child's. I recommend investing in several different toys to start your dog's toy collection: a ball, something that squeaks or makes another fun noise, and a chewable item should all be included on your initial shopping list. Over time, you can add to your dog's toys, rotating items in and out of the toy box to keep your pet's interest level high. It is also important to throw away any items that could be dangerous—for instance, a chew toy that your pet has whittled down to a size that makes it a choking hazard.

Bear in mind that some toys require a human partner. That ball, for instance, won't be much fun for your dog without someone to throw it for him. For this reason, make sure your pet has items that he can use to entertain himself when you cannot participate. Some dogs especially enjoy educational toys, such as balls that dispense treats when rolled just the right way and complex puzzle toys that offer similar edible rewards when solved; these "brain games" will help exercise your dog's mind.

Whatever type of toys your dog prefers, make sure that the ones you offer him are size-appropriate and sturdy. Be sure to keep a few of his favorites on hand. They will be especially useful when it comes time for teaching your dog the Drop It and Leave It commands; favorite toys are also excellent alternatives to edible training rewards.

Gates

Safety gates are among the most important tools for creating a safe environment for your dog. Puppies, in particular, can be inquisitive to the point of placing themselves in danger. Many adult dogs, too, have a tendency to get into trouble at times, whether in the form of rummaging in the trash or chewing on their owners' belongings. While you should puppy-proof as much of your home as possible, you will inevitably find gates helpful in one way or another, whether or not your dog also uses a crate.

Sometimes you don't need to crate your dog, but you want to keep him out of a single room or part of your home for a while. Maybe you've just had your wall-to-wall carpeting cleaned and need to keep little feet off it while the fibers dry. Perhaps you are having a bathroom remodeled, and workers will be leaving exterior doors open for extended periods of time as they carry items inside and out. Whatever your reason, a gate can afford your pet with more space than a crate while still protecting him from harm.

If you will be using a gate instead of a crate for your dog, you may consider investing in a model that can be permanently affixed to a doorway. These swing-style gates allow pet owners to walk through quickly and easily, without having to reposition anything but a handle. Of

A strategically placed gate limits your dog's access to certain parts of the house.

course, if you need a gate in more than one area of your home, a pressure-mounted unit (or multiple gates) may be the better choice. Pressure-mounted gates offer pet owners the flexibility to move them wherever they want without having to install any hardware.

Secure Fencing

No matter how much you play with your pet inside, getting outdoors for exercise and fresh air is good for both your pet and you. Daily walks, or jogs for more athletic dogs, are a great way to keep your pet fit and happy. Still, nothing can replace the thrill a dog feels when he can run outside freely. A fenced yard can make it possible for your pet to enjoy exhilarating off-leash playtime every day without putting his safety at risk. Having a fenced yard can also provide your dog with a safe potty spot that he can access with just the opening of the door. If you choose to install a doggy door, he could even head to his potty spot in the fenced yard without any assistance.

Before you allow your dog to spend time in your yard unsupervised, you must make certain that every part of your fence is secure. This structure must not have any gaps through which your dog could escape. It also must not have crossbars that could offer your dog a leg up in climbing over it. Larger breeds can jump over fences that aren't high enough. Certain breeds, such as terriers, have a talent for digging under fences. Even when you have done everything

Your fencing should have no gaps where your dog might squeeze through.

Equipment Checklist

You may find a few additional items helpful once your dog has settled into your home. For example, if you will be performing extensive grooming, you might choose to invest in a grooming table. This piece of equipment, which you can collapse when not in use, makes brushing and trimming a dog's coat considerably easier on an owner's back. Likewise, you may decide to use a nail-grinding tool for your dog's pedicures instead of a set of manual clippers. When used properly, this item helps owners avoid injuring their pets' nail beds. Exactly which items you purchase is strictly a matter of personal preference, but the following list of gear will start you off on the right paw.

- ✔ Crate
- ✔ Crate Pad/Liner
- ✔ Leash
- ✔ Collar or Harness
- ✔ Bowls
- ✔ Toothbrush and toothpaste
- ✔ Brush
- ✔ Flea Comb
- ✔ Clippers (for longhaired dogs)
- ✔ Nail Trimmers
- ✔ Toys
- ✔ Safety Gate(s)

correctly in securing your fence, you shouldn't leave your dog unsupervised outside for too long. In addition to keeping your dog safe, your joining him for outdoor time will make the experience a more enjoyable one for your pet.

Cleaning Supplies

One of the most important steps in the housetraining process is cleaning up thoroughly after your dog has an accident. Dogs have incredibly sensitive noses, so if your dog detects any trace of urine or fecal matter left behind after a housetraining mishap, it will encourage him to continue using the area as a potty spot.

The first step to removing pet stains and odors is removing the urine or feces. Solid waste can be flushed down your toilet, but urine is a much more complicated matter, especially when your dog pees on a carpet. Clean up puddles as soon as you notice them to prevent the urine from seeping too far into the rug. You may use old towels, rags, or paper towels for this step. Once you have absorbed the majority of the liquid, place a fresh towel over the area and step on it (with a shoe on, of course!). This additional measure will allow you to reach as much of the urine that has soaked into your carpet fibers as possible. Repeat this step until you absorb no more liquid from the soiled area.

The second and equally vital phase of the cleanup process is cleaning the area with an enzymatic cleaner. This type of cleaner will help remove any odors that are still left behind—the ones that a human nose cannot sense. While all enzymatic cleaners rely on proteins to break down stains and odors, it is important that you choose a product made specifically for pets. Whatever you do, never use a cleaner that contains ammonia to clean a housetraining mishap. Because urine itself also contains ammonia, your dog will be even more likely to revisit the spot!

You will also need to clean up after your pet when he eliminates in his proper potty spot outdoors. Any fecal matter left on the ground can breed bacteria. If you or your dog step in excrement, you can transport a variety of dangerous germs into your home. Your pet may even ingest germs this way, placing him at risk for several serious illnesses.

The most efficient way to clean up your dog's potty spot is with a "poop scoop." Some are one-piece, hinged units, while others include a small hoe and separate shovel for transporting waste to your garbage can. You may find it helpful to keep a designated lined trash can in your yard for depositing dog waste; be sure to replace the liner each week after trash day.

Although poop scoops are ideal for backyard cleanup, they are typically too cumbersome to bring with you when you walk your dog. For this purpose, you will need to bring along cleanup bags. You can buy rolls of plastic cleanup bags from a pet-supply store, but many owners find that plastic grocery-store bags work perfectly. Whichever style you prefer, the most important thing is remembering to take them with you whenever you walk your dog. Many municipalities have laws about cleaning up after pets. If you don't remove your dog's waste from a public place, you could be fined. Since no one enjoys stepping in dog poop, cleaning up after your pet is simply the right thing to do.

A good veterinarian will take care of your dog in sickness and in health throughout your pet's life.

Finding a Veterinarian

If you already have other pets, you also likely have a veterinarian to whom you take them for checkups and when problems arise. If you are new to dog ownership, though, finding a vet may be one of the tasks on your to-do list. Or, you may be looking for a new veterinary hospital even if you have dealt with other vets in the past. Finding the right match is important because this person, more than any other, is your best resource for your dog's health. If you don't feel 100-percent comfortable with a veterinarian, you should keep looking.

Make all introductions low key, and supervise any children with your new puppy.

You can probably get the names of half a dozen veterinary hospitals in your general vicinity instantly simply by asking the digital assistant on your smartphone. What the automated voice can't tell you, though, is which vets are the best. A better way to choose a vet is by asking for recommendations from your breeder, rescue group, or local humane society. You can also ask dog-owning friends or family members for their vets' names.

Once you have narrowed down your search to one or two veterinarians, head to the Internet to research them further. Most veterinary hospitals today have websites or social media pages that offer basic information about the practices, including photos of the staff and facilities, hours of operations, the types of animals they treat, and maybe even brief bios of the doctors. You can also look for reviews posted by other pet owners. Read all of this information, and if everything looks good, plan to stop by for a visit.

Dropping by unannounced to make your first appointment may seem like a sneaky trick, but it gives you the opportunity to make sure that the hospital is indeed what it seems. I do recommend avoiding the busiest times of the day—typically first thing in the morning and just before closing time—out of consideration for the staff, however. If the waiting room is filled with patients when you arrive, simply let the person at the front desk know you would like to schedule a well visit for your dog and patiently wait until someone can speak with you.

Take a look at your surroundings. Is the facility clean and well organized? Is the staff friendly to both the pets and their owners? Do you feel welcome and at ease? The answers to all of these questions should be *yes*.

Preparing a Safe Place in the Home

Owners aren't the only ones who can feel a bit overwhelmed by the new dog's homecoming. As you worry about whether you might have overlooked an important step or item, your new dog may feel scared or stressed on his way to his new home. Bear in mind that he does not yet know where he is going or what he might encounter there. It is your job to help him feel as relaxed as possible.

Your new dog will fit into the family in no time!

One of the best ways you can accomplish this task is by limiting how much you expose him to right away. On his first day home, try to keep the hoopla to a minimum. As excited as you surely are, more commotion means more for your pet to process. Meeting his other household members is a must, but introducing them one at a time can make it easier for your dog to see that there is nothing to fear. If extended family, friends, or neighbors want to meet your new pet, hold off on those introductions until the next day, again introducing just one new person at a time.

Giving your dog free run of your entire home right away may be too much too soon. For his first day home, it might be wiser to provide your pet with access to just one or two rooms. He will surely find plenty of new objects and scents to explore in this limited space as you keep an eye on him and how he is adjusting. Don't be surprised if he sniffs around for a few minutes and then proceeds to take a nap. Puppies in particular wear out quickly, but even an older dog may need to recharge after a long car ride to this new environment.

What matters most is that you make sure that the room you choose for your pet's homecoming is safe and comfortable for him. Tidy up before your dog's arrival to make sure that personal belongings, such as shoes, children's toys, and anything else you don't want chewed, are put away. Any items small enough to fit in your pet's mouth should likewise be removed from his space. Like human babies, puppies have no way of discerning safe objects from the ones that pose a choking hazard.

Many owners opt to keep their dogs in the kitchen for the first day or two to make it easier to clean up any housetraining mishaps as they begin the training process. If this is the case for you, either place your dog's crate in the kitchen or offer your dog a pet bed or folded blanket for comfort. A few toys will also be soothing to your pet as he settles into his new home.

Puppy-Proofing

Before your dog can begin exploring the rest of his home, you should make sure that each new room he enters has been properly puppy-proofed. Do not assume just because your dog has been well behaved in the kitchen that he won't get into trouble in your family room or bedrooms. Puppies have a knack for finding items that people didn't even realize they left out, so, as mentioned, intentionally inspecting your living areas and removing potentially dangerous items is a necessity.

Begin puppy-proofing each room with a general cleanup. The saying "a place for everything and everything in its place" can be mighty useful for new dog owners. Similarly, you will find it easier to keep your rooms puppy-friendly by establishing basic house rules, such as:

- Coats and shoes get placed in closets as soon as they are removed.
- School and work supplies get placed on desks—never on the floor or in chairs where your dog can reach them.
- Leftover food gets covered and placed in cupboards or the refrigerator.

The exact rules you choose for your home depend on your individual circumstances, but a neat home is the safest place for your new dog. In order for the rules to work, all household

Expect a few accidents during housetraining and be prepared to clean up the mess.

Pet Insurance

Somewhere between buying your dog's crate and selecting a veterinarian for his first checkup, you may wonder whether you should purchase pet insurance. In addition to the cost of your dog's yearly physical exams, he may need emergency care at some point during his lifetime. Even if you take the best possible care of your pet, he might also develop a chronic condition that requires either frequent trips to the vet or regular medication. In either case, having pet insurance could help. This doesn't mean that it is definitely the right choice for you and your pet, though. Much depends on the unknown.

I had no way of knowing that I would experience both veterinary emergencies and chronic health issues with my own pets. My first Cocker Spaniel, Jonathan, slipped on the ice one winter, tearing his anterior cruciate ligament. Surgery to fix this relatively common injury is costly, and it comes with a lengthy recovery period. To avoid the long recovery, my vet treated my dog with acupuncture instead of surgery. This plan worked wonders for Johnny, who was running around again long before he would have been with the surgery, but I spent about the same amount of money on the weekly acupuncture treatments as I would have on the operation.

Another one of my Cockers, Molly, has idiopathic epilepsy. The word "idiopathic" means that the cause of her condition is unknown. Molly's vet and I manage her seizures with anticonvulsant medication, which recently doubled in price at the pharmacy. Although Molly is on a very low dose, this medication can also damage her kidneys and liver over time. For this reason, her vet must run blood tests periodically to make sure that all her levels are where they should be.

members must respect the protocol. Among the most insidious threats to your pet's safety are board games and other children's toys. Small to medium pieces pose a choking hazard to dogs, and a swallowed object can cause a bowel obstruction—or worse. Magnets are of particular concern because their attraction to one another doesn't stop after they enter an animal's digestive system. Magnets have been known to rupture a dog's stomach or intestines due to the objects' strong magnetic force, putting the dog's life in jeopardy.

Even after you have removed all of the obvious risks to your dog, you still have a few more steps in the puppy-proofing process. One of the best ways to identify the dangers that still lurk in a room is by getting down to your pet's level, literally. Lower yourself down to your pet's height and look around. Do you see any exposed nails or sharp edges on furniture? Is that your favorite pen under the sofa? Is there a web of tangled power cords behind your television or computer?

I am happy to pay for whatever care my pets need, but not everyone is fortunate enough to have this choice. Still, pet insurance doesn't necessarily make veterinary care more affordable for everyone. The cost of pet insurance can vary dramatically based on certain factors, including your dog's age and even his size. Your plan may cost more or less depending on where you live, as well. The more a plan covers, the more you will pay for your premium. The least expensive plans cover emergency care only, while others will pay if your pet gets sick. Even plans that cover illnesses may not pay for treatments for hereditary or pre-existing conditions. The most thorough plans, however, even cover preventive care, such as vaccinations and flea control.

So, is pet insurance worth it? Like health insurance for humans, pet policies have deductibles and copays. You must consider the cost of your premiums, the amount you must pay out of pocket if your dog needs care, and the costs of your hospital's services before deciding if pet insurance is right for you. If your dog is a puppy, his insurance will be relatively inexpensive, but many premiums increase as the pet get older—when they are more likely to have health issues.

Some owners prefer to use a savings account for their pet's healthcare costs. If your dog doesn't require any veterinary treatment other than preventive care for several years, this strategy could work well. If, on the other hand, he ends up needing emergency surgery before his first birthday, you could come up short. Conversely, you could pay hundreds or even thousands of dollars over the course of several years for insurance that your dog never needs. However, pet insurance can be helpful if you accumulate large veterinary bills for covered services.

Most fixes are simple. A hammer can drive a nail back into the underside of a chair in just seconds. Childproofing kits made for human toddlers come with soft corner covers for furniture. You'll find enclosures at your local office-supply store that keep electrical cords organized and out of the reach of teething pups. Whichever tools you use, taking proactive steps is vital for your pet's safety.

As you get to know your new dog, you may discover additional puppy-proofing steps that are necessary for your individual pet. For instance, some dogs have an impressive talent for getting into cupboards or trash cans. Safety kits also contain childproof locks for securing cabinets and cupboards, which will keep your pup away from dangerous food items, toxic cleaning chemicals, and even medications.

Your dog may show no interest in your pantry or garbage, but he might enjoy drinking from the toilet. This behavior isn't just unpleasant for owners, but it can also allow the dogs to ingest deadly cleaning chemicals. The solution here is as easy as making sure that everyone closes the lid before leaving the bathroom. Make this simple step a new house rule and post a note near your commode as a polite reminder for guests.

Identification Options

As much as we all like to think it won't happen to us, dogs slip out doors from time to time. If owners are lucky, it happens after they have had a chance to train their dog to come back to them when called. Many times, however, our excited canines run away before we can catch them. If you spend any time online, you have surely seen the numerous posts about lost animals. While social networking has given us a wonderful new way to spread the word, the sad fact is that many of these dogs never find their way back home.

The most effective way you can protect your dog from becoming one of those dogs is to keep a close eye on your pet whenever doors and windows are opened. The next is to start teaching him the Come command on the day you bring him home—and practicing it every day thereafter. Even the best plans, however, need a fail-safe. In the case of a lost pet, this important safeguard means providing your pet with identification.

Owners have several choices when it comes to ID. A traditional dog tag may seem obsolete to some people, but a tag is actually one of the smartest, easiest, and cheapest ways of identifying your dog. If your dog ever becomes lost, anyone who finds him will check his collar first to see if that tag is there.

Tags can be purchased at pet-supply stores or online. You can find them in every color of the rainbow, shaped like dog bones or fire hydrants (or other clever shapes), and ready to be inscribed with several lines of text. Your dog's name is always a good start, but the most important information to include is your name, address, and phone number. Affix your dog's tag right away—ideally, even before you leave the store. Your dog's tag will lead others to you if he is wearing it when he gets lost, and history has taught us that we never know when this might happen.

A dog tag is a simple and effective means of identifying your dog.

Some companies make personalized collars with the dog's name and his owner's contact information printed right onto the collar. These are just as effective as tags. If you go this route, just be sure that the letters and numbers do not wear off or otherwise become illegible over time. A collar with the information embroidered onto it is ideal.

Another effective means of identifying a dog is microchipping. This method of inserting a small chip just under a dog's skin has been around for years, and it has become extremely popular. The chip itself is about the size of a grain of rice,

A GPS tracker fits on the dog's collar.

and the procedure to insert it just behind the dog's shoulder blades is as quick and painless as a vaccination. The chip provides the dog's and owner's information when scanned; veterinarians, humane societies, and even local police departments have embraced microchips and likely have scanners with which to scan your dog.

If you choose to microchip your dog, be sure to register your chip with the provider and keep your contact information up to date. If you move or change your phone number without alerting the microchip company, the employees will have no way of getting in touch with you if your dog is ever found by a helpful stranger.

Unfortunately, not all strangers are indeed helpful. However, if your dog is ever stolen, a microchip can serve as a way to prove ownership of your pet. A thief may be able to remove a tag or collar from your dog, but a microchip is a different matter. While there is no guarantee that the person who finds your dog will have him checked for a chip, having one in place increases your pet's chances of making it back to you.

Another form of technology that will help you locate your pet if he is ever lost is a GPS tracker. Like an ID tag, this device attaches to your pet's collar. It then allows you to track your dog's whereabouts using an app on your smartphone. Some brands even alert owners as soon as an escape happens.

Whichever form of identification or tracking device you choose for your pet, never rely on it to keep your pet safe. Lost dogs face many dangers outside the safety of their homes. Automobiles, wild animals, and harsh weather conditions are just a few of these threats. Nothing replaces your careful supervision.

CHAPTER 3

YOUR DOG COMES HOME

Y ou've picked out your dog. You've waited for the breed rescue to approve your application or for your puppy to be old enough to leave his mother. And you've bought all the necessary supplies that your new pet needs. You may have even puppy-proofed every square foot of your home in preparation for that date on the calendar that you circled in red marker. Now, as they say, the real fun begins.

You may worry that you've forgotten about an important task or item, but rest assured that this feeling is normal in your excitement to pick up your new pet. Take a deep breath and repeat after me: "It's OK." In just a short time, you will officially become a dog owner.

After your new dog arrives home, you will soon learn exactly how long it takes to drive from your home to the nearest pet-supply store, and you will also start learning how to communicate with your new dog through training. Most importantly, though, you will provide the best home possible for your furry new housemate.

Picking Your Pet's Name

Choosing a name for your new dog can be one of the most fun tasks of pet ownership. For some new owners, though, this step can also be one of the most daunting. If this dog will be a family pet, you must all agree on the name—and this can take both time and a certain amount of compromise. Even if your new dog will be yours alone, the sheer number of possibilities can seem overwhelming.

Pick a name that suits your dog's personality.

Maybe you are a traditionalist who prefers old standards, such as Jake and Max, which have been among the most popular names for male dogs for decades. Likewise, Maggie and Molly have ranked at the top of the list for female dogs. I chose the name Molly for one of my dogs in honor of a previous dog whose dam's name had been Molly. Using this name felt like keeping a small part of my Johnny with me. In the years that I have spent with my Molly, though, this independent and vivacious gal has added much to my connotation of the name. It is now unequivocally her own.

Pop culture has added Bella and Marley to the ranks of popular dog names, and naming dogs after famous dogs—fictional or otherwise—has also become a common practice; a fair share of pups answer to Balto, Scooby Doo, and Shiloh. Some owners even enjoy naming their dogs for one of their own favorite people or pastimes. A Beatles fan might choose Ringo, and a soccer fan might go with Beckham. I named one of my dogs Damon, because he was born the night Johnny Damon and his Boston Red Sox teammates won the World Series.

Your dog's tag should list his name, your name, and at least your cell phone number.

Some owners prefer to take some time to get to know their dogs before choosing a name. Sometimes a dog just looks like an Abby or a Sam. Or an owner may go with a more descriptive name, based on the dog's personality or looks, such as Einstein, Freckles, or Romeo. What matters most is that you like the name you pick, but it might also be helpful to go with something short and easy to say. Longer or more formal names are fine for a dog's American Kennel Club (AKC) registration, but a shorter nickname will be more practical for everyday use.

Set a goal of choosing a name as soon as possible, so your dog can start learning it. If you are adopting a dog, he likely already has a name. Should you keep it or change it? While there is no universal answer to this question, I can offer you a few guidelines. First, consider how long the dog has had his name. Second, is there anything disparaging about the dog's current name? And third, how do you feel about it yourself?

The more time he has had with his name, the harder and more confusing it may be for him to learn a new one. My dog Jemma was already named when I adopted her. Although she was only five months old at the time, I thought that she had already lost enough; I wanted her to be able to keep this one thing. I also think that Jemma's name suits her. I might never have considered it on my own, but I quickly came to adore both it and her.

If you truly dislike your adopted dog's name, it may be better to change it. Names that are in any way belittling should also be replaced. Many dogs have an innate talent for sensing people's feelings, so names like Puddles or Stinky, even if they were given in fun, come with negative implications that your new pet may pick up on. Dogs may not be able to comprehend all the subtleties of language, but they often know when they are the object of ridicule.

First Introductions

Whether your pet is a new puppy or a seasoned adult, homecoming day can be both exciting and a bit scary for him. A little patience and planning can help keep any anxiety he may be feeling to a minimum, though.

To Your Home

Upon arriving at your home with your new dog, take him directly to his potty spot before doing anything else. Whether you've been in the car for a long or short time, this should be standard protocol each time you return home with your pet following an excursion. If he doesn't relieve himself after a few minutes, try again a short time later.

Next, take him into the main room of the house in which he will spend most of his time that day. For many households, this is either the kitchen or living room. Even if you have already

Some pups will make themselves at home right away.

puppy-proofed your entire home, it is smart to limit your pet to a smaller area initially. Doing so will allow him to get the lay of the land without feeling overwhelmed.

Be sure to show your dog where his water bowl is located, as he will likely be thirsty. A few treats may help calm your pet's nerves by giving him something fun to focus on, but be careful not to overdo the edibles. Toys may also serve as enjoyable distractions from stress, but limit him to one or two toys, again to prevent overstimulation. If the breeder or rescue volunteer sent you home with any of your pet's prior belongings—such as a toy or blanket, it is smart to keep this item nearby. Just the scent of something familiar may comfort him as he acclimates to his new environment.

A trick I've used is leaving a toy with the breeder or foster family for my dog to play with prior to taking him home. Keep the item with you for a day or two before dropping it off to help acquaint your new pet with your scent, so your home won't seem completely foreign to him on homecoming day. Additionally, this item will absorb the scent of his prior residence, increasing his feeling of security as he makes the transition to his new home.

To the Family

As tempting as it may be to have numerous family members and friends in attendance for your dog's homecoming, it is wiser to limit the number of people present on the first day. Although you have been looking forward to his arrival, your new pet didn't realize he was moving to a new home until this very moment. He simply needs some time

Have your puppy's area ready for him when he first comes home.

to adjust. It won't be long before he is greeting visitors with an exuberant spirit and a wagging tail, but give your dog some time to get to know your immediate family and take in his new surroundings before inviting company to meet him.

If your household includes numerous family members, it may better to stagger the introductions rather than approach your new pet all at once. Children, in particular, can overwhelm a dog just from their excitement over meeting the new canine family member. Parents can help guide kids by creating a few rules beforehand, such as:

- Encourage the dog to come to you, but never chase him.
- Touching and petting the new dog is fine, but do not try to pick him up.
- Use "indoor voices" so as not to scare the new family pet.

Puppies have an incredible amount of energy, but they also need to rest often. Following the trip home and a quick meet-and-greet with the family, a young pup will likely need a nap. Rest assured that when he wakes, he will be raring to go once again. Even an adult dog may feel tired after moving to his new home, but he too will be more playful once he has had a chance to rest and settle in.

On the second or third day, you may begin inviting guests over to meet your new addition. Use the same protocol for these introductions as when your family members met the new dog. A friend or two at a time is fine, but hold off on hosting a party until your pet has adjusted to his new home and family.

To Other Pets

Introducing your new dog to any pets who already live in your home can be a bit more complicated, but it doesn't have to be difficult. For safety's sake, the best place to arrange a meeting between two dogs is outdoors, preferably away from your yard. A dog who has lived with you for some time might feel threatened by the arrival of a new canine, and he might react by trying to defend his territory or you from this strange new animal. Using a neutral setting for the first meeting, however, can prevent an aggressive reaction.

Many dogs get along surprisingly well with cats. Others may chase a feline housemate from one end of your home to the other whenever the opportunity arises, and this behavior could cause a trip to the emergency animal hospital. For the time being, the best approach may be separation. Keep your cat in another room with the door closed. Once your new dog has settled in a bit, you can then introduce him to the cat—with careful supervision, of course.

When I rescued Jemma, the woman who had been fostering her told me that Jemma loved cats. She certainly didn't exaggerate. Jem indeed loves my cat Autumn, but the ways she shows her affection is often too much for my kitty's taste. Autumn has never once tried to scratch Jemma, but she has hissed at her when Jemma has tried to pin her, lick her, or play with her. Over time, Jem's infatuation with the cat has lessened, but not as much as I would like.

I found a simple solution to this problem: I gave Autumn my home office. It isn't hers alone, of course; I still use it, too, but by installing a walk-through pet gate in the doorway and placing Autumn's dishes, a cat tree, and a litter box on the other side, I have given her a place where no dogs are allowed. I think she would post a sign saying as much if she could! She

Once a dog and cat get used to each other, they can become good friends.

still has free run of the rest of my home whenever she wants it, but I no longer worry about Jemma and Autumn potentially hurting each other.

To the Crate

If you plan to use a crate with your new dog, set it up before your pup's homecoming. Leave the door open so he can go inside freely to inspect the enclosure as he explores the rest of his new home. If he does venture inside on his own, reward him at once with either a toy or an edible treat. A heartfelt "good boy!" can also go a long way in helping your pet form a positive association with his crate.

If he doesn't enter his crate independently, place him inside with a treat. Do not close the door at this point because you are simply introducing him to the enclosure. Slow and steady steps will show him that he has nothing to fear from the crate. Once he links going inside the crate with rewards, he may start to go in on his own. If so, treat him and offer praise again.

With soft bedding inside, the crate becomes a comfortable spot for your dog to rest.

Once your dog is entering his crate voluntarily, you can begin closing the door and gradually increasing the length of time you leave him inside it. Some dogs may protest at this point, but others accept the closed door quickly and easily. If your dog is among the former group, the most important thing to remember is not to let him out while he is fussing. Even if he stops only for a mere moment, this is the sweet spot during which you can let him out. If you open the door when he is protesting, you will reinforce the wrong behavior, teaching him that fussing effectively leads to an open door.

Crate training can take time, so be patient with your new pet. For now, your biggest goal is to make the crate an inviting space where your dog will enjoy spending some of his time. The best way to accomplish this goal is by keeping the payoffs big and the pressure low.

The First Day and Night

Although you may feel overcome with happiness that your new dog is home with you, it can take your pet a little longer to feel at ease in his new living situation. He may be missing his littermates or his foster family members. He might even feel a bit scared. Remember, your dog doesn't understand that the bright lights that keep shining through your window are from cars driving past your home or that the odd sound he keeps hearing is just your refrigerator's icemaker.

Once your dog seems comfortable in the first space to which you introduce him, you may gradually widen his access to the rest of your home. If you live in a multilevel house, it may be best to stick to the first floor for your pup's first few days at home. If he is still small, or if he's not used to stairs, just learning how to navigate stairs may take some time and practice. Rest assured that there will be plenty for your dog to explore without giving him the grand tour of his new residence just yet.

Stairs can be confusing for a puppy or dog who has never used them before.

Puppies, and even older dogs in new environments, are a lot like small children. They often need comfort and patience. Your new pet may even cry during the first few nights. The old advice about wrapping a ticking clock in a towel and placing it in a puppy's bed can indeed help. The sound, which mimics a mother dog's heartbeat, often soothes a tired, scared pup.

Your dog's first night in your home will set the tone for much of his future routine. Certainly, you may end up making some changes if needed, but it is best to make as many decisions as possible in advance so that any changes are few and minimally disruptive. Dogs are creatures of habit, and they learn and settle in quickly, making it especially important for you to choose the best spot for your pet to sleep before bedtime rolls around on that first night home.

Allowing your dog to sleep in your bedroom does not mean that your pet has to sleep in your bed. Many owners teach their dogs to sleep on their own beds, a compromise that allows the animals to be close to their people yet sleep independently. Some dogs, particularly those with heavy coats, actually prefer to sleep in their own beds, where it is cooler. If your dog does jump up on your bed, you must redirect him to his own space until he stays there. Training your pet to sleep on his own bed can take time, but it will take even more time if you give in and let him sleep with you just once.

If you do allow your dog to sleep with you, it is a good idea to establish boundaries right away. You may expect your pet to stay at the foot of the bed, for example, or you might not want his paws on your pillow. Whatever your rules are, just be clear about them from the beginning.

Whether your dog sleeps in your bedroom or another area of the home, many owners find that comfortable padding, such as a crate liner, makes the dog's crate an ideal overnight spot. Place the crate in a quiet location that is neither too warm nor too cool or drafty.

Starting a Schedule

One of the simplest ways you can help your new dog adapt to your home is by maintaining a consistent schedule. Most households already have a routine in place before a dog joins the family, and in most cases only small changes will be necessary to accommodate the new arrival.

The Everyday Routine

The best schedules begin with a set time to wake up every day. If your morning alarm allows for a fairly leisurely pace, you might not even have to get up earlier—although giving yourself an extra half hour might not be a bad idea. Even if you prefer to sleep in on weekends, it is important that you get up early enough to take your pup to his potty spot in a timely manner.

Household routines do not have to revolve around your dog. In fact, you shouldn't change some aspects of your schedule to accommodate your new pet. In most ways, your dog needs to adjust to your routine, not the other way around. For example, impromptu play sessions are among the best parts of owning a dog, but your new pet needs to learn that bedtime is not playtime.

Two aspects of your routine that you may want to schedule around your dog's needs are meals and exercise. Eating at the same times each day is good for both you and your pet. While your dog is still a young puppy, he will need to eat three meals each day. Scheduling these feeding times around your own breakfast, lunch, and dinner will keep him satiated, and it will also help teach him that he needs to eat his own food, not beg at the table for yours. Exercise, too, is a practical pastime to share with your pet. Regular walks in the morning and evening are a terrific way to de-stress and add physical activity to your routine.

Consistent mealtimes for your puppy lead to consistent potty times, too.

Housetraining

Scheduling meals for the same times each day is important not just to establish a routine, but it will inarguably make housetraining your pet easier. Even if you adopt a dog who is already housetrained, staying true to a routine is the best way to ensure that he doesn't regress in his behavior. Take an adult dog to his potty spot:

- First thing in the morning
- Twenty minutes after he has eaten a meal
- Promptly after a vigorous play session
- Whenever he awakes from a nap
- Right before bedtime

Puppies should be given more frequent chances to relieve themselves. Most pups can "hold it" for about an hour for each month of their age. For example, a two-month-old puppy should go to his potty spot about every two hours. When he reaches three months old, you can most likely extend this schedule to every three hours. This formula will gradually reach its limit once your dog is between four and six months of age.

An adult dog should never go longer than eight hours between trips to his potty spot—and this is the maximum, not the norm. If you work full time while no one else is home, arrange for a neighbor or petsitter to stop by to take your dog outside midday. Imagine what it would be like not to get a single bathroom break all day! Your dog wouldn't like this restrictive schedule, either.

Take your pup outside and lead him to the appropriate potty spot first thing in the morning.

Setting Boundaries

Setting boundaries—and sticking to them—is one of the most important things you will do for your new pet. For your dog to behave the way you want, you must show him what you expect from him. Few dogs can maintain consistent behavior in an inconsistent environment. It simply isn't fair to allow your dog to sit on the furniture for several weeks and then abruptly create a new rule that forbids him from doing so. It is your job, as your dog's owner, to set him up for success.

Going Out for Potty

Before your dog comes home, choose a spot where he will be able to relieve himself outdoors. He will probably eliminate on walks as well, but he should have a set place on your property where you take him when you don't have time for a stroll. While you are housetraining, taking him to the same spot every time can help trigger elimination. Dogs have incredibly sensitive noses, and they are more likely to relieve themselves in a spot where they have previously done so.

If one of your doors serves as a primary entrance and exit to your home, it may surprise you to know that it will actually help your dog with housetraining. If you routinely use more than one door, make a concerted effort to use just one when your dog is with you. You might even consider hanging a noisemaking device, such as a cowbell, near this door or on the doorknob. Each time you head to your pet's potty spot, stop and ring the bell—doing so can help teach your dog to ring the bell when he needs to go outside, and rewarding this behavior will encourage him to repeat it. As much as schedules help with housetraining, nothing is as valuable as a well-trained dog who has learned to communicate his needs.

One of the most common mistakes new pet owners make is allowing a new puppy to sleep with them in their bed for the first few nights if they don't want this to become a habit. I personally see nothing wrong with cosleeping, providing the bed isn't so high that a dog can get hurt climbing up or jumping down. And even then, a simple set of doggy stairs easily solves this potential problem. There is nothing wrong with not wanting to cosleep, either. You simply must make up your mind before your pet's arrival so you don't send him mixed messages.

Other boundaries are far less open to personal preference. One of them is biting. Puppies need to chew. Much like human toddlers, most pups will put almost anything in their mouths. Teaching a dog the Leave It and Drop It commands, as well as keeping potentially dangerous items out of your pet's reach, will help prevent inappropriate chewing. Still, many teething pups will try to gnaw on whatever is nearby. If your pup bites your hand or any other body part—even in play—you must stop him immediately.

Allowing a puppy to chew on your finger may seem harmless, but it actually teaches him that it is acceptable for him to place his teeth on human flesh. If your pup starts biting, say the word "no" as you offer him a toy instead. When he takes the toy, praise him immediately. You must let everyone who lives in or visits your home know that any type of biting is not allowed so that no one inadvertently allows your pet to cross this nonnegotiable boundary.

Dog-Safe Areas

Even after you have thoroughly puppy-proofed your home, you may want to limit your new pet's access to a smaller area until he is reliably housetrained and past the teething phase. Choking hazards and poisonous plants, for instance, can be moved out of your puppy's reach, but you won't be able to relocate your wall-to-wall carpeting or large pieces of furniture. To protect these and other immobile items, set up at least a couple of dog-safe areas (other than his crate) for your new pet.

A puppy in the midst of housetraining is bound to have accidents, even when his owners are in the room. This reality makes a kitchen or other tiled room a perfect area for your pet during his first few days and weeks at home. No one enjoys cleaning up a potty accident, but it's undoubtedly easier if it happens on a hard floor rather than on a carpet.

Safety gates can be invaluable for creating dog-safe areas, but gates aren't always usable in homes with open floor plans. In this situation, an "ex-pen" (short for exercise pen) works especially well. Some owners like to situate the ex-pen around the puppy's crate; this type of setup gives the pup a safe place to eat and play—and to rest when he is tired.

Location, Location, Location

Dog ownership isn't limited to people who own sprawling farms or other expansive properties in the country. Owners can also make excellent homes for dogs in the busiest cities, providing the owners know how to fulfill their pets' needs in an urban environment. Likewise, suburbanites can provide wonderful homes for dogs. Each of these settings offers its own unique set of circumstances.

City Dwellers

Bringing a dog home to an apartment or other home in the city isn't much different from introducing him to any other type of dwelling. Once you venture outside with your new pet, though, you will notice certain challenges almost immediately, the most noticeable being the number of people you encounter. Crowded sidewalks make it necessary to teach your dog to walk politely on a leash right away. On the bright side, all of the people—and likely some pets, as well—will make socializing your pet much easier. Just walking a dog in a city is in itself a social experience.

Initially, some dogs may be intimidated by the many sounds of city life. Blaring car horns, rumbling subway trains, and beeping signs that tell pedestrians when it is safe to cross the street are just a few of the noises that your new pet will hear. Most dogs just need some time to adjust to the hustle and bustle. Puppies are often the quickest to acclimate to city life because everything is new to young dogs anyway. A puppy will likely accept the commotion as just another facet of his new home. A rescued animal from a different type of living environment may take more time to adjust, but your patience and training will help.

Find out where the nearest public park that allows dogs is located before bringing your new pet home. This will be your go-to area for walks and outdoor playtime. Many cities also have dog parks or off-leash areas within larger parks, created specifically for canine exercise and socialization. While dog parks can be a lifesaver for responsible pet owners in cities, always use caution when visiting. Only friendly animals should be taken to dog parks, but you have no way of knowing if other owners are respecting this important protocol.

Cleaning up after your dog is necessary no matter where you live, but you will need to dispose of your pet's solid waste immediately when walking him in public. Nearly all cities have pooper-scooper laws to keep the streets as clean as possible. You needn't carry an actual poop-scoop for this purpose; clean-up bags or plastic grocery-store bags work just as well and are much easier to transport. Even living in the suburbs, I keep clean-up bags in the pockets of all my jackets so I am never caught unprepared.

While some cities are remarkably clean, you will surely encounter some litter or other debris on the sidewalks where you walk your pet. The Leave It and Drop It commands are

Dogs of all sizes can adjust to city living when given adequate activity.

invaluable in these situations. Preventing your dog from picking up just one discarded cigarette butt or piece of chewed gum will make the minimal amount of effort that teaching these commands requires well worth it.

Country Dogs

Dogs and rural settings may seem like they go hand in hand, but country living, too, comes with its share of challenges—the most obvious being the wildlife that your dog may encounter in this setting. Depending on where you live, a range of animals—from deer to raccoons to bears or even alligators—may venture onto your property when you least expect it. For this reason, it is important to supervise your pet when he spends time outdoors.

Although I live far from the country myself, my backyard abuts a heavily wooded area. For this reason, I am very cautious when taking my dogs outdoors at night. I always bring a flashlight with me on nighttime walks, and I always turn on the light in my fenced-in yard before letting my dogs out after dark.

Space to run is one of the biggest advantages of living in the country. Leash laws may not be a concern in a rural area, but owners must understand that their dog must be taught to come when called before they can trust him off lead. You cannot simply bring a puppy home and assume that he knows that he isn't supposed to run off when an enticing sound or smell beckons. Dogs become lost every day because owners take for granted that their dogs won't run away. In a rural setting, wild animals often find and kill these innocent pets. Fences can help prevent this tragedy.

Country dogs are likely to meet a lot of different friends.

Suburbanites

Living in the suburbs offers pet owners the best—and sometimes the worst—of both worlds. Suburban dogs have plenty of opportunities for socialization and considerably more space than city dogs, but they can also be subjected to many of the same dangers as pets in both the city and country. Dogs escape their homes in suburban neighborhoods every day, either by slipping out doors or being allowed off leash without proper training. With cars around every corner, these pets face additional risks to their lives. As society encroaches on wildlife more and more, pets in the suburbs can also come face to face with dangerous animals.

I have seen a surprising variety of wildlife in my peaceful neighborhood over the years. As an animal lover, I often delight in watching dozens of blue jays fill the trees outside the sunroom on the back of my house. One afternoon, as I was preparing to leave my driveway, a large red fox appeared from those same woods on my side lawn. I sat quietly in my vehicle,

Suburban dog owners can have plenty of fun right in their own backyards.

both mesmerized and a bit shaken by the encounter. After pausing for a moment, he darted across the street into a neighbor's yard. Although I never saw what it was, he was clearly chasing something. I remember hoping that my neighbor's kitty was an indoor cat.

Many dangers in suburban homes can be prevented with a little forethought. Garages are often filled with chemicals that are toxic to pets, so keeping your dog out of your garage will help keep him safe. If your home has a deck, be sure that your dog cannot slip through the railings and fall. Similarly, if you have a pool, make sure that your new pet does not have access to this area without supervision.

Your Puppy's First Year: Developmental Stages

Like a human baby, a puppy goes through several developmental stages during his first year of life. Two of these stages will already be behind your pup when he comes home with you. For his first two weeks, your pup was completely dependent on his mother. A newborn pup has only two senses—touch and taste—and they are essentially his whole world during this period, called the neonatal stage. The mother dog nurses her pups and cleans them meticulously during this time. Without her, the pups would be unlikely to survive.

The transitional stage begins at the end of these two weeks and lasts until the pups are about four weeks old. As its name implies, this period is all about change. This is when your dog opened his eyes and began hearing and smelling the world around him. Pups in the transitional phase continue to rely on their mother for nourishment and care, but they also become more aware of their siblings and their own physical independence. They stand, take their first steps,

Teething

When you bring your new puppy home, he will have twenty-eight astonishingly sharp teeth. Around the age of four months, though, he will start losing these teeth, and permanent pearly whites will replace them as this happens. You probably won't notice when your pup has a loose tooth. More likely, you will find the tooth after it has fallen out, but you probably won't find all of them. Between six and eight months of age, your dog's molars will come in, bringing his new total to forty-two.

Teething can be just as painful for a puppy as it is for a human infant, and you can take a page from the child-care guides when it comes to this problem. When babies teethe, parents offer them teething rings, and you can find similar toys for teething puppies at your local pet-supply store or online. Often, these comfort items can be placed in the freezer beforehand to make them especially soothing to sore gums.

and discover that they can bark. Their vision is relatively poor at first but is fully developed by the time the pups head into the next stage.

The socialization stage is one of the most influential periods of a dog's life. Overlapping with the end of the transitional stage, this stage begins at the age of three weeks and lasts until the pup is twelve weeks old. Instead of merely becoming aware of the world around him, a puppy in this stage can start interacting with other pets and people and benefitting from these experiences; these early encounters lay the foundation for his future social skills.

One of a young puppy's most important means of interaction is play, through which he learns basic boundaries and consequences. *If I bite my sister, she might bite me back.* He also learns to overcome basic fears. *Hey, that big round object isn't as scary as it looks. It is even fun to play with when I roll it.*

The socialization stage is also a time of ongoing physical and mental development. Pups become more coordinated in their movements during this period. Their early relationships with people also make it possible for the pups to begin simple training. Many breeders will start the housetraining process during this

Puppies learn a lot about play and social behavior during their time with their littermates.

Newborn puppies don't open their eyes until one or two weeks after birth.

time. Some even teach their pups to sit for treats. You can then pick up where the breeder left off when you bring your new pet home.

The ranking stage is the first stage your puppy will enter after joining your family. During this period, which lasts from your dog's third month to his sixth month, he will begin to understand the hierarchy in your home. Owners must walk a careful line during this stage. A puppy this age is highly impressionable. While it is important for him to understand that you are the boss, it is also essential that you help him overcome any new fears and provide him with plenty of positive reinforcement to bolster his confidence and encourage good behavior. A pup is also most prone to engage in inappropriate chewing during this stage, so providing your pet with plenty of safe chew toys is a must.

The adolescent stage begins where the ranking stage leaves off, but it can last far beyond your dog's first birthday. The rate at which a pup matures differs dramatically between breeds. Owners often describe larger breeds, such as the German Shepherd Dog, Greater Swiss Mountain Dog, and Labrador Retriever, as "puppylike" for the first few years of their lives. Smaller breeds, like the Lhasa Apso and Miniature Schnauzer, tend to mature more quickly. However, even members of the same breed can take vastly different amounts of time to reach maturity.

Your dog is much like a human teenager during his adolescent stage. He may challenge your rules, try to venture out on his own more often, and make mistakes. The good news is that you and the other people and animals in your home will be his biggest influences throughout his adolescence. If you remain committed to training and caring for him, he will leave this stage a pleasant, reliable companion.

CHAPTER 4

SOCIALIZING YOUR DOG

Socializing your dog is one of the most important, yet one of the easiest, training tasks you will undertake as a pet owner. People feel more comfortable around dogs who are friendly and at ease in social situations, and socializing also benefits the animals in myriad ways. A well-socialized dog will experience less anxiety and stress when he encounters new people, animals, or situations. The best way to start socializing your dog is simply by introducing him to the people and dogs you come into contact with each day.

Introducing Your Dog to Adults

You may think that stopping briefly to say hello to neighbors while walking your dog is a small act, but, to your dog, these greetings are ripe with social opportunity. Encourage your friends to speak to your pet and offer him small rewards for his good behavior. Carry bite-sized treats on your walks specifically for this purpose.

Make sure that strangers approach your dog gently.

Make sure that no one inadvertently rewards your dog for poor manners. If your pet indulges in boisterous behavior, such as barking or jumping, rewards will only reinforce these actions. Many dog lovers might be quick to tell you that they don't mind your dog's exuberance, but remember that proper socialization means teaching your dog polite behavior. Tolerating or dismissing rowdy behavior will only do your dog a disservice. People can, however, offer praise and treats as soon as your dog stops behaving badly. In fact, after just a little training, most dogs quickly learn to sit when they see a treat.

Interacting with people of all ages is essential to a dog's socialization.

It is also important that you use a certain amount of discretion when socializing your pet. Do not ask someone who doesn't like dogs or is fearful of them to help you socialize your dog. In addition to making the person uncomfortable, you won't be doing your dog any favors by forcing him on someone who is uneasy around dogs. Animals are deeply intuitive beings; they can sense discomfort and may react negatively to it. Unless you are certain that a person is open to interacting with your pet, always ask before you approach him or her with your dog. Rest assured that you will encounter many people who are willing to say hello to your new pet. Some may even ask you first if it is OK to pet your dog.

Introducing Your Dog to Kids

Kids and dogs seem to go together like peanut butter and jelly, but you must use caution when socializing your dog to children. The younger the child is, the more cautious you must be. Larger dogs, even the friendliest ones, can injure a small child without meaning to.

Kids often display their excitement over seeing a dog by running up to the animal immediately. Some kids may also be too young or inexperienced with pets to know how to treat them respectfully. Part of your job as a dog owner is protecting your pet in these kinds of situation. A dog may become frightened if a person of any age approaches him too quickly. He might also growl or even bite if a toddler pulls on his ears or tail.

This doesn't mean that your dog shouldn't be socialized to children; rather, it means that everyone involved in the process must remain vigilant. Especially if there are no kids in your

Don't Share!

Be careful that a child doesn't share food with your dog without your knowledge or permission. Chocolate, one of the most popular treats among kids, is toxic to dogs. A sugar-free sweetener called xylitol has become an especially common ingredient in children's snacks in recent years. Unfortunately, xylitol can trigger a sudden release of insulin in dogs, which can cause hypoglycemia. The best way to avoid these problems is not allowing your dog to interact with kids until they are done eating.

household, your dog may not know how to react to a child the first time he sees one. Some dogs seem to understand that kids are simply younger people, but other dogs need more time to learn how to interact with these energetic new friends.

Most pet-supply stores welcome friendly, leashed pets.

Meeting Other Dogs in Your Home

If a friend asks to bring his or her dog to your home, consider the visit a valuable opportunity to socialize your pet. This doesn't mean that you should agree in all situations, however. Have you met the dog yourself? Is he reliably trained? Is your friend a responsible pet owner who will help you make the interaction a safe and positive one? Ideally, the answers to all three questions will be *yes*, but there may be some gray areas here, too. Puppy playdates can be a great way to socialize young dogs, so a lack of training or familiarity with the animal isn't as important as the answer to the last question.

While every dog is different, certain breeds tend to be more gregarious than others. Border Terriers, Pembroke Welsh Corgis, and Shetland Sheepdogs are among the breeds known for getting along well with other dogs. Basenjis, Chow Chows, and Shiba Inu tend to be more aloof with other dogs. This isn't to say that a Chow Chow will instigate a fight—or that a Border

Introducing Your Dog to Your New Baby

When I was pregnant with my son, I worried that my dog, Jonathan, would feel hurt when the new baby arrived. Up until then, after all, Johnny had essentially been the baby of the household. He hadn't had to share his time with my husband and me with anyone, least of all with a little person who required 'round-the-clock care. Although Jonathan had always been friendly when children approached him, he had only seen a baby a few times. What would I do if he saw my new son as a rival?

Concerns like the ones I felt are typical among expecting parents who are also pet owners. In extreme cases, these concerns even turn to panic, leading some people to consider rehoming their dogs before their babies' births. While the pet owners in these scenarios may think they are simply acting like responsible parents, they are definitely putting the cart before the horse. Most dogs deal with the arrival of an infant quite well.

Parents-to-be can certainly take some proactive steps to help ensure that things go as smoothly as possible, however. One of the easiest things you can do to give your dog a heads-up is introduce him to your baby's scent prior to the baby's homecoming. Have someone take a piece of the baby's clothing or a burp rag from the hospital home, where your dog can sniff it under controlled circumstances.

Shortly before you bring your baby home for the first time, have someone take your dog for a long walk to help him burn off excess energy. Who holds the baby during the introduction is less important than the person's emotional state at the time. If you are overly worried, your anxiety may influence your dog's reaction. Allow the dog to see and sniff the infant from a reasonable distance. You can let him come closer gradually over the next few days or as you feel more comfortable.

Oh, and if you are wondering how I made out with Johnny, he never did display any jealous behavior with my son. On the contrary, he enjoyed helping me care for my new baby. When Alec would wake up crying at 2 a.m., Jonathan would accompany me to the nursery and sit dutifully by my side until the middle-of-the-night feeding was complete.

From first meeting to playmates to all smiles!

Terrier won't—but it can be helpful to know a bit about a breed's characteristics before planning a playdate.

Just as you may have introduced your dog to other pets in your own household on neutral territory, this approach is often the best one for welcoming a new canine guest. Even if you aren't worried about your dog's reaction to the other pet, he may better accept the new animal as an equal if they meet outside your home before heading inside. And always keep both dogs leashed until they demonstrate friendly behavior toward each other.

Don't worry if the dogs tussle a bit at this time. A small amount of roughhousing is normal among pups, but do watch out for signs of impending aggressive behavior. This can manifest itself in the form of a stiff posture, a fixed gaze, or prolonged growling. If either dog behaves in any of these ways, separate them at once. You can try again after the dogs have had a chance to calm down, but if the negative reaction continues, it is probably better to cut the visit short.

Meeting Other Pets in Your Home

Owners of other kinds of pets usually don't take their animals for outings as often as dog owners do, but certain circumstances may bring your dog under the same roof with a member of a different animal species occasionally. Perhaps a friend with a cat needs a place to stay for a night or two, or maybe your daughter has volunteered to care for the class guinea pig over school vacation. Whatever the details, the most important thing is the safety of all creatures involved. With a little planning, however, this, too, can serve as a great socialization exercise for your pet.

The old stereotype about dogs naturally hating cats is usually just that, an oversimplified—and often untrue—image that needs to be dispelled. The Beagle, Golden Retriever, and English Setter are just a few dog breeds that typically adore cats. A few breeds, though, do have deeply ingrained predatory instincts: Alaskan Malamutes, Norwegian Elkhounds, and Bedlington Terriers need careful supervision around cats and other small animals for this reason. Some breeds, like the Plott and Whippet, can cohabitate with a cat if the dog is raised with the feline, but these same dogs may still act out if a strange cat comes into the household.

In many cases, a cat will tolerate an enthusiastic canine's advances.

Always use caution when introducing your dog to any animal, but be especially careful when there is a considerable size difference. Sometimes, though, size is far less important than prey drive. The terrier group includes dogs of all sizes—from the tiny Yorkshire Terrier to the gigantic Airedale Terrier, and nearly every one of these dogs will hunt a rodent if given the opportunity. While you may view your gerbil or hamster as a beloved family member, a terrier is unlikely to overcome his urge to hunt these pocket-sized pets. For safety's sake, it is best to keep small animals out of your home if you own a terrier breed.

Meeting Other Dogs in Public

Taking your dog to public places, like the pet-supply store, is an excellent way to work on his social skills. Virtually everyone you'll encounter at such a dog-friendly business enjoys the company of animals. This doesn't mean that you should allow your dog to approach every

You never know how a dog will react to small furry creatures, so supervision is necessary.

Bringing your dog along is part of the fun at some cafes and restaurants with outdoor seating.

person or animal he sees, though. You should be just as respectful of others' space in these public places as you would be anywhere else.

If you do take your dog to the pet-supply store, ask if the business offers puppy playtimes. These informal get-togethers are another practical way to help your dog meet new people and animals. Unlike training classes, which focus on teaching commands, these fun sessions simply allow young dogs and their owners a chance to spend time together in a relaxed setting. If you enjoy the experience, though, you might consider enrolling in a puppy kindergarten class as well. While puppy kindergarten includes basic training, socialization is the biggest emphasis for this introductory course.

Always ask before entering an establishment if you aren't certain whether it allows dogs. Some libraries, for instance, allow well-behaved pets, but others have strict no-pet policies. One of my favorite places to take a dog is a seasonal seafood restaurant where I live in Maine. In addition to the indoor seating, it offers its guests dozens of picnic tables spread across its sizable lawn. The tables are far enough apart that I know my dog won't make anyone feel uncomfortable, but whichever dog I take along inevitably makes a new friend while we are there.

It's very likely that your dog will encounter other pets at the veterinarian's clinic. A veterinary appointment can serve as a wonderful yardstick for measuring your dog's social progress. He will see healthy dogs who are at the vet's office with their owners for well visits, and he may also see dogs who are feeling under the weather. The veterinary hospital might

Dog Parks

A dog park can be an ideal setting for your pet to meet and play with other dogs. When owners take untrained or unreliable animals to these locations, though, a dog park can also be a dangerous place for both people and pets. For this reason, owners should always keep their wits about them when visiting a dog park. Most importantly, watch your dog for any signs that he is uncomfortable or frightened.

Always read a park's rules thoroughly before entering. In addition to following this protocol, owners should use common sense. Balls and flying discs can be fun toys for a dog park, but avoid taking any item that your dog is inclined to guard. Likewise, edible treats should be dispensed with great care because they, too, might trigger a protective reaction if other dogs are nearby. If you notice an aggressive animal or feel that the dog park is too crowded, leave and return another time.

An owner should never take a dog younger than four months to a dog park, and it's preferable to wait a little longer. The final booster shot of a puppy's vaccination series is usually administered around four months, and it then takes another couple of weeks before the pup reaches optimal immunity. While owners should only bring healthy animals to a park, you have no way of knowing if a sick pet has visited the space. It only takes one dog with an illness such as parvovirus to pass it on to any animal still vulnerable to this potentially deadly disease.

You would never allow another dog to bully or hurt your pet in any way. Likewise, you have a responsibility to leave a dog park at once if your own dog is acting aggressively toward others. While dogs might play by barking at or chasing one another, it is essential that owners interrupt play that becomes too rough. Often, all that is needed is a little redirection, but if that doesn't solve the problem, call it a day.

even be the first place your dog runs into a cat. He needn't get up close and personal with any of these animals—in fact, it is better that he doesn't, unless the other animal is both healthy and friendly. If your dog behaves properly despite the variety of distractions, however, it is a great indication that he is on the right track with socialization.

Be an Ideal Guest

Inviting dog-owning friends to your home with their pets can be a fun way to socialize your dog. Likewise, you and your pet may be on the receiving end of a similar invitation. This, too, is a terrific opportunity for socialization. If your friend has a dog, don't assume that the resident dog will be as excited about the visit as you might be. Ask if the dog has had other canine company before. If he has, your dog's arrival may not cause any problems, but just to be safe, you may want to propose introducing the two animals in a neutral setting first.

Keep your dog on his leash until you are confident that the two animals are getting along well. The resident animal is usually the more likely to act out, but this isn't always the case.

You will also want to keep an eye on your pet even after the dogs have appeared to accept each other. You are always responsible for your dog's behavior.

Don't be surprised if your dog follows you around at your friend's home. If this is his first time paying someone a visit, the experience will be a new one. Staying close to you may help him remain confident during the visit, but do encourage him to interact with your friend and any other people who are present as well.

Introductions to New Experiences

Socialization isn't just about introducing your dog to people and other animals. You should also expose your dog to a variety of sights, smells, noises, and surfaces. Many experiences, such as walking your dog on the beach, will stimulate all of his senses.

You may choose to take your dog to many different places, but it is smart to socialize him the most to the ones he will be visiting often. For example, if you take your dog with you to your child's baseball or soccer games, make a point of walking him up and down the bleachers. Aluminum bleachers in particular can be noisy—and scary—for dogs, but you can head off fear by exposing him to the stands in a positive way. He will likely enjoy the experience even more if you ask a fellow spectator to offer him a treat while you are there.

If you feed your dog from a stainless steel bowl, you can use this simple item to prevent him from developing a fear of loud noises at home. Inevitably, you will drop his bowl or another item on your kitchen floor. Making a point of doing so early on will expose your dog to the noise, so he doesn't panic when it happens by accident. Some dog trainers even use this technique as a way to teach dogs to deal with distractions when their owners instruct them to sit and stay. You can adjust the exercise to include any sounds your dog may hear regularly at home, such as the alarm clock, doorbell, or vacuum cleaner. The greater the variety of experiences your dog has at a young age, the less likely he will be to fear those same things as an adult.

There's plenty for dogs to experience at the beach.

PART II

EVERYDAY CARE

CHAPTER 5

FEEDING
YOUR DOG

Providing your dog with sound nutrition is one of the most important things you can do for his health and well-being. Dog foods have come a long way in recent decades—from just a few brands sold at supermarkets to a wide range of specialty diets sold exclusively at pet-supply stores. Certain foods are even available by prescription only through veterinarians. Some owners opt to prepare their dogs' food themselves instead of buying prepackaged formulas.

There is no such thing as one perfect food for all dogs. Two different animals may have vastly different nutritional requirements. Age, activity level, and health conditions can all play a part in determining what type of food is best for your pet. You may even find that several different options can fulfill your pet's needs.

Although the choices may seem endless, having numerous options can be a lifesaver for many pet owners. Some dogs develop allergies to certain ingredients, for instance, making a dietary change necessary. You might end up switching to a new food as a means of providing your dog with some variety. Or you may not think your pet is thriving on his current food. Choices come in handy in all these situations.

Puppy formulas are designed to promote healthy growth.

Commercial Food Varieties

Commercial pet food is by the far the most popular choice among dog owners. The most obvious advantage of this type of diet is the convenience it offers. Pet owners can simply open a package and serve the ready-to-eat contents to their animals—no muss, no fuss. An even more important benefit of a good-quality commercial food is that it is specifically formulated to offer your dog an ideal balance of nutrients. An adult dog food is designed to maintain your dog at a healthy weight and provide balanced nutrition, and there are specialized food varieties for other life stages and situations, too; the types that follow represent some of the more common variations.

With the wide selection of foods available, how will you choose?

Puppy Formulas

Puppy food differs from adult-dog food in several important ways. Because they are still growing, puppies need more protein than they will as adult dogs. Protein is responsible for growing and repairing your pup's body tissue. It also plays an important role in bolstering his immune system. For this reason, most puppy-food formulas are made up of between 25 and 30 percent protein. Puppy food also contains more fat than adult food; a good puppy food will offer between 10 and 25 percent fat.

In addition to offering your pup more of the nutrients he needs most, some dry puppy food formulas—usually called "small breed" or "small bite"—come in smaller pieces. Toy breeds, such as the Affenpinscher and the Manchester Terrier, have an easier time eating these tiny pieces of kibble made specifically for smaller pups like them.

Smaller breeds reach their adult size earlier than larger dogs do. In most cases, small and medium pups reach their adult size between nine and twelve months of age, at which point owners can transition them to adult food. It takes larger breeds, like the Bearded Collie and the Giant Schnauzer, much longer to reach full size. Some large breeds don't reach their adult size until they are two years of age. They, too, need to eat puppy food until they reach their adult size, but owners need to be careful not to feed their larger breeds too many calories. Large-breed puppy formulas are made with the right balance of nutrients and calories to promote proper growth. Growing too quickly can create orthopedic problems, so foods designed specifically for large breeds contain fewer calories and a fat content of just 8 to 12 percent.

Senior Formulas

As a dog gets older, his metabolism will begin slowing down. Even dogs who have been slim most of their lives may start gaining weight more easily as they enter their senior years. Most dogs are considered seniors when they enter the final third of their projected life span, but the age at which this happens can vary greatly according to a dog's breed or size.

Smaller breeds, such as the Chihuahua and Pomeranian, typically live longer than larger ones. My great-grandmother owned a Toy Fox Terrier who lived to the ripe old age of nineteen. A few toy breeds have even been known to make it into their twenties, but a more realistic lifespan is around fifteen years. With proper care, larger breeds often live from eight to twelve years or longer. Feeding a healthy diet is the best way to help any breed of dog make it to the far side of his life expectancy.

As with people, another common side effect of aging in the canine species is arthritis. Although this orthopedic condition can strike any dog, it is most common in overweight dogs. A specialized senior diet can help with both of these problems. Senior dog foods contain fewer calories than adult formulas, and many also contain glucosamine, chondroitin, and methylsulfonylmethane (MSM), compounds that have been shown to help relieve the pain and stiffness of arthritis. It should be noted, though, that the amounts added to most food formulas are negligible, so you may want to ask your veterinarian about adding these supplements to your older dog's diet to get the highest possible benefit from them.

The amount of protein that older dogs need has become a highly debated topic. For many years, veterinarians recommended lowering the protein content of a dog's food once he enters his senior years. The reason behind this was that many commercial dog foods contain rendered protein. Rendering is a process that separates fat from the meat and bone. Rendered protein becomes difficult for dogs to process as they age, and a food high in rendered protein can even lead to liver or kidney damage over time. While it makes sense to avoid rendered protein in general, it is especially important

In addition to a graying muzzle, your senior dog's activity level may decrease.

to avoid it if your dog is a senior. If a food label includes the terms "meat meal" or "bone meal" on the ingredient list, this means that the food contains rendered protein.

Some dog food companies have reduced the amounts of protein in their senior formulas to lessen a senior dog's rendered protein intake, but many canine nutritionists contend that avoiding rendered protein in all dog food formulas is a better strategy. An adult dog's need for protein doesn't change as he gets older, and the best senior dog food formulas contain the same levels of protein but more fiber and fewer calories than adult formulas. Added fiber will help your dog avoid constipation, another common side effect of the aging process.

Whether in organized activities or backyard sports, active dogs need food to fuel them.

Just as there is no single food that is right for every dog, you won't find one senior formula that is ideal for every older dog. If your dog has remained active, his weight may not be a concern as he ages. Likewise, if your dog has no issues with constipation, he may not need added fiber in his diet. In fact, too much fiber can block your dog's absorption of certain nutrients. No rule states that you must transition your dog to a senior formula at any age. Foods geared toward the most common needs of senior animals are just among your many options if you own an older dog.

Formulas for Active Dogs

If your dog joins you regularly in physically demanding pastimes such as running or hiking—or even if he just plays vigorously and enjoys especially long walks—it may be a good idea to feed him a food formulated for active animals. Dogs who participate in organized activities, such as agility, dock jumping, or flyball, can also benefit from the extra protein and calories offered by these foods.

The most important thing to remember when considering a food made for active pets is that it must contain complete and balanced nutrition. Companies that simply up the fat and rely on by-products to increase protein levels aren't worth your time—these are the canine equivalents of fast food. Athletes, even the four-legged kind, need to eat nutrient-dense foods that provide their bodies with the energy they require.

If you notice that your dog is putting on weight from eating an active-formula food, it may be time to switch back to a healthy regular food. You can also use an active formula only during the times when your dog is most active—in the summer months, for example. If your long walks tend to be cut short when the temperatures drop, switch back to a regular food during the cooler months. What matters most is that your dog gets the extra calories when he needs them but not when he doesn't.

Prescription Formulas

If your dog ever suffers from a serious health issue, such as diabetes or kidney disease, your veterinarian may suggest placing your pet on a prescription diet. The advantage of these food formulas, which are available exclusively through veterinarians, is that they offer the limited or specific ingredients that dogs with certain health conditions require until their health improves. Some dogs must even stay on specialized feeding regimens long-term.

Like low-protein senior formulas, prescription diets have their share of critics. At one time, only a single dog food company provided vets with medical diets, but several manufacturers have since added products to this market. As with foods sold in pet-supply stores, prescription diets can vary in quality dramatically. Always read the label of your dog's food thoroughly, paying special attention to the ingredients list. By-products, chemical preservatives, and filler ingredients are all warning signs that a food isn't as healthy as it should be. If you're not happy with the quality of a veterinarian-recommended food, ask your vet about cooking for your pet instead. Your vet should be able to help guide you in this increasingly common feeding choice.

Consult your veterinarian before making changes to your dog's diet.

Types of Food

Once you have narrowed down your choices of dog food brands and you have an idea of what kind of formula you wish to feed your pet, the next step is deciding between canned food, dry food, and moist food.

Canned Food

Even finicky dogs will usually gobble up canned, or "wet," food. Its enticing aroma can be intensified if you heat the food up before serving it to your pet. Canned fare also has some clear nutritional advantages. First, wet food typically contains more meat-based protein and fewer carbohydrates than dry food. Second, canned food also doesn't need preservatives because the canning process creates an airtight seal. Additionally, dogs

Choose a quality food suitable to your dog's age and size.

likely appreciate the taste of canned food because its ingredients—particularly the meats it contains—are closer to their natural state than those found in kibble.

Older dogs, in particular, may appreciate canned food because it is kinder to pets with dental problems, such as missing teeth. Your dog may also do better on canned food if he needs to lose weight. The calorie content of a wet food may be comparable to that of a dry food, but the higher water content of wet food can help your dog feel fuller because the same amount of nutrients take up more space in liquid form.

The biggest disadvantage to canned food is that it can contribute to dental problems if owners aren't meticulous about brushing their dogs' teeth. A dog eating canned food needs his teeth brushed daily. Wet food particles can accumulate surprisingly quickly in a dog's mouth, increasing his risk for periodontal disease. This is especially true of toy breeds, who are prone to dental problems due to crowding in their smaller mouths. However, opting against canned food won't get you out of brushing your dog's teeth. All dogs need regular dental care—wet food just seems to morph into plaque and tartar more quickly.

Canned food is a bit more expensive than dry dog food, but it can be stored for longer periods of time before going bad. Once a can is opened, however, its contents need to be eaten rather quickly. Your dog's wet food should be thrown away if it sits uneaten for more than four hours, and the bowl needs to be cleaned before his next feeding. Depending on the

Variety, convenience, and affordability make dry dog food the most popular choice with owners.

brand and formula you choose, you may be able to cover and refrigerate leftovers for up to a week. Another option is freezing leftover canned food in meal-sized portions that you can thaw as needed.

Dry Food

Dry food is by far the most popular variety among dog owners for numerous reasons. While kibble's shelf life cannot match that of an unopened can, a large bag of dry dog food will usually last long enough for even a small breed to finish it. When you consider how much money you can save by feeding kibble, it is easy to understand why you see so many dog owners walking out of the local pet-supply store with bags on their shoulders.

Among kibble's biggest liabilities are the nutrients lost during its cooking process. The heat and pressure involved in manufacturing those crunchy bites also rob the food of many vitamins and minerals. Dog food companies compensate for this unavoidable loss by adding synthetic nutrients back into the food.

A bowl of dry food won't spoil quickly even during the hottest months of the year, but larger amounts of kibble must be stored in a sealed container for several important reasons. First, air can cause dry food to go stale over time. High temperatures, humidity, and direct sunlight will also shorten the shelf life of kibble. Living in New England, I store my dogs' food in the mudroom between my house and my attached garage for three seasons out of the year. Before the summer months begin, however, I move the food containers inside, where the air conditioning will keep them reasonably cool even when the outside temperature soars.

Another reason to transfer dry dog food from its bag into an airtight container is to keep pests, such as ants and moths, from infiltrating your pet's kibble. Just because a container has a lid does not mean that it is airtight. Look for a seal around the inside of the cover or opening to make sure that no air, moisture, or critters can make their way inside. Use all of the food in the container before adding more, and clean the container thoroughly first. And always save the UPC barcode and expiration date from the food package until your dog has finished the food in case of a recall.

Moist Food

There are different types of moist dog food, which owners might see as a compromise between canned food and kibble. One type, which is sold in pouches and made to look like chunks of meat in gravy, has so much salt and sugar that it is not recommended for regular feeding.

Another popular type, sold in rolls that resemble sausages, is a tasty and healthier alternative to add some variety to your dog's diet. Since its moisture content is lower than that of canned fare, this option is slightly kinder to your dog's dental health.

If your senior dog has any loose or missing teeth, pieces of dog-food rolls will be easier for him to chew than kibble. Swapping to a softer food can be especially important following a dental cleaning if your veterinarian had to extract any of your dog's teeth. Your pet's gums will be sore for a few days, and he may have a harder time crunching through dry food in the long term as well, although some dogs with just a few teeth seem to manage kibble just fine. Moist or canned food can also help revitalize the appetite of an older, finicky eater.

I find that moist food serves as a valuable resource for training. Some trainers advise owners to use food from their dogs' regular meals as rewards during training so as not to exceed the animals' daily calorie limit with training treats. Many trainers also recommend using high-value treats for training. The premise here is that human foods, such as bite-sized pieces of chicken or steak, work especially well for capturing a dog's attention and inspiring him to work as hard as possible during a training session. I buy smaller rolls of moist food specifically for training time because they are extremely easy to cut into small pieces, and, because they are so soft, the pieces don't distract my dogs from their training as much as crunchier training treats, which take longer to chew.

Like canned food, dog-food rolls offer a long shelf life until they are opened, but they, too, must be eaten quickly afterward to avoid spoilage. Pound for pound, moist food tends

Certain types of moist food, while very palatable to dogs, are not the most nutritious choice.

to be more expensive than kibble. If cost is a concern, you can always use dog-food rolls as supplements to your dog's dry diet. My dogs definitely appreciate eating this type of moist food as a special treat.

What to Look for on Food Labels

Reading a dog-food label can be a bit confusing at first. After all, the nutrition labels on pet foods look a lot different than the ones printed on human products. The label on your dog's food is required by law to list the ingredients in descending order. This means that the first ingredient listed is the most prevalent. For example, if the ingredient list begins with duck, there is more duck, pound for pound, in the food than any of the other ingredients listed. The second ingredient listed is the second most prevalent, and so on down the list.

It is important to understand that the weight of an ingredient does not necessarily equal its nutritional presence. Take that duck, for example. Raw poultry has a high water content, so typically about 80 percent of this type of meat is actually water. A common second ingredient in many dog foods is meat meal. If the word "duck" is immediately followed by "duck meal" on your food label, then the next most prevalent ingredient is this duck concentrate, which is a product of rendering. Duck meal usually has about 300 percent more protein than raw duck.

Debates about the nutritional value of meat meals are common. Many canine nutritionists equate the nutritional benefits of meat meal to that of protein powder—this is essentially what meat meal is. The highest quality meat meals can increase a food's protein levels in a healthy way, but lower quality sources, such as those derived from meat by-products, are a different

Many dogs aren't picky about what they eat, so dog owners have to be.

AAFCO Guarantee

With all of the pet food brands available today, narrowing the choices down to the healthiest options can be a lengthy undertaking. Nearly every dog food brand seems to claim that it is the best choice in one way or another, but what do terms like "clinically proven" and "human grade" actually mean? And how do you know that the claims on the outside of the package are backed up by the ingredients on the inside?

Certain words and phrases are regulated by the Association of American Feed Control Officials (AAFCO). This organization oversees the sale and distribution of food and medications for animals. A label stating that a food is "all-natural" indicates that the ingredients all come from plant, animal, or mined sources. Nothing else, such as artificial preservatives, has been added to the product. A food containing natural ingredients can end up being a healthy option, but it is important to note that an all-natural food can also be highly processed. It can be subjected to rendering or extraction, for example, and still legally be labeled as all-natural.

The AAFCO does not regulate the use of the word "organic" on dog food labels. The US Department of Agriculture (USDA) oversees this word's use with foods for human consumption, and you may find a USDA seal on certain organic dog food packages. In these cases, the pet food companies follow the same rules that apply to human food products. The ingredients of an organic food have been farmed without any pesticides or chemical controls for at least five years.

Perhaps the murkiest word often seen on dog food packages is "holistic." Because the AAFCO has not legally defined the term, consumers have no way of knowing exactly what this word means when describing a particular food. The word *holistic* means "to treat as a whole." Holistic medicine, for example, takes a person's entire body into account when treating a specific illness in one part of the body. But what is holistic dog food? Was it formulated with a dog's whole body in mind? This seems to be the implication, but, without any parameters, it is tough to say for certain.

Many terms, such as "human quality" and "new and improved" also aren't regulated by the AAFCO, so companies can use them without being held to a specific standard. The term "proven," on the other hand, must be backed up with research. If a food's label states that it has been "proven to improve coat appearance," the company must have evidence that the product has been tested on dogs and that it was shown to do what it claims.

matter. Also, the best meat meals always specify their source—"duck meal" or "salmon meal," for instance, as opposed to the more generalized term "meat meal."

Beware of foods that contain meat by-products in any form. By-products include parts of the animal, such as bones, beaks, and feet, which are not considered fit for human consumption. By-products are a cheap way for pet food companies to boost a food's protein content. Also, avoid foods that list chemical preservatives on their ingredient lists. These additives, which extend shelf life, may be listed as butylated hydroxyanisole (BHA), butylated hydroxytoluene (BHT), or ethoxyquin. Nutritionists have questioned the safety of these preservatives for years, but many manufacturers still use them.

Another thing to watch out for is the separate listing of similar ingredients. Savvy companies have figured out a way to make it seem as if the most prevalent ingredient in a particular food isn't the main ingredient after all. If you see phrases like "corn" and "corn gluten meal" listed on a product label, it is entirely possible that their combined weight is more than that of the ingredients listed higher up. Corn gluten meal, in particular, is not ideal as a dog food ingredient. Although this corn derivative increases the amount of protein, it is low in the essential amino acids that dogs need in their diets.

Finally, don't forget to check the expiration date on the package each time you buy dog food. Never buy an expired product, of course. If you want the freshest possible food, I recommend doing a bit of research regarding shelf life before heading to the store. Most pet food companies list the shelf life of their products on their websites. Obviously, the closer to the expiration date a bag of food is, the longer it has been sitting around in a warehouse. And although the food may be perfectly safe for your dog to eat, I personally would rather feed my pets food that was produced as recently as possible.

Cooking for your dog means preparing the proper balance of protein, fat, and other essential nutrients.

Homemade Diets

An increasing number of dog owners have begun cooking their pets' meals themselves instead of buying prepackaged food. Although this approach definitely isn't for everyone, it can be a practical way to make sure that your dog is getting

Some owners feel that raw diets are the healthiest alternative.

all the nutrients he needs. Owners who go this route must do a certain amount of research, however. If you miss an essential nutrient, or do not include enough of it, you could compromise your pet's health despite your best intentions.

Dogs need and enjoy many of the same foods that you probably buy every week for your human family members. Lean meats, vitamin-rich vegetables, and whole grains are tasty and healthy choices. You may even feed your dog many of the same recipes you make for your own meals, providing you avoid human foods that are toxic to pets. Onions, for instance, can cause anemia in dogs. If one of your favorite dishes calls for onions of any kind, simply skip the ingredient altogether or make your pet a smaller portion without this root vegetable.

Your dog also should not eat foods that are high in salt or sugar. A certain amount of salt is necessary for good health, but remember that many foods made for people contain a surprising amount of sodium. If you buy canned vegetables for your pet, opt for varieties labeled "reduced sodium" or "no salt added" and rinse them before use. Even better, buy fresh or frozen veggies instead.

It is wise to consult your veterinarian before beginning a home-cooked feeding regimen for your dog. Your vet can offer advice and insight into how you can best fulfill your pet's nutritional needs. However, if your vet discourages you from cooking for your pet due to your dog's health or lifestyle, listen carefully—your dog may do better eating a high-quality prepackaged food. If you still want to offer him home-cooked food, you may be able to supplement his commercial diet with a few prepared meals here and there. Most importantly, learn as much as you can before you start cooking so you can offer your dog the healthiest food possible from the start.

Raw Diets

Raw diets have also become more popular in recent years. The premise of this type of feeding plan is that raw food most closely resembles the diets of wolves, the species from which all domesticated dogs descended. You can feed a raw diet in one of two ways—by preparing the

What Not to Feed Your Dog

Numerous human foods can be dangerous for your dog. Keep these food items out of your dog's bowl, as well as out of his reach.

- Alcoholic beverages
- Apple seeds
- Avocados
- Bread dough
- Caffeinated beverages (including coffee, tea, and cola)
- Candy or other foods containing xylitol
- Chocolate
- Fruit pits (such as those from cherries or peaches)
- Grapes or raisins
- Gum
- Milk and other dairy products
- Nutmeg
- Nuts (especially macadamia nuts and walnuts)
- Onions (or any derivatives, such as onion powder or onion salt)
- Salt

Also, if you have a vegetable garden, bear in mind that the leaves of potatoes and tomatoes are poisonous to dogs.

food yourself or by purchasing a prepackaged raw formula. Of course, you can also use a commercial raw diet to supplement one you prep at home, or vice versa.

Sometimes referred to as the BARF (bones and raw food) diet, this type of feeding regimen includes uncooked meat or fish, bones, and vegetables. Some owners who feed raw diets also give their dogs eggs, often with the shells for added calcium.

The proponents of raw diets note that their pets thrive on this type of feeding plan. Many owners quickly observe that their dogs have shinier coats, cleaner teeth, and more energy on a raw diet. Critics of raw feeding point out that the risks of this type of diet can be serious. Dogs who consume raw bones and raw food can suffer from broken teeth, abdominal blockages or punctures, or bacterial infections like *E. coli* or *Salmonella*. Dogs can also choke on bones. While these occurrences might be rare, most veterinarians who oppose raw diets report that the conditions they treat as a result of raw feeding are often life-threatening. It should be noted, however, that a fair number of vets approve of feeding raw food.

If you are considering a raw diet for your dog, talk to your veterinarian. Together you can decide whether this type of regimen is right for your pet. Compromise is also possible with this type of plan. For instance, you might choose to feed raw vegetables and eggs along with cooked meat and no bones. A friend of mine even buys prepackaged raw food and then cooks the individually wrapped portions before feeding them to her pet. While this may go against the very premise of feeding raw food, she likes the fact that raw brands contain such healthy ingredients, but worries about bacteria. Whatever type of feeding plan you choose for your pet, you should feel completely comfortable with it.

Supplements

Vitamins and minerals play an important part in your dog's health, happiness, and even his appearance. Vitamin B5, also known as pantothenic acid, has been shown to reduce stress and anxiety in animals. Vitamin E oxygenates the blood, improves the immune system, and helps correct skin problems. As with people, calcium helps dogs grow strong bones and teeth. The best way for your dog to get these and the other nutrients he needs is through his food, but occasionally supplementation is necessary.

If your dog has a deficiency of a particular vitamin, supplements can be a practical way to increase this nutrient in your dog's body. Perhaps you are concerned that your pet is not absorbing enough vitamin D from sunlight because he spends his days indoors while you work and only gets outside for walks when it is dark.

Some dogs would never stop eating if given the choice!

The first thing you should do, before beginning supplements, is schedule an appointment with your veterinarian. If the vet determines that your dog indeed needs more calcium, for example, a vitamin supplement isn't necessarily the best solution. While milk and other dairy products aren't good for dogs, you can add a bit of cod liver oil to his food to increase his calcium intake. Your vet can advise you on the amount of calcium your dog needs, recommend other foods that are rich in calcium, or point you toward a quality calcium supplement if one is necessary.

Some vitamins are water soluble, meaning that amounts that aren't used by your dog's body are flushed away through his urine. Other vitamins, though, are fat soluble, meaning that unused portions are stored in the body with your dog's fat. The latter kind can be especially dangerous if owners do not know which vitamins—and how much—their dogs need. If you must give your dog supplements, make sure that you know the proper dosages. Too much calcium, for example, can cause kidney stones. To prevent an overdose, talk to your vet before giving your dog any type of supplement.

Portion Control

According to a study by the Association for Pet Obesity Prevention, more than half of pets in the United States are overweight. The reasons for this problem include offering too many treats, sharing "junk food" with our animals, and not giving our dogs enough exercise. Another reason is poor portion control. Do you know the right amount of food to give your dog each day based on his size, age, and activity level? If you don't, you're not alone. But you can find out and start using portion control to your dog's advantage.

Many dog food packages include instructions for how much to feed an animal based on his size. While these directives can be a great start, they do not take all factors into consideration. Like people, pets have individual metabolisms, habits, and sometimes health problems. The best way to determine how much dog food to feed your pet is by weighing him regularly. Once a dog reaches his adult size, his weight should vary only slightly. Of course, a slight weight gain for a Great Dane could equal the entire weight of a Yorkshire Terrier, so the amount is relative. If your dog starts gaining too much weight, reduce his portions and make a point of exercising him more until the scale returns to where it should be.

I keep a scoop inside each of my dog food containers so that I am sure to dispense the correct amount of food at each meal. A set of stainless steel measuring cups works great if you have dogs of more than one size, like I do. Just be sure that you are giving your pet a level scoop every time you feed him. A well-rounded portion could lead to a well-rounded dog.

Carrots are healthy, crunchy treats that many dogs enjoy.

Treats

One of the best parts of owning a dog is handing out treats. Whether you are trying to teach your pet a trick or you just feel like spoiling him a little, offering your dog an edible goody can make you as happy as it makes him. Since too many treats, or the wrong kinds, can lead to unnecessary weight gain, though, it is smart to have a plan. Some owners limit their dog's caloric intake from treats by breaking larger ones in half before placing them in a treat jar. Others skip the biscuit-style treats altogether and opt for using fresh veggies, such as baby carrots, as dog treats instead. Owners of overweight pets may even set aside a small amount of their dogs' daily food portions to use as treats.

It doesn't take much to make most dogs happy. While you may feel that a cupcake is a more tantalizing indulgence than an apple, your dog will likely enjoy a slice of your apple just as much as a small bit of cake or frosting. And while the apple contains some sugar, it will surely be less than the amount in that cupcake. The notion that dog owners shouldn't share their food with their pets is antiquated. What matters is that owners make healthy choices for their dogs as often as possible.

Food Allergy or Intolerance?

Just like people, dogs can suffer from allergies and intolerances to foods. For dogs, the most common triggers are certain ingredients in commercial foods, with beef, corn, and wheat among the most prevalent offenders. While any dog can suffer from a food allergy or intolerance, a few breeds, including the Cocker Spaniel, Dachshund, Golden Retriever, and Labrador Retriever, seem to be more prone than others.

Dogs can have a wide range of reactions to problem foods—from runny eyes or sneezing to diarrhea, vomiting, or breathing trouble. Some dogs experience hair loss, while others suffer from recurrent ear infections. An overwhelming number of dogs, however, react by itching. If you notice your dog scratching incessantly and see no signs of fleas or another obvious cause, make an appointment with your veterinarian. Your vet will need to rule out other health problems that could be behind your dog's symptoms, but be sure to discuss his diet with your vet.

The good news is that true allergies are extremely rare. If your dog is allergic to a certain food, eating it will cause a swift immunological response. You may have heard of anaphylactic shock, in which a person's or animal's airway starts closing up in response to an allergen. If your dog ever appears to be having difficulty breathing, get him to the nearest veterinary hospital immediately because this is a medical emergency regardless of the cause.

Food intolerances, while undeniably unpleasant, are a less serious—albeit much more common—situation for dogs. Sensitivity to a particular food is ten to fifteen times more likely than an allergy for the canine species. The most important thing owners can do if they suspect a food sensitivity is to get their pets some relief. Ask your vet about giving your dog an antihistamine to stop the itching or other symptoms while you try to identify the cause.

Water

When it comes to planning your dog's diet, don't forget that water is one of the most vital nutrients. Water makes up about 80 percent of your dog's body and is responsible for numerous functions, from transporting other nutrients and regulating his body temperature to digesting food and removing wastes. Your dog should have clean, fresh water available to him at all times. The one exception may be if you decide to remove his water bowl overnight while he is housetraining, and I don't recommend taking his water away at night if the weather is extremely hot.

When dogs don't drink enough water, they can become dehydrated, so it is smart to carry water with you whenever you go out with your dog. Your pet will appreciate a drink on a

Most vets recommend an elimination diet to narrow down the causes of food allergy or intolerance. Allergies and food sensitivities are among the most common problems for which a prescription diet is recommended, but you can also prepare an elimination diet at home. This process typically begins with switching your pet to a hypoallergenic diet—that is, one with limited ingredients that seldom cause allergies or sensitivities in dogs. Once your dog has shown that he is tolerating the hypoallergenic food well, you then gradually introduce other foods, one at a time, keeping a careful eye on his reactions.

The process of identifying the problem ingredient can be a long and frustrating one. Adding a new food too quickly can make it difficult to know which ingredient is the issue, so sticking to your vet's recommended timetable is essential. If your dog has a true allergic reaction, ask your veterinarian about allergy testing. Although expensive, this process can help you identify foods that your dog should never eat. In some cases, however, even allergy testing can yield no results.

Some owners assume that food isn't the problem if their dogs' diets haven't changed recently, but it is important to realize that sensitivities aren't always triggered by a new ingredient. The longer your dog has been eating a certain type of food, the more likely it could be that an ingredient in that food is the culprit. Remember that most dogs eat the same food each and every day. Over time, your dog can develop an intolerance from ingredients that at first didn't bother him at all. Some owners try to prevent sensitivities of this kind by changing their pets' food at regular intervals. In addition to lessening the chances of an intolerance, this strategy can also offer a dog a pleasing amount of variety in his diet.

short walk during the summer as well as anytime you go somewhere in the car at any time of year. You can find collapsible bowls at your local pet-supply store; some even come with convenient clips that allow you to carry them from a belt loop or backpack.

Certain situations make dogs more vulnerable to dehydration. If your dog has vomited or suffered from diarrhea recently, he will need to drink more to make up for the fluid his body has lost. If his appetite wanes or he acts lethargic, seek medical help right away because these are signs of serious dehydration. Sometimes dehydration is a symptom of an underlying health issue. Dogs with diabetes, kidney disease, or an infectious disease face the highest risks of dehydration.

CHAPTER 6

GROOMING
YOUR DOG

When you hear the term "dog groomer," you may envision a smocked individual who works in a pet salon. Grooming is indeed a profession specializing in the canine shampoo, cut, and blow-dry, but professional groomers are not the only people who perform these important tasks. Everyday pet owners are groomers, too. Whether your dog is a longhaired show champion or a smooth-coated mixed breed, you will need to perform at least a small amount of grooming yourself. You might even discover that it's a whole lot easier and surprisingly more fun than you imagined.

Coat Care

Keeping your dog's coat in proper condition doesn't just keep him looking good. It also helps keep your pet happy and healthy. Brushing removes dirt and dead hair. It can also alert you to any problems with your dog's skin. Bathing your pet on a regular basis keeps him clean and smelling fresh, and regular haircuts make all of these jobs much easier.

Even shorthaired breeds benefit from regular brushing to remove dead hair and debris.

Brushing

How often your dog needs to be brushed depends on the length and texture of his hair. Dogs with long or medium-length hair need to be brushed more often than shorthaired animals to prevent mats and tangles; fine hair and thick undercoats are also more prone to matting or tangling without regular brushing. However, don't assume that you get a free pass if your dog has a smooth coat. Often, shorthaired pets are the most profuse shedders, making brushing just as necessary for them.

The types of tools you need also depend on your dog's coat type. A wire slicker brush or wire pin brush is much too harsh for a smooth-coated breed but essential for a dog with long, thick fur. Shorthaired dogs usually do best with a soft-bristled brush, although some home groomers prefer using a grooming mitt. Owners of dogs with longer fur may also find a metal comb and a mat splitter helpful.

To make sure that you cover all the important areas, brush your dog systematically from head to tail, paying special attention to being gentle while working near your pet's eyes, ears, and face. For smooth or fine coats, brush in the direction of the hair's growth. For dogs with thick fur or undercoats, begin by brushing a small section of hair in the opposite direction and then brushing the same section of hair in the direction in which it grows. Repeat these steps until you have brushed your entire pet.

A pin brush's stiff wire pins are usually set in rubber.

A slicker brush has flexible wire bristles set close together and is good for removing dead hair from the coat.

If your dog has longer hair, always be on the lookout for knots on his chest, belly, and the undersides of his legs. These are the spots most vulnerable to matting. Minor snarls can usually be untangled with a brush or comb alone, but larger mats may need to be removed from your pet's coat with a mat splitter or clippers. Avoid using scissors to remove mats whenever possible because you are more likely to injure your pet; even with clippers, use extreme care not to cut your pet's skin.

Bathing

The frequency of your dog's baths depends on his hair type as well as on his individual lifestyle. Pets who spend a lot of time outside may need more frequent baths than those who get most of their exercise indoors. Just because a dog has long or medium-length hair doesn't mean that he needs to be bathed more often than a shorthaired pup. The Great Pyrenees, for example, has a tremendous amount of hair, but bathing this breed too often can destroy important natural oils that keep his hair and skin in proper condition and help his coat repel water. Basset Hounds, on the other hand, have short yet excessively oily coats that make weekly baths a smart idea for many members of this breed.

For most dogs, a monthly bath is the way to go. You can extend the amount of time between your dog's baths by brushing him often. A German Shepherd Dog, for instance, may not be prone to matting, but weekly brushings can reduce his need for baths to just a couple of times a year, providing he doesn't get into anything particularly messy.

Owners can choose from a wide selection of shampoos and conditioners for their dogs, but keep in mind that the best shampoo for your pet is whichever product gets him clean and rinses from his coat easily. A fresh smell is a bonus, but remember that your dog's nose is much more sensitive than your own, so avoid products with especially strong scents. If your pet has dry or itchy skin, consider a product made with oatmeal. You can keep a white dog's coat from yellowing with a shampoo made specifically for this hair color.

When the time comes for bathing your dog, gather all of your supplies before you start running the water. Once your dog is in your sink or tub, don't leave his side. A large bath towel (or two, if your dog is a larger breed), a washcloth for his face, cotton balls for his ears, and his shampoo are all you need. Finally, turn up the thermostat a few degrees so that your pet is not chilled after the bath and then take him out to his potty spot right before his bath.

The most efficient way to bathe a dog is to give him a shower instead of a conventional bath. A doggy bubble bath isn't many dogs' idea of a good time. Even pets who tolerate bath day well

Be careful to keep soap away from the dog's eyes.

can get bored waiting for the tub to fill and drain. To avoid boredom, and the misbehavior that can accompany it, I recommend filling the tub with just a few inches of water. Make sure it is warm enough, but not too hot. That old-fashioned elbow test for a baby's bath water works great for dogs as well. A skid-resistant mat is also smart for safety.

A rubdown with a soft, dry towel will remove a lot of moisture from your dog's coat.

After inse0rting a cotton ball in each of your dog's ears to keep water from entering his ear canal, place him in the tub. Next, use a cup or sprayer to saturate his coat with plain water. Be careful not to get water in your pet's eyes. Using your washcloth, gently wipe your dog's head and muzzle. It is best to wash the face without shampoo to reduce the chances of getting it in his eyes.

Once you have finished washing your pet's face, squeeze a small amount of shampoo into the palm of your hand. Rub your hands together, working the product into a gentle lather, before applying the shampoo to your dog's coat. Pet shampoo does not create a lot of suds like human products do, so don't be concerned if you don't see many bubbles. You will be grateful for the lack of suds when it comes time to rinse your dog.

You can use your hands or the washcloth to shampoo your dog's body. As you did when brushing him, be sure to reach all of the important areas. Follow the directions on your shampoo's label for the amount of time to leave the product in his coat before draining the basin. Then, pick up that cup or sprayer and begin rinsing the product out. The biggest mistake most pet owners make when bathing their dogs is not rinsing thoroughly enough. Any residual soap left in your dog's coat can cause dryness and itching. To prevent this problem, I recommend rinsing twice.

Trimming

Giving their dog a haircut is often the grooming task that owners prefer to leave to the professionals. If you plan to keep your Poodle in a continental clip, which is the traditional Poodle 'do, it might indeed be smart to visit a professional groomer. If, on the other hand, you decide to keep your dog in a pet-style clip, you may be able to handle it yourself without much difficulty. You might even find that a more complicated hairstyle isn't as difficult to master as you imagined. Grooming a dog simply takes practice—and paying someone else to do it can be expensive.

Not all dogs need haircuts. Some dogs with heavy coats actually should not be clipped, even during the hottest months. For example, double-coated breeds, such as the Chow Chow, Pomeranian, and Siberian Husky, do not need summer haircuts because their fur helps them stay cool and helps prevent sunburn. Plus, trimming a double coat can alter the look or feel of the fur as it grows back in. In many cases, the new hair growth is frizzy or much sparser than before.

If your dog's coat needs to be trimmed regularly, and you will be performing this task yourself, invest in a set of good-quality clippers. Many owners find rechargeable cordless clippers to be the handiest choice. In either case, a trusted brand is usually best. The old adage about getting what you pay for is often true when it comes to most grooming tools.

Most longhaired breeds need a trim every four to six weeks, which means that your clippers will be getting a lot of use. A quality brand can handle this continual wear, but do keep in mind that you will need to replace the blade when it becomes dull. Depending on your dog's hairstyle, you also may need various blades in multiple sizes. The higher the number of the blade, the shorter it trims the hair. Many owners can get

Pliers-style nail clippers.
Inset: Guillotine-style nail clippers.

by with just one or two blades—a #4 or #7 for the body and a #10 for the face and ears, for instance.

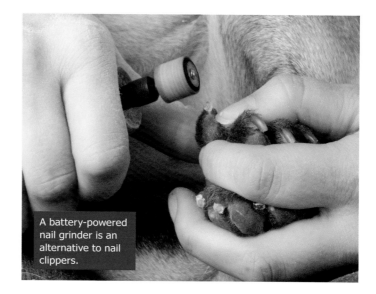

A battery-powered nail grinder is an alternative to nail clippers.

Go slowly when it comes to clipping. You can always remove more fur if needed, but putting it back on isn't an option. Brush your dog thoroughly before beginning the clipping process, and keep plenty of treats nearby, especially if your dog is new to grooming. You want him to enjoy the experience, not be stressed by it.

Just as you brushed your dog from head to tail, perform his haircut this same way. Gradually move from one area of his body to the next, never rushing.

Be mindful of the rising temperature of the clippers. More than one well-intended owner has "clipper-burned" a dog with trimmers that had become too hot for their pets' skin. A little trick I have learned is keeping a cookie sheet in the freezer. By placing a hot blade directly against the cookie sheet's cold metal surface for about thirty seconds, you can drastically reduce the time it takes the blade to cool down. And, as your dog would tell you himself if he could speak English, anything you can do to reduce the amount of time for which he needs to stand still for a haircut is always a plus.

Finish your dog's trim by giving him one final brushing. This important step will help remove any stray hairs left clinging to his coat.

Don't expect miracles the first time you clip your dog. It may take you a while to get the hang of this task, but your technique will improve with repetition. The good news is that your dog will be happy to have spent the time with you instead of at the grooming salon all day. Grooming your dog yourself can also serve as a trust-building exercise between you and your pet. Once he sees that he has nothing to fear from grooming, he will likely behave better when the time comes around again.

Nail Care

If your pet is heading to the grooming salon for a haircut, ask the groomer to trim his nails at the same time. Likewise, veterinarians often perform this simple grooming procedure for pet

Dogs and Sunburn

Few parents would consider heading outdoors on a sunny day without arming their kids with sunscreen, yet many dog owners do not even realize that they should be protecting their dogs' skin as well. Just like people, dogs can suffer from sunburn if they spend too much time in direct sunlight. Shorthaired breeds and lighter-colored dogs—including Dalmatians, Weimaraners, and Pit Bulls—face the highest risk, but even a shaggy or dark-haired dog can end up with a sunburned nose or ear tips. Dogs can also suffer from skin cancer.

Owners can protect their dogs from the sun by applying sunscreen to them before spending time outside. You must not use a product containing zinc oxide, however, because it is toxic to dogs if it is ingested. If you cannot find a sunscreen made specifically for dogs, use one for human babies or sensitive skin. Also, shield your dog from direct sunlight whenever possible. A little shade can go a long way in keeping your pet safe. I avoid taking my dogs on walks or outings between 10 a.m. and 2 p.m., when the sun poses the greatest risk to everyone.

owners when they visit the clinic for their pets' routine checkups. The problem with relying on a groomer or vet exclusively to trim your dogs' nails, however, is that the dog's nails will need attention far more often than the dog requires coat trims or well visits. Most dogs need their nails trimmed about every three weeks.

Owners have several choices of canine nail-trimmer types. Pliers-style and guillotine-style clippers are by far the most popular types due to their ease of use. An electronic version of the guillotine trimmer can even detect your dog's "quick" (the vein that runs through each nail and will bleed if cut) and alert you before you accidentally cut into this sensitive area. Scissor-style nail trimmers work best on toy breeds, such as the Italian Greyhound, but they are not strong enough to cut through the nails of larger breeds, like the Rottweiler. A fourth option is a nail grinder. This battery-powered rotary tool reduces the length of your pet's nails much like an emery board, only faster. While this tool can't cut your dog, the high-speed rotation of the grinder can still injure your pet. Care must be taken with whichever nail-trimming tool you choose.

The two biggest hurdles to trimming your dog's toenails are fear: yours and his. You can reduce your pet's fear by exposing him to the process as often as possible—although you can't actually trim his nails more often than needed, you can help your dog become more comfortable with the trimmers by letting him touch and sniff them. You can also help acclimate your dog to nail trims by touching his feet frequently; half the battle of nail trimming is that many dogs dislike having their feet handled. You can prevent this problem by touching your dog's toes at various times throughout the day to get him used to it. The more comfortable he gets with this part of the task, the easier nail trims will be.

The only way to ease your own fear is through practice. First, take a deep breath and try to relax before you trim. Next, gently press on your dog's paw pad to extend the nail you plan to clip. You needn't trim off too much; simply snip off the hook-like end of the nail. You can always take off more if needed, but in most cases only a single snip is necessary. Repeat this process until you have trimmed all of your pet's toenails.

If you do cut the quick, it will bleed. Do not panic. Instead, remain as calm as possible while applying styptic powder to the wound. This product, which can be purchased at your local pet-supply store, will speed clotting. In a pinch, you can substitute cornstarch, a bar of soap, or a wet tea bag instead. Nearly all owners nip the quick at least once. Go easy on yourself if it happens to you. Just be more careful next time.

Ear Cleaning

As with many canine grooming products, owners now have a variety of options when it comes to ear cleanser. Many products contain alcohol, which helps ears dry more quickly after a cleaning. The problem with this ingredient is that it can be too harsh, particularly for dogs prone to ear infections. If an ear is sore, a cleaner containing alcohol will burn. For this

Use a cotton ball or pad rather than a cotton swab to clean the ears.

Choosing a Groomer

I encourage owners to groom their pets themselves whenever possible. Many owners find that grooming offers a wonderful opportunity for bonding with their animals. If you do not have the time or ability to perform certain grooming tasks yourself, however, you will need to employ a professional.

It is essential that you trust your groomer with your dog, so careful selection is a must. While online reviews can be helpful, nothing beats a more personal recommendation. Ask your pet-owning friends for the names of their favorite grooming salons. In addition to the cleanliness of a facility, other factors to consider include the experience level and pet-friendliness of the grooming staff, whether the groomers use cage dryers, and how many dogs a particular salon serves each day.

A small business is often the best choice because a high volume of clients often means that dogs must wait for long periods in cages for their turns. Many busy salons also rely on cage dryers. While there is nothing inherently wrong with a cage dryer, the lack of attention that can accompany its use can lead to heatstroke and even death. By taking the time to interview a groomer before scheduling an appointment, you can be sure that your philosophies about pet care match the person or company to whom you entrust your dog's grooming.

reason, many owners prefer to use alcohol-free products instead. The key is not to use too much cleanser because it will keep the ear wetter longer.

Squirt a small amount of cleanser into one of your pet's ears and then gently massage the ear from the outside; repeat with the other ear. Many dogs resist the first step but relish the second, often leaning into their owners' hands during the ear rub. It is also common for a dog to shake his head as soon as he feels the cleanser enter his ear canal. Either reaction will help distribute the cleanser and also loosen any wax or other debris in the ear.

Next, wipe the inside of each ear with a cotton ball. Never use a cotton swab because you can accidentally injure your pet with this item, especially if he resists the cleaning process. Most ears need several wipes with fresh cotton balls, but you don't have to remove all of the wax. A small amount of wax is actually good for the ear, but if the cotton ball reveals dark-colored residue, keep cleaning.

How often you must clean your dog's ears is somewhat dependent on your individual dog. Breeds with pendulant ears tend to get more ear infections—and therefore need more frequent cleanings—but other factors also play a part. Dogs who swim regularly are also prone to infections because dampness creates an ideal setting for bacterial growth. Despite having shorter ears, Labrador Retrievers and Bulldogs produce more wax than many other breeds, so their ears also need a little extra attention. Every dog should have his ears cleaned at least once a month; if your dog is prone to ear issues, weekly cleanings are better.

Brushing Teeth

The most overlooked of all canine grooming tools is the toothbrush. Many owners still don't realize that, just like people, pets need regular dental care. Others buy the toothpaste and toothbrush with the best intentions but always seem to put off brushing their dogs' teeth until a vague time in the future. Let's be honest: there is never a convenient time to perform a task that so many dogs resist. This is why the most important step in brushing your dog's teeth is simply beginning the process.

It doesn't matter if your dog hates having his teeth brushed. It doesn't matter if you don't reach every single pearly white in one session. And it doesn't matter if your dog hides from you for an entire hour afterward (trust me—he will forgive you). What matters is that you make time for toothbrushing as often as possible. Brushing your pet's teeth daily is best, if you can manage it, but even once or twice a week is significantly better than routinely procrastinating.

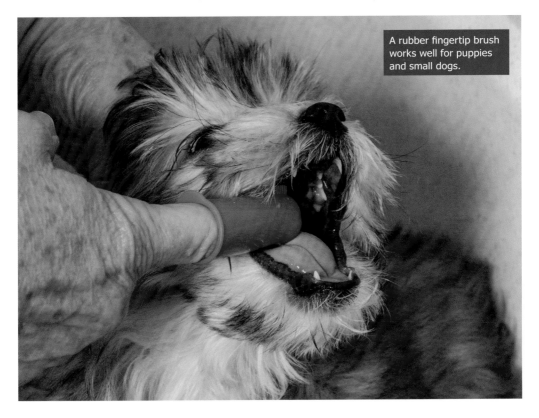

A rubber fingertip brush works well for puppies and small dogs.

Regular brushing keeps your dog's teeth white and healthy.

Begin by placing a small amount of doggie toothpaste on your finger and allowing your dog to sniff and taste it. Canine toothpaste comes in meaty flavors, so your pet will likely be drawn to it; it's usually the brush that scares him off. With that in mind, allow your pet to inspect the toothbrush, too. If he balks when you try to place it in his mouth, skip the brush altogether and simply substitute a smaller, softer fingertip brush or even a piece of damp gauze.

Work in an oval motion, beginning at the area where the tooth meets the gum. Move from one tooth to the next in this way until you have cleaned all of your dog's teeth or until his resistance indicates that it's time for a break. You can always return to the task later.

Because canine toothpaste is safe for your pet to swallow, you needn't rinse his mouth after brushing. Your dog may appreciate a cool drink when you are finished, though. I also recommend giving him lots of praise for his compliance. A heartfelt "good boy!" should never coincide with resistance, but when offered during a cooperative moment (however short), praise can encourage your dog to tolerate this important grooming task better.

If you have let dental care fall to the wayside for too long, you may need to schedule an appointment with your dog's veterinarian for a professional dental cleaning. Owners cannot remove calculus, the official term for tartar, with toothpaste alone. Because tartar must be scraped away, your vet will need to anesthetize your pet for his cleaning. As safe as it is for most dogs, though, going under anesthesia always poses a certain amount of risk. It is highly preferable to start brushing your dog's teeth while he's young to make this elective procedure unnecessary.

Deskunking

While proactive grooming can do a lot to keep your dog smelling fresh, a chance encounter with a skunk can undo all of your hard work in just seconds. If your dog ever ends up on the receiving end of skunk spray, he will need a bath as soon as possible. Unfortunately, regular dog shampoo will do little to rid him of the pungent odor. Thankfully, there is an efficient home remedy for this common problem. Before you start running the bath water, however, you must perform a quick health check.

1. Since skunks can carry rabies, the most important thing to do after a spraying is make sure your dog has not been bitten by the animal. If your pet is injured, head to the nearest veterinarian immediately.

2. Once you have ruled out a bite, make sure that the spray did not get into your dog's eyes. If they look red or otherwise irritated, flush them with plain water immediately.

3. If possible, keep your pet outdoors as you move on to Step 4. If you think getting skunk odor out of your dog's coat is challenging, wait until you try to remove it from your carpeting and furniture.

4. Mix 1 quart of 3-percent hydrogen peroxide with ¼ cup baking soda and 1 teaspoon liquid dish soap. *Note*: Do not cover this mixture. Although it is perfectly safe to use on your dog, the contents could explode under pressure.

5. Apply the peroxide mixture to your dog's coat, rubbing it in as you go along. Once you have thoroughly saturated the fur, rinse your pet completely with warm water. Keep in mind that peroxide is a bleaching agent. It will lighten your dog's hair if it is left on too long.

6. Bathe your dog with his regular shampoo, continuing as you would for a routine bath.

You may have heard that bathing a dog in tomato juice will help remove the smell of skunk spray, but the peroxide mixture has proved to be more effective—and considerably more pleasant. It may take more than one bath to rid your pet of the skunk smell completely. If you find that your clothes have absorbed the odor, add some baking soda to your laundry detergent when you wash them. This household staple is remarkable at removing all types of odors.

CHAPTER 7

EXERCISE
AND ACTIVITIES

Exercise is among the biggest contributors to a dog's health and happiness. Whether your pet is long-legged and muscular or petite and pampered, fitting some physical activity into each day is essential for his well-being. Exercise isn't just good for your dog's body; it also improves his mental health. Staying active even affects an animal's behavior in positive ways. Pets who stay at home all day while their owners work may act out or become depressed. A regular walk around the neighborhood or a fun daily play session in the backyard can make a world of difference.

How Much Exercise Does Your Dog Need?

The exact amount of exercise your dog needs depends on his breed, age, and health. Most dogs do best with between thirty and sixty minutes of physical activity each day. You must also factor your pet's current fitness level into the equation, however. Overweight pets can benefit immensely from an exercise regimen, but their owners must introduce exercise slowly because overexertion can cause orthopedic or other health problems. Even a thinner dog who presently spends most of his time napping will need a gradual increase in activity before he will be ready to go for runs or long hikes.

A long lead allows your dog to explore new sights and smells safely.

Some of the most active dog breeds may surprise you. Many Pembroke Welsh Corgi owners learn quickly that these small animals can keep up remarkably well with owners who take them jogging. This breed can also be an impressive contender on the agility course. Another small dog who requires significant exercise is the Boston Terrier, and not just any type of activity will do—Bostons require activities that are both physically

You don't have to have a retriever to play fetch!

and mentally stimulating, such as playing hide-and-seek with their owners. It's important to note that no matter what kind of dog you have, your dog should always be the "seeker" in hide-and-seek games because you never want to encourage your dog to hide from you.

Among the more obvious canine athletes, you will find the Border Collie, Boxer, and Siberian Husky. Mixed breeds who have these and other active breeds in their lineage also need a good amount of exercise. On the other end of spectrum, some breeds—such as the Basset Hound, Cavalier King Charles Spaniel, and Old English Sheepdog—require only a minimal amount of physical activity.

The ways in which you provide your pet with the physical activity he needs may be as different as your individual dog. If running isn't your thing, but you have a large yard, your Weimaraner may be able to get enough exercise chasing a ball every afternoon. Just be sure to buy one of those nifty throwing wands, or you may end up needing to ice your arm by the time evening rolls around. A Shih Tzu might get enough of a workout from a daily game of fetch in your living room, although he will surely enjoy a fun walk or trip to the park occasionally.

Games to Play with Your Dog

Games of fetch and hide-and-seek are just the beginning when it comes to playing with your dog. Playtime is an opportunity to indulge your pet's personality. Some dogs may like to chase balls at the dog park while other dogs might prefer to jump and catch flying discs at the beach. Other pets may favor playing indoors with toys that make noise. Whatever your dog's style, you can usually find a game to match it.

If your dog enjoys running around, your fenced-in yard could be the perfect setting for a game of chase. As with hide-and-seek, your dog should always be the one to pursue you. In the event that your dog ever slips out of his collar in public, you do not want him to think that it is a fun game to run away from you—instead, you hope he will chase you, just like he does when you play this exhilarating game.

If your dog doesn't seem interested in the game at first, try tempting him with some treats as you initiate the play session. Few dogs can resist any game that ends in an edible reward. Of course, not all dogs are as food motivated. Some dogs are instantly engaged by an impromptu game of bubbles. This old standard from your childhood is a fun and inexpensive way to entertain your dog; many dogs delight in chasing the shiny spheres, even jumping into the air to burst as many as they can before the bubbles float away. Just be sure to buy a brand of bubbles that is nontoxic for your pet. Some companies even make special meat-scented bubbles for canine enthusiasts. Other canine bubble brands claim that their products land without popping, making the game even more interesting for pets.

When the weather is warm, consider turning on the sprinkler for your dog. Many pups enjoy chasing water as the jets spray it in various directions around the yard. You can easily mimic this kind of spray by holding your thumb over the end of a garden hose if you don't have a sprinkler attachment. If you'd rather not let the water run, you can find toys designed to be filled with water instead. A simple kiddie pool can also be fun for dogs who love water. You might want to slip into your bathing suit before heading outdoors for water play with your pet because you'll probably end up as wet as he does!

Provide your dog with a place to cool off on a hot day.

Playing with You versus Playing Alone

Some toys and games are meant for two players. A flying disc is simply no fun for a dog without someone to throw it. Other playthings, though, were designed to amuse your pet when you cannot. One of the best behaviors you can instill in your dog is how to pass time with a toy independently. A dog who relies on his owner for all of his entertainment will do one of two things when the owner leaves the house: either he will feel sad and lonely, or he will find a way to entertain himself, usually through some type of destructive behavior. For these reasons, it is necessary that you provide your dog with toys to keep him busy when you are not with him.

The first type of toy that may come to mind when you think of autonomous play is the chew toy. Made to ease the pain of teething—and to save your possessions from certain destruction—chew toys are among the most popular single-player toys. Many dogs enjoy chewing well into adulthood, and the toys at their disposal have come a long way from the simple rubber bones of the past, although these old standards remain popular. Today, chew toys also come in a wide array of materials and flavors. Some have hollow centers that dog owners can fill with tasty treats like peanut butter or pieces of kibble. Chewing also helps maintain your dog's dental health, with some chews made specifically for this purpose.

Chew toys aren't the only type of toys that your dog can play with alone. Dogs who enjoy mental stimulation often love puzzle toys. You hide a food reward inside this type of toy, but in order to reach it, a dog must perform a series of maneuvers to solve the puzzle. Your pet doesn't have to be at the head of his training class to play with puzzle toys. In fact, many animals may appreciate a demonstration from their owners before going solo with one of these educational playthings.

In general, though, the way to make the most out of single-player toys is to save them for the times when your dog must entertain himself. If he can play with certain items only at these times, not only will their stock rise in his eyes, but they may also make "alone time" a bit less dreary for him. It is also smart to rotate the toys you give your pet when he's alone so that nothing becomes boring.

If your dog has a curious mind and a strong nose, you may be able to take a game of hide-and-seek to the next level to challenge your dog's brain. Instead of hiding from your pet, place a treat under one of two plastic cups when your dog isn't looking. Next, encourage him to sniff the cups to determine which one holds his reward. As your dog catches on to the objective of this game, you can then add more cups to make it more difficult. You might even vary the game by hiding treats or toys in different places around the room. The key to holding your dog's attention is keeping the game exciting yet not too hard.

Flyball practice is even better on the beach!

Organized Sports for Competition or Fun

You may buy your dog his first ball, assuming that it will simply serve as a way to pass some time with your pet, but, during your daily games, you just might discover that your dog has an innate talent for catching. Similarly, you may enroll in a basic training course and find that your pup can perform a sit-stay longer than any other dog in the class. If your dog shows an aptitude for a particular sport or obedience training, he could be a good candidate for an organized activity. Some owners even select a certain breed or type of dog with a pastime like this in mind.

Participating in a sport like flyball or rally obedience can be a great way for you and your dog to spend time together, meet other dog owners and their pets, and get some physical activity as well. You needn't compete formally to enjoy any of the following pastimes. Many dog owners set up small agility courses in their own backyards strictly for their own enjoyment, and some of the best trained pets have never taken part in an obedience trial.

Agility

Agility is by far one of the most popular canine sports. Modeled after equestrian jumping events, dog agility competitions take place on a course with a variety of obstacles. The canine contestants must navigate chutes and tunnels, hurdles, seesaws, suspended tires, and weave poles while being timed. Owners are allowed to direct their dogs through the course, using hand signals, verbal commands, or a combination of the two.

Training a dog to master agility obstacles is no simple task. Even when an animal shows great potential for the sport, owners must spend hours practicing the various obstacles with their pets. Many people start teaching their dogs the basics while they are still puppies, although dogs must be one year old or older to compete in agility due to the delicate nature of their growing bones, which can be injured too easily before the one-year mark. For some larger breeds, who continue growing past their first birthdays, it may even be smart to postpone jumping even longer.

Border Collies, Parson Russell Terriers, and Australian Shepherds often win numerous titles in agility, although any breed or mixed breed is allowed to compete in this fun sport. Active breeds with medium builds tend to perform the best at agility, but what matter most are a high energy level and an outgoing temperament. Dogs with shy personalities may enjoy practicing their agility moves at home but then falter when they must perform in front of other people and dogs.

Because agility equipment can be expensive, many owners recommend attending events as a spectator before deciding whether this sport is indeed for you and your dog. If you want to try it before buying, so to speak, you can sometimes rent time at an agility ring. In the beginning, you can also use makeshift items that mimic the equipment used by serious contenders. A child's play tunnel, for instance, can serve as a great substitute for the real thing while you see if you can teach your dog to run through it. You can also create hurdles and weave poles from PVC pipes.

Dogs just starting out in agility compete in the Novice Class, and they earn the title of Novice Agility Dog (NAD) when they complete this level. Depending on your dog's abilities and your own interest in further competition, your pet may earn three additional agility titles at progressively more difficult levels:

A German Shepherd Dog nagivates the weave poles.

Open tunnel success!

Even the smallest dogs can compete, using obstacles suitable for their size.

- Open Agility Dog (OAD)
- Agility Dog Excellent (ADX)
- Master Agility Excellent (MAX)

To earn each title, a dog must earn a qualifying score at three different agility events at the given level. These scores must be given by at least two different judges. A dog who earns ten qualifying scores in the Agility Dog Excellent class is awarded the MAX title.

Obedience

Some dog owners might say that calling obedience a sport is like calling the game of chess a sport—it's much more mentally challenging than physically challenging. However, it is an activity that involves physical exertion. And, as anyone who has ever taught a dog to sit knows, the victory an owner feels when that furry little bottom first hits the floor is akin to how David Beckham must have felt when he scored his first winning goal.

If your dog learns commands quickly and you enjoy the training process, the two of you might enjoy formal obedience trials. Certain breeds are known for their intelligence and trainability; this list is long, but the Border Collie, Poodle, and German Shepherd Dog frequently occupy the top spots. It is important to note, however, that any dog can learn with an owner who is willing to teach him.

Like agility, obedience has several levels of competition at which dogs can earn titles. These include:

- Companion Dog (CD)
- Companion Dog Excellent (CDX)
- Utility Dog (UD)
- Utility Dog Excellent (UDX)
- Obedience Trial Champion (OTCh)

For advanced levels of obedience, dogs must learn to retrieve a dumbbell.

The Companion Dog class is the beginning level of obedience, but some of the commands a dog must demonstrate to earn his CD title may seem advanced to owners new to training. Dogs must know how to heel both on and off leash, come when called, and remain in the sit and the stay positions for three minutes each. Once a dog has mastered these commands and received his CD title, the next step is Companion Dog Excellent, which includes additional exercises such as jumping and retrieving.

The next three obedience titles are increasingly difficult to obtain. Dogs competing in the Utility Dog class must respond to hand signals, demonstrate scent-discrimination skills, and perform directed jumping and retrieving maneuvers. Dogs are bestowed the UD title when they earn qualifying scores at different shows from three different judges. Only about five dogs out of every thousand who begin in the CD class make it to this point. Going on to achieve the title of Utility Dog Excellent or Obedience Trial Champion is considered a truly rare and distinguished accomplishment.

Rally

If your dog enjoys both physical and mental stimulation, rally may be an ideal sport for him. Sometimes called rally obedience or simply "rally-o," rally combines the fast pace of agility with the discipline and intelligence required for obedience trials. Dog-and-handler teams move from one station to another, performing a different task at each one. A course consists of between ten and twenty stations, depending on the level of competition.

Rally includes many moves and combinations not seen in conventional obedience trials. For example, a team may be asked to spiral right with the dog on the outside. In this exercise, the handler walks in three increasingly smaller circles, with the dog keeping pace at the handler's right side throughout the task. Other rally exercises include drop on recall, send over jump, and sit-down-sit.

Like agility and standard obedience, rally is open to all dogs, regardless of pedigrees. Many owners utilize rally as a stepping stone to other canine sports. Some start participating in rally after they have accomplished all of their goals in another sport and would like to pursue a new challenge. And others turn to rally after their dogs have experienced physical injuries that rule out agility and other more physically demanding sports.

Rally is an incredibly inclusive sport. It offers classes for puppies as young as six months of age, adult dogs, and senior pets. Likewise, dog lovers of all ages are welcome, with junior titles available for handlers younger than eighteen. Rally even offers special provisions for dogs with certain handicaps.

Both the AKC and the Association of Professional Dog Trainers (APDT) sponsor rally events. Rally teams can earn three titles from the AKC—Novice, Advanced, or Excellent. The APDT offers fourteen different titles that rally participants can pursue.

Flyball

Some dogs have one-track minds when it comes to playing ball. These dogs will chase a ball across a field, into a lake, or virtually anywhere else a person throws it. These dogs also often enjoy a canine sport called flyball. When my son played soccer in elementary school, a fellow soccer mom often brought her Labrador Retriever, Sierra, to the practices. This dog wasn't at all interested in chasing soccer balls, though. Instead, she played fetch with tennis balls—for the entire two hours, every single night. My friend would always bring along her throwing wand, but even with this helpful tool, her arm would inevitably tire. The other parents and I took turns keeping Sierra entertained, and each one of us also got an upper body workout. The family moved away, but I always thought that Sierra would enjoy flyball as much as our boys loved soccer.

In flyball, the dog races over a set of hurdles after catching the tennis ball.

While its name conjures images of a pop fly to right field, the course for flyball is nothing like a baseball field, but rather a long, straight strip of land. When a signal is given, the dog's owner releases him onto the course. The dog then jumps over four hurdles on his way to the other side, where a box with a foot lever is positioned. As soon as he reaches the box, the dog jumps on the lever, releasing the ball into the air. His job at this point is to catch the ball and return over the hurdles to his owner without dropping it. Since he is being timed, he also must be fast.

Flyball is a relay sport, meaning that four dogs compete on each team, taking turns to achieve the best possible combined time. Either two or four teams may compete against each other. This, too, is a sport that is open to all breeds or mixes, although herding and sporting dogs often make the best flyball players. Purebred dogs often compete on single-breed teams, but multi-breed teams are also allowed.

Breed-Specific Activities

Today, most dogs are first and foremost treasured companions. Originally, however, many dogs were bred for specific purposes—such as herding, hunting, or ridding the family home of pests. Many of these breeds still enjoy performing these jobs because the drive to do so remains strong among their instincts. Some dogs even participate in organized activities that allow them to indulge in and further develop these deeply ingrained skills.

Herding

Herding dogs, such as the Australian Cattle Dog and the Briard, were first bred to round up and protect farmers' livestock. The instinct to herd remains so strong in many herding breeds that the dogs will sometimes try to herd children—and sometimes even adults—if they get too rambunctious. Many herding-dog owners have their hands full with these driven and intelligent breeds. These highly focused dogs often need a purpose in addition to serving as loving companion animals, and this is where competitive herding comes in.

Some of the luckiest herding dogs live on expansive farms where they enjoy roles as both beloved pets and capable farm workers. But, alas, not every herding-dog owner is fortunate enough to have several acres of land complete with grazing cows or sheep. Both farmers and owners who live in the suburbs, however, can participate in competitive herding with their dogs. This program helps dogs explore the special function for which they were bred.

If your herding dog has never even seen a farm animal, you might assume that he wouldn't even know what to do in a herding trial. After all, you wouldn't expect your dog to know what to do on an agility course without some training, right? As surprising as it may seem, many herding breeds have a natural ability to move and control livestock. If you are curious whether your dog falls into this group, consider taking part in a noncompetitive herding test. Many breed clubs offer this evaluation, called an instinct test, which measures an individual dog's predisposition and trainability for herding.

If you wish to compete in competitive herding with your puppy in the future, you can get started training him right away even if there isn't a farm animal in sight. Begin by playing chase with your pet, encouraging him to chase you and other family members. As soon as he catches on to this game, start teaching him to stop chasing on command. Next, teach him to sit and stay when you throw his favorite toy. The reward for his compliance will be your "OK" command, after which he is allowed to chase after the toy. Both of these training exercises will help him learn to be directed during more complex herding tasks.

The next step is exposing your dog to livestock, perhaps during a noncompetitive herding test or maybe at a local farm. Either way, if he is going to compete in herding, he must learn to follow your commands despite the distraction of these new and interesting creatures.

A Border Collie moves the sheep into a pen at a herding trial.

Lure coursing gives sighthound owners the chance to see the elegance of their dogs in action.

Lure Coursing

Sighthounds, such as Greyhounds and Salukis, possess an exceptional ability for chasing and catching prey. If you own one of these lightning-fast breeds, you can indulge this deeply rooted instinct through lure coursing, an AKC sport limited to purebred sighthounds. For a complete list of the breeds that are eligible to participate, visit the AKC's website (www.akc.org).

Lure coursing simulates a hunt with mechanical lures, so no animals are hurt while participating in this pastime. A field is typically between 500 and 1,000 yards (457 and 914 m) long, although some are even longer. Instead of moving in a straight line, the faux prey is carried by an intricate pulley system, which allows for unexpected zig-zagging and turns. The changing directions more closely mimic the route a prey animal might take when being pursued, keeping the contest as authentic and challenging as possible for the canine participants.

If you think your dog may enjoy lure coursing, attend an event as a spectator and watch your dog for signs of interest. Although a sighthound must be a year old to compete in this sport, owners often see potential for lure coursing long before this time. Puppies may need a bit of time to mature before competing, however; lure coursing requires an enormous amount of focus on the dog's part.

Dock Diving

I may be a bit biased, but, in my opinion, one of the most enjoyable canine sports to watch is dock diving. My family and I regularly attend an event of this kind each summer in Maine, and I always leave the competition with a smile on my face. Sometimes that smile comes from witnessing the powerful canine athletes defy what I thought were the limits of a dog's jumping ability. Other times, a giggle accompanies my smile when I think of how there is always that one dog who changes his mind at the very last moment, not unlike a hesitant child on a diving board.

The sport of dock diving combines a dog's retrieving skills with his ability to jump as far as possible from a dock into the water below. For the sake of convenience, competitions are held in above-ground pools set up specifically for this purpose. Owners who would like to participate in this pastime with their pets, either for practice or just for fun, can practice wherever they like, however. I have no doubt that this activity is even more enjoyable outside a lakeside cabin with a scenic view.

Dogs are judged on the distance of their jumps, measured between the edge of the dock and the base of the animals' tails. In some cases, distance is evaluated by the human eye, although most competitions utilize cameras to ensure the most accurate measurements possible. A single jump may even be captured by cameras in several different locations.

Handlers can place their dogs anywhere they like on the dock before throwing a ball or bumper, although giving the dog the dock's full length for a running start usually offers the best chance for his longest jump. The dog then runs to the end of the dock and jumps into the water after the airborne object. Some competitions award extra points to dogs who catch the object as well.

Water-loving breeds such as the Chesapeake Bay Retriever and the Labrador Retriever are often naturals at dock jumping, but an individual dog's personality also comes into play here. No matter how much your dog may enjoy swimming, he must also be fearless when it comes to leaping off that dock to excel at this sport. You'll also see a good number of Belgian Malinois and Border Collies at dock-diving events. Smaller breeds may lack the ability to jump the farthest, but some of them still take great enjoyment from the water sport. Many crowds will cheer the loudest when they see a Yorkshire Terrier on deck—even if he jumps only one-fifth the distance of the larger dogs competing in the event.

Hunting

One of the oldest pastimes that people and dogs have shared is hunting. If you are a hunter, you have a wide selection of dog breeds to assist you; there are many hounds and sporting dogs who both enjoy and excel at hunting. Your breed of choice may depend on the type of game you hunt and the type of assistance you require.

A German Shorthaired Pointer, doing what he does best.

A pointing breed helps his owner by locating birds and other game. When a pointer finds his prey, he takes up a distinctive stance to alert his human companion. The dog will raise one of his front legs while extending his tail straight back. His whole body seems to point toward the prey. Pointing breeds include such dogs as the aptly named Pointer, German Shorthaired Pointer, and German Wirehaired Pointer as well as the Brittany, Spinone Italiano, and Vizsla. Setters, such as the English and Irish Setter, also point game.

Another type of hunting dog is the retriever. As this name suggests, a retriever assists in hunting by running or swimming toward the downed game bird and bringing it back to his owner without crushing it. Since most retrievers love to swim, they won't hesitate to swim out to game that has fallen into the water. These dogs' webbed feet and wide tails help make them powerful swimmers. Their thick coats, which repel water, are also made for this type of work. In addition to the more common retriever breeds, hunting retrievers include the Curly-Coated Retriever, Flat-Coated Retriever, and Nova Scotia Duck Tolling Retriever.

Some hunters prefer working with spaniels because these dogs flush game into the air. Birds such as pheasants often hide in dense brush, but spaniels rush into these areas, forcing the birds to fly up into the air, where hunters can see them. One might say that spaniels do double duty because many of these dogs also retrieve the game after it has fallen. Popular spaniel breeds for hunters include the Boykin Spaniel, English Cocker Spaniel, and English Springer Spaniel. The American Cocker Spaniel is not used as much for the sport today as it was in years past, although many dogs have retained their "birdiness"—that is, their excitement for chasing after birds.

When it comes to hunting, no dog has a more powerful nose than a scenthound. These dogs help their human companions find game by relying on their finely tuned sense of smell. Many will also chase foxes or rabbits from their dens. All dogs have significantly more scent receptors than the average human—about 200 million versus about 5 million—but certain scenthounds have even more; in fact, Basset Hounds, Beagles, and Bloodhounds have as many

as 300 million, making them ideal hunting companions. American Foxhounds and English Foxhounds also excel at scenting, although both breeds are rare as pets.

If you want to hunt with your dog, share your plans with the breeder. Many of the best hunting dogs show potential for this activity when they are quite young, so the breeder can help match you with the best pup for you. Some breeders specialize in either show lines or hunting lines, and significant differences

Therapy Certification

Therapy Dogs International (TDI) is one of the organizations that certifies, insures, and registers therapy dogs. Many organizations require your dog to pass the AKC's Canine Good Citizen® (CGC) test, which is a good place to start your training. Although becoming a Canine Good Citizen will not guarantee your dog certification as therapy dog, passing this test opens the door. It also shows that your pet possesses many of the necessary skills needed for therapy work. Not all dogs pass the test the first time around, and this is OK. Sometimes a dog just needs a little more work to meet the therapy program's standards. Dogs who are younger than a year old when they pass the CGC test are even encouraged to take it again as adults to ensure that their temperaments have remained consistent. Only dogs one year of age or older can take the TDI certification test.

TDI certification consists of two phases with a total of thirteen different tests in addition to a temperament evaluation. Evaluators observe the dog as he performs commands and responds to a variety of simulated experiences—from checking in at a hospital's front desk to moving around patients using crutches, walkers, and wheelchairs. During the first phase, dogs are tested as part of a group, but in the second phase, each dog is evaluated individually. Owners of dogs who pass the test are then able to apply for local volunteer opportunities that interest them.

can exist between these two types of the same breed. The English Springer Spaniel, for instance, is divided into bench (show) dogs and field dogs. While they may look similar to the uninitiated, the field version of the breed has shorter ears and a shorter, wavier coat that's more conducive to working in brush and woods. Marked differences in temperament also exist; hunting dogs are usually considerably more independent.

Even the most natural hunting dogs still need training, so be sure that you are willing to put the necessary time into teaching your new pet his hunting duties. A good breeder can point you toward the best resources in your area. Be sure to start your future hunting dog's training early because waiting too long can result in a dog's becoming gun-shy (fearful of the loud noise a gun makes) when he is finally exposed to the sound. Many hunters insist that this gun-shyness cannot be overcome once it appears.

Earthdog

If you own a terrier, you probably already know that the instinct to dig runs deep in these dogs. Dogs like the Cairn Terrier, Rat Terrier, and Silky Terrier were developed to rid homes, farms, and factories of vermin. Often, doing so required these breeds to "go to ground," or dig into the earth to capture their burrowing prey. The instinct to perform this work remains so deeply

The Cairn Terrier is among the talented earthdog breeds.

ingrained in most terriers that they should never be kept in homes with pet rodents of any kind; their hunting drive is simply too strong for this kind of cohabitation to be safe. As many terrier owners have also learned, these dogs sometimes aren't the best match for homes with gardens or decorative landscaping, either.

Earthdog trials, sometimes called go-to-ground events, offer terriers a chance to put their hunting skills to use in a fun and practical way, with no harm coming to either flora or fauna. These competitions simulate hunts using safely caged quarry and measure a dog's ability to move through an underground system of tunnels to reach his prey.

Because an earthdog trial is a pass-or-fail event, this canine sport is considered a noncompetitive activity. No points are awarded at these events, so every dog who successfully completes a trial is on equal footing with all others who have achieved the same goal. For this reason, most of the owners at earthdog tests cheer as enthusiastically for the other dogs as they do for their own. The result is an overwhelmingly positive environment of camaraderie and encouragement.

As with most canine pastimes, the best way to learn about earthdog trials is attending an event. Talk to handlers after their dogs have completed their trials to learn more about the activity. Many terrier owners train their pets at home, using long, narrow cardboard boxes or wooden tunnels that they build specifically for earthdog practice. If this activity seems like something both you and your dog might enjoy, consider participating in an upcoming event at the entry level.

Therapy-Dog Work

Have you ever noticed how just spending time with your dog can make you feel better after a bad day? Numerous studies have revealed the incredible health benefits of the human–animal bond, but did you know that a person doesn't have to have a history with a particular dog to reap many of these rewards? Simply spending time with a friendly dog can lower a person's blood pressure, diminish pain, and trigger a release of endorphins that produce a calming effect on the entire body. Animals can also have a positive effect on a person's mental health—relieving anxiety or boredom and adding valuable socialization. For all of these reasons, training dogs to become therapy animals has become increasingly popular among pet owners.

Therapy dogs accompany their owners to hospitals, nursing homes, and even special-education classrooms to offer people a break from whatever challenges they are facing. In hospitals, these animals may spend time with patients as they recover from an illness or surgery, or they might help family members of patients pass time as they wait for their loved ones to return from lengthy operations or testing procedures. Some therapy dogs are even trained to listen to children reading aloud. Because dogs neither correct nor judge people when they make mistakes, therapy animals often make an ideal audience for self-conscious readers.

Any purebred dog or mixed breed can become certified as a therapy dog, but some breeds are more commonly seen performing this important volunteer work. Golden Retrievers, Poodles, and Pugs can make excellent therapy dogs, but so can German Shepherd Dogs, Pit Bulls, and Rottweilers. What matters most is that your dog is friendly, well behaved, and comfortable in a variety of settings. You may notice that your dog has a special affinity for a particular age group—senior citizens, for example. If this is the case, I highly recommend taking advantage of it. Just as animals often know when particular people like them, people, too, can feel kinship with a dog who possesses a genuine fondness for them. And in these situations, the benefits of therapy work can be even greater.

Therapy dogs bring comfort to those who need it.

CHAPTER 8

KEEPING YOUR DOG OUT OF DANGER

As soon as you become a dog owner, you'll start noticing that danger can lurk around some surprising corners. The kitchen where you prepare your family's meals suddenly becomes rife with hazards like garbage cans, household cleaners, and foods that, while perfectly safe for people, can be life-threatening to your new pet. Bathrooms, living rooms, and bedrooms are no different. They can expose your dog to medications, choking hazards, electrical cords, and a number of other hidden dangers.

By systematically removing or managing as many risks as possible, you will help keep your new pet safe. Puppy-proofing is half the battle. It is important to note, however, that the other half of the battle is remaining watchful. You must keep an eye out for any new threats that may arise if you want to keep your dog as safe as possible.

Household Dangers

In the process of puppy-proofing your home, you will discover that some dangers cannot be removed. Open windows and doors, for example, pose an escape threat to your dog, but keeping them closed permanently isn't a practical solution. Instead, you must figure out how to manage these threats to keep your pets safe.

Escapes and Falls

If you allow your dog on your furniture, as I do, he may discover that the back of your sofa is a rather comfortable napping spot, as my dog Damon has. But if your sofa is positioned in front of a window that you enjoy opening during the warmer months, this arrangement could allow your dog to get out if you aren't careful. As much as I love fresh air, I don't enjoy letting insects into my home, so I always have my window screens in, but these thin coverings can easily pop out of their frames if too much pressure is applied to them. In this situation, the best thing to do is either move your sofa away from the window or choose another window to keep open on warm days.

Doors are a bit trickier, but they too can be managed. I have a small mudroom between my kitchen and garage. This setup inspired my family to establish a simple rule: one door closes before the other door opens. By following this simple guideline, we never risk an animal slipping past us. If you do not have two doors at your primary entrance, a better rule might be that your dog remains crated whenever someone is carrying grocery bags from the car to your kitchen. You can also use an interior door or safety gate in your home to your advantage by placing your dog behind one in a specific room while you perform tasks that require you to leave an exterior door open for any length of time.

Other spaces that pose escape hazards include balconies, decks, and patios. Balconies and decks can be especially dangerous because they include the added danger of falling. Unless you are absolutely certain your pet cannot fit through the openings between the rails on your balcony or deck, your dog should not be there—period. Some pet owners affix netting to their deck railings to make these outside areas safer. If you go this route, be sure to check for any loose spots or openings from time to time.

An open door is an invitation to escape.

Drowning Hazards

Whether you own a toy breed who only enjoys water when he's drinking it on a hot day or a large dog who enthusiastically retrieves tennis balls from the ocean, you must be extremely careful if you have an in-ground pool or hot tub. Even dogs who are capable swimmers can have trouble climbing out of pools—and smaller dogs can face similar struggles exiting a hot tub. Ironically, soft-sided covers for these tubs can be one of the most dangerous devices when it comes to pets because animals can become caught in the fabric and drown before their owners even realize that they have fallen into the water.

Protect your dog around water as you would a small child—the two are actually remarkably similar when it comes to water safety. Never leave your dog in a pool, bathtub, or sink unsupervised. Tragic accidents can take just moments to occur, but the consequences can last a lifetime for pet owners.

While most dogs are born with an innate ability to swim, it is also important to note that certain breeds' physiologies work against this natural instinct. Bulldogs, for instance, have large

Heavy-bodied Bulldogs are not good swimmers, so a fall into the pool could have tragic results.

heads, thick bodies, and short legs—all of which make swimming a much too difficult task. Boxers, Dachshunds, and Pugs may also have a hard time keeping themselves above water for long periods of time.

The chemicals for cleaning pools and hot tubs pose an added concern. Bear in mind that your dog doesn't have to swallow these caustic products to be hurt by them. Pool-maintenance chemicals can burn your pet's skin or eyes if he simply comes into contact with them. And inhaling them can harm his throat, nasal passages, or lungs. Keep these products in a secure location away from your pet, and keep him out of the area when you use them.

He Ate What?

You probably don't think that you use many dangerous items during your personal care routine, but bear in mind that you know the proper uses for the products that keep you looking and feeling your best. A dog with a penchant for garbage does not. Household trashcans can hold some remarkably

The enticing odor of dirty laundry can prove too much for some dogs to resist!

dangerous materials for pets. Your dog may simply be searching for the empty tube of mint-flavored toothpaste you tossed into the trash earlier this morning, but if someone else threw away a disposable razor, you could soon be on your way to the veterinary emergency room with a bleeding dog. Another item that can cause serious injuries for pets is dental floss, which can become tangled around a dog's intestines if swallowed. And it too often comes in appealing flavors that can entice pets. Since abstaining from activities like brushing and flossing isn't terribly convenient or hygienic, I recommend investing in trash cans with secure lids to protect your dog from these and other dangers.

Some dogs are drawn to objects that truly perplex their owners. A family I once knew had a Labrador Retriever named Jack who delighted in eating socks. The last I heard, he'd had three separate surgeries after eating nonedible items—two to remove socks and one to remove the contents of an entire box of facial tissues from his digestive system. You just never know what will appeal to a mischievous dog. Although the Lab's owners often joked about their dog's peculiar tastes, they were actually quite fortunate that their vet had been able to save Jack's life repeatedly in these situations.

Special Considerations at Holidays

Certain times of the year present specific kinds of dangers to pets. As we celebrate holidays and other special occasions, we often bring items into our homes that can be toxic or otherwise harmful to our pets.

Candy and Chocolate

We often celebrate Valentine's Day, Easter, and Halloween with copious amounts of candy, and chocolate is one of the biggest concerns for dog owners. This popular sweet treat contains a caffeine-like compound called theobromine, which dogs cannot metabolize as easily as people can. Dark chocolate contains the highest levels of this ingredient, but any type or amount of chocolate is unhealthy for your canine companion. If you enjoy eating chocolate, be sure to keep it out of your pet's reach.

Another dangerous substance to look out for during the holidays is xylitol. This sugar-free sweetener is a common ingredient in gum, candy, and even certain gelatin, peanut butter, and pudding brands. If a dog

Keep the holiday happy by sticking with dog treats for your four-legged Valentine.

eats food containing xylitol, it can cause an acute and life-threatening case of hypoglycemia. As much as you might want to share your holiday treats with your pet, the safest thing to do is limit his treats to the healthiest foods made from the simplest ingredients. If you are unsure of an item's ingredients, never share it with your dog.

Decorations

If you celebrate Christmas, one of your favorite things may be decorating and displaying a Christmas tree. Dog owners must be extra careful, however, that their Christmas trees don't compromise their pets' safety. If your dog is rambunctious, he could knock your tree over. In addition to breaking precious ornaments, your dog could also injure himself in the process. If your pup is a chewer, electric lights pose a risk for electrocution. And even the best behaved dogs may be tempted to drink from the tree's water basin, so be sure not to add any chemicals to it. If you can't always supervise your dog around your tree, the safest thing to do is either keep him out of the room in which you place the tree or set up an exercise pen around the tree to keep your pup a safe distance from it.

Edible ornaments, such as strands of cranberries or popcorn, can tempt dogs to jump up on Christmas trees. While these foods aren't poisonous to pets, the string that holds them together can have a similar effect on your dog's intestines as swallowed dental floss. Another decoration that you might not think of as being dangerous is tinsel. Numerous dogs end up in emergency

Christmas ornaments or shiny playthings? Your dog may not know the difference.

surgery each year after eating these thin strips of metal foil. The intestinal blockages that this popular decoration—as well as the faux grass used in many Easter baskets—can cause can be life-threatening.

If your holiday traditions include burning candles, consider swapping to the flameless kind for the sake of safety. Dogs simply do not understand the danger and destruction that fire can cause. All it takes is one misstep for your entire home to go up in flames, placing both pets' and human family members' lives at risk.

Plants

For many years, the media has warned dog owners that poinsettias are a deadly poison to animals. I remember my own mother instilling this information in me so that I would never bring one of these plants into my childhood home around Christmas. Even though I had never seen our family dog eat plants of any kind, I dutifully shared the warning with pet-owning friends, who likewise shared it with their friends. From the frequency and intensity of the warnings, one would have thought that poinsettias tasted like sirloin steak to dogs.

Mistletoe is a holiday favorite that can lead to a trip to the emergency vet.

In recent years, I have learned that the alarm over poinsettias was largely unnecessary. I won't say it was unfounded, though, because the leaves of this plant can indeed cause nausea and vomiting if they are ingested, and consuming a large amount could indeed be toxic. The good news, however, is that the leaves are armed with an incredibly unpleasant taste and sap that irritates a dog's mouth and esophagus, making it highly unlikely that an animal will eat it in the first place. If you still aren't comfortable with poinsettias, a Christmas orchid is a completely safe alternative.

Other popular holiday plants that are much more dangerous than poinsettias include holly, mistletoe, and their berries. Dogs who consume these plants may experience diarrhea, vomiting, and abdominal pain. Mistletoe in particular can also cause a severe drop in blood pressure and breathing problems.

The amaryllis is a popular holiday gift, but great caution must be taken with this plant around animals. The flowers, stalk, and bulbs are all highly toxic to dogs. Like holly and mistletoe, amaryllis can cause gastrointestinal upset as well as lethargy and even tremors in your pet if ingested.

Of course, iholiday plants are not the only plants that pose a risk to your dog's health. Many other plants, including both indoor and outdoor varieties, are considered toxic to pets. Before adding any plant to your home or garden, check with your veterinarian to make sure that it is among the safe choices. The American Society for the Prevention of Cruelty to Animals (ASPCA) and the Humane Society of the United States (HSUS) also offer detailed lists of dangerous plants on their respective websites.

Fireworks

Although you may want to include your dog in your summertime celebrations, you should know that the thunderous noise from fireworks can have a devastating effect on an otherwise well-adjusted pet. Many dogs who are frightened by thunderstorms experience similar reactions to this popular Fourth of July pastime. Two of my dogs greatly enjoy walking on a local beach on warm summer evenings, but I make a point of not taking them on Thursday nights because the town holds weekly fireworks shows every Thursday between Independence Day and Labor Day.

In some states, fireworks can be used only by licensed professionals, but in others, virtually anyone can buy these explosive items. If you live where fireworks are permitted, your dog may become frightened if your neighbors decide to put on a fireworks show of their own. In this situation, the best thing you can do for your pet is distract him from the noise. Turn on your radio or television, offer him one of his favorite toys, or give him a special treat. If none of these things helps, try taking him for a short car ride and returning when the festivities are over.

Fireworks or other loud noises can make some dogs fearful.

In Case of Emergency

If you suspect that your dog has ingested a dangerous substance, seek veterinary help immediately, and call the nearest veterinary hospital to let the staff know you are on your way. Many times, this advance notice can help the veterinarian prepare to treat your pet. Calling ahead can also enable the vet to advise you about what you should or shouldn't do both before and during transporting your pet.

Many pet owners keep ipecac syrup in their canine first-aid kits. While one might assume that this vomit-inducing medicine would be helpful in the case of a poisoning, using it after your dog has swallowed a caustic substance can actually be dangerous because a corrosive material can burn an animal's throat both when going down and when coming back up.

If you cannot reach a veterinarian in an emergency, call the Animal Poison Control Center's hotline, run by the ASPCA, at (888) 426-4435. You will need to have a credit card ready to pay the consultation fee, but the advice you receive could quite possibly save your pet's life in this dire situation.

Chewing and Mouthing

Owners must be especially watchful while their puppies move through the teething phase. Even more important than protecting your belongings from your pup's razor-sharp teeth is protecting your pet from the harm that can come to him from chewing on the wrong objects. Training can help, but you must never trust your dog to know which items are safe and which ones are not.

Cords

In modern homes, you can't just pack away your electrical appliances until your dog outgrows the inappropriate-chewing phase. Certainly, you can remove unnecessary items, but lamps, air conditioners, and many other items you use on a daily basis may be far less expendable. You can shield your dog from electrical cords by using cord organizers made specifically for computers or other electronics to enclose the cords. For most people, though, it simply isn't feasible to cover each and every power cord in the home.

If your pup remains intent on chewing these dangerous objects, a bitter-tasting spray made to deter chewing may help. This useful product can be found at most pet-supply stores. Begin by unplugging each item before you spray its cord with the solution. Then either wipe the cord with a rag or allow it to air dry before plugging the item back into the electrical outlet.

For items that you use less frequently, unplugging can help prevent electrocution. Even if you use an item often, consider unplugging it each time you are done using it. So-called "vampire"

Chewing on forbidden objects can be both dangerous and destructive.

electronics are known for using energy whenever they are plugged in—even when they are turned off—so pulling that plug can be good for both your dog and your wallet. Remember, though, that while unplugging can prevent a tragedy, it won't stop your pet from destructive chewing; you will still need to treat all cords with the repellent to deter a voracious chewer.

Chemicals

When many pet owners think of chemicals that could harm their pets, they picture the collection of bottles that we all seem to have assembled under our kitchen and bathroom sinks. If yours is anything like mine, it probably includes at least one furniture polish, window cleaner, and multi-surface spray as well as an array of specialized products made for smooth-top ranges, copper cookware, and hardwood cupboards and floors. Certainly, all of these products pose a health risk to your dog if he ingests any of them. Owners must look beyond the cleaning cupboard, though, when protecting their pets from dangerous chemicals.

If your hardwood floor cleaner would poison your pet if swallowed directly, consider the effect that using this product on your floors—where your dog spends most of his time—could be having on him. Dogs are meticulous self-groomers, and the only tools they have at their disposal for this instinctual activity are their tongues. When they clean their coats, they can ingest any substance with which their hair and skin have come into contact. For this reason, many owners prefer to use only nontoxic cleaners on their floors, carpets, and other household areas. Many stores now carry environmentally responsible—and animal-friendly—products. In many cases, you can even make your own cleaning products from natural ingredients, such as olive oil or vinegar.

Also, consider the chemicals you use outside your home. Garages often serve as storage areas for automotive chemicals, lawn treatments, and even pest-prevention products. The best way to keep your dog safe from these poisonous hazards is by not allowing him in the garage. Bear in mind, though, that products like antifreeze can sometimes make their way onto the surface of your driveway, where your pet can easily lick them up.

Antifreeze is in fact one of the deadliest of all chemicals to dogs. Just a tablespoon can lead to acute kidney failure in a small dog. To make matters worse, the smell and taste of this product appeals to pets, increasing their chances of ingestion if owners aren't careful. Conventional antifreeze is made with ethylene glycol, but a safer alternative is a product made with propylene glycol. While your dog shouldn't ingest this substance either, he is much less likely to be poisoned from it if he does ingest it.

Also, bear in mind that any product you use on your lawn can also make its way into your pet's mouth by way of self-grooming. Insecticides and pesticides are of particular concern. In addition to refraining from using these chemicals yourself, be sure that anyone you hire to do property maintenance doesn't use any products that could harm your pet.

Keep cleaning products and supplies locked away, out of puppy's reach.

Cold and Hot Weather

Few things influence our everyday routines as much as the weather. If you live in a colder climate, simple tasks like walking your dog can become more complicated in the midst of a snowstorm, for example. Likewise, the heat can play a role in which outdoor activities you participate in with your pet during the summer months, especially if your breed is sensitive to warmer temperatures. Knowing what to look out for in all types of weather is the first step to making sure that your pet stays safe whether the forecast is calling for rain or sunshine.

Cold Concerns

Some dogs love nothing more than romping in freshly fallen snow. The Akita, Bernese Mountain Dog, and Keeshond are just a few of the breeds that will happily walk or play outdoors when their owners can barely feel their own noses. These dogs have thick coats that keep them warm in even bitterly cold temperatures, so never cancel your daily walk with one of these breeds over a little—or even a lot of—snow. If you enjoy cross-country skiing, you can even teach a winter-loving breed to run alongside you.

No matter how adventurous or athletic they are, though, certain other breeds are unlikely to appreciate winter sports of any kind. Greyhounds, Whippets, and Italian Greyhounds are sleek breeds with short hair and very little body fat, which means that they feel the cold rather quickly. Toy breeds also tend to get cold fast because their shorter legs situate them closer to the ground. Even some large and tougher looking breeds, like the Doberman Pinscher and Great

Dane, can start shivering if the temperatures dip too low. If you own any of these breeds, it is best to limit outdoor time on the coldest days. I also recommend investing in a sweater or fleece coat for winter walks or trips to the potty spot on the coldest days.

No matter how thick your dog's coat is, you must protect his paws from salt, sand, and other de-icing agents. When buying a product to make your own outdoor stairs or walkways safer, look for a pet-friendly brand that won't burn your pet's feet. Nonetheless, if you walk your dog in the winter, he is sure to encounter corrosive de-icers in one place or another along the way. Paw wax can help. This genius product not only shields your pet's paw pads from salt and chemicals but also helps keep him from falling on slippery ice.

Heat

While many people consider summer their favorite season, this hottest time of the year in the Northern Hemisphere can be brutal for thick-coated dogs. Don't be surprised if your American Eskimo Dog or Great Pyrenees doesn't seem to have as much energy when the mercury rises. Other breeds that have poor heat tolerance include the Bulldog, Japanese Chin, and Pekingese. If your dog has a thick coat or a short muzzle, the best thing you can do for him on a hot day is keep him indoors where it is coolest, preferably with air conditioning running.

Although exercise is important for your dog's health, avoid performing any strenuous activities with him during the hottest parts of the day. Walk him early in the morning or after the sun has set, and keep the excursions short even at these times during heat waves. Always take along fresh water and a collapsible bowl, and stop in the shade to offer your pet a drink as needed.

The French Bulldog is among the bracycephalic breeds and doesn't tolerate heat well.

Plant Caution

If you enjoy keeping live plants, it is essential that you know which ones are safe to keep around your dog. Never assume that just because your dog doesn't touch your plants, he won't in the future. All it takes is one incident for you to have a tragic outcome on your hands. This is undoubtedly a situation in which it is better to be safe than sorry.

Popular plants that are poisonous to dogs include:

Autumn crocus	Hyacinth	Tulips
Azalea	Iris	Wisteria
Daffodil	Rhubarb leaves	
Foxglove	Sago palm	

If you have any of these plants in your yard, you may choose to remove them completely, or you might relocate them to a part of your property to which your dog doesn't have access. It is never advisable to keep a plant that is poisonous to dogs inside your home where your pet can reach it.

A recent addition to most no-no lists, though technically not a plant, is cocoa mulch. Made from cocoa beans, this landscaping material is as toxic to pets as chocolate because it is derived from the same source. And because cocoa mulch smells like chocolate, many dogs and other animals are drawn to it.

Plants that are safe to keep around dogs include:

African violet	Dwarf palm	Petunia
Bamboo palm	Hollyhock	Spider plant
Begonia, climbing or trailing	Impatiens	Sunflower
Daylily		

Other ways to keep your pet cool on hot days include offering edible frozen treats, adding a kiddie pool to your backyard, and investing in a cooling mat. You can also place one or more of your dog's toys in the freezer for an hour or two before playtime. For longhaired breeds, regular brushing will also help prevent overheating. And when bathing your dog in the summer, skip the blow dryer and let him air dry instead whenever possible.

Finally, don't forget that dogs can suffer from sun damage just like people can. Whether they have long or short hair, their ears, noses, and any other body parts with little to no hair are vulnerable. Even when the temperature is mild, too much time outdoors can lead to sunburn and raise your dog's risk of skin cancer. You can find dog-friendly (free of zinc oxide) sunscreen at your local pet-supply store.

CHAPTER 9

YOUR
DAILY ROUTINE

Becoming a dog owner changes a person's life in many ways. One of the biggest changes is the necessity to juggle your schedule for the sake of your new pet. For households with multiple people, caring for a dog around work, school, and activities can usually be easily managed, providing a little planning goes into the process. People who live alone may need to ask for help from family members, friends, or neighbors at times to meet all of their dogs' needs. If you have just moved to a new area where you don't know many people yet, you can utilize dog-care professionals such as dog walkers or doggy daycare providers to help you make sure that your beloved pet gets enough exercise, socialization, and playtime.

Your Daily Schedule—and Your Dog's

Whether you have a traditional nine-to-five job, work the graveyard shift, or are self-employed, you have certain responsibilities you must handle each day. Dog owners who work from home may have the most flexibility in their schedules, but even these people often have deadlines

and other time-sensitive work obligations. In addition to work, you may also exercise, volunteer, or enjoy an active social life. Whatever your typical day entails, you will now need to add caring for your dog into the mix.

One of the easiest ways to meet your dog's needs is to tend to him before you move on to other tasks. For example, your dog will need to go to his potty spot first thing every morning. If you decide that making your bed or taking your shower should come before taking your dog out, he may decide to relieve himself inside your home instead. Most housetrained dogs can wait long enough for their owners to brew a cup of coffee before heading outside each morning—although this is too much to ask of a young puppy—but making your pet wait for you to become perfectly coiffed is too much to ask of even a well-trained adult dog.

When your new puppy or dog first comes home, I recommend setting your alarm a half hour earlier each morning and allowing an extra hour before bedtime each night for pet care. Your dog will also need additional attention during your normal waking hours, but this extra hour in the evening can prove enormously helpful to new pet owners. As both you and your pet adjust to your new routine, you may be able to whittle this extra time down to a half hour or less each day.

Get in the habit of walking your dog before you start your day.

It can be helpful to take a look at your schedule, either on paper or on an electronic device, to see where you might need to make changes. If you have a meeting that runs late every Thursday, for instance, you may need to enlist some help in caring for your dog each Thursday evening. Likewise, if you travel for work or pleasure regularly, you will need to make arrangements for pet care while you are away from home. Reviewing your schedule can also help you identify the best times for important tasks like exercising, grooming, and training your dog.

Getting Some Help

Family or friends who live nearby can be lifesavers when you cannot get home to feed or walk your dog. Make sure the person you entrust with these tasks is up to the challenge; don't rule out a responsible teenager. Many kids adore animals and are surprisingly dependable. A retired neighbor who likes dogs may also be willing to help you out in this type of situation. Don't wait until the last minute, though. If you know that you will need help later in the week, make your arrangements as soon as possible. The more notice you offer, the better your chances will be of finding someone willing to help you.

Make sure you give your dog's caretaker(s) all of the necessary tools and information. Show him or her where you keep your dog's food, bowls, leash, and cleanup materials. Also, be clear about what you need him or her to do, including specific times for feeding, potty breaks, and exercise.

Post the name, address, and phone number of your pet's veterinarian, as well as info about the nearest emergency veterinary clinic, in a convenient location, and make sure that the caregiver knows where to find it. Anyone caring for your dog also needs your mobile number or work contact information so that he or she can reach you in case of an emergency. Finally, share any important information about your pet that is relevant to his care—for example, if he has a food allergy or doesn't get along with the dog down the street.

Hiring a Dog Walker

Hiring a stranger to help you care for your pet can be a scary undertaking. After all, you must entrust this individual with both your precious pet and the keys to your home. It is imperative that you check references and perform a personal interview before adding this person to your dog's list of caregivers. Increase your chances of finding a dependable dog walker by asking for

A professional dog walker should like and be able to handle all types of dogs.

Questions to Ask a Dog Walker

There are no universally right or wrong answers to the following questions, but asking them—and listening carefully to the interviewee's answers—will give you valuable information for choosing the best dog walker for your pet.

- ✔ Do you walk the dogs yourself, or do you hire other people to do it?
- ✔ Are you bonded or insured?
- ✔ What kind of experience and training do you have?
- ✔ How many dogs do you schedule for a given day? Is there a limit?
- ✔ How much time do you allow for each walk?
- ✔ How many dogs do you walk at one time?
- ✔ Do you ever stop at dog parks or allow dogs to be off their leashes?
- ✔ What are your typical pick-up and drop-off procedures?
- ✔ How do you handle behavior issues?
- ✔ Do you know canine CPR and first aid?

Finally, ask the dog walker if you can go on a short test walk together. Beware of anyone who is hesitant to agree to this simple activity.

recommendations from other pet owners. If someone you know has had a good experience with a particular person, you will likely feel more comfortable hiring him or her.

As their job title suggests, dog walkers generally stop by your home once or twice a day to take your pet for a walk. They should also give your dog a chance to relieve himself while outdoors, clean up after him if he does eliminate, and make sure that he has enough food or water before leaving him alone again. You might also ask a dog walker to perform other small tasks, such as leaving a light or radio on for your pet.

In addition to being prompt, a dog walker should have a genuine affinity for the canine species. When you interview someone for this job, include your pet in the process. Observing the way the dog walker interacts with your dog can tell you a lot about how he or she treats animals. Likewise, watch your pet to see what he thinks of the person. Animals are often the best judges of character. If your dog clearly doesn't like someone, it doesn't matter if that person is the best dog walker in the tri-state area—he or she clearly isn't the best choice for your pet. Keep looking until you find someone of whom both you and your dog approve.

Doggy Daycare

Doggy daycare centers offer a wide range of services to busy pet owners who don't want their dogs spending their days at home, alone. From providing your pet with exercise and

What to Look for in a Doggy Daycare

✔ Solid health criteria and temperament testing prior to admission
✔ Groupings based on size, age, and/or activity level
✔ Well-trained employees who know canine CPR and first-aid
✔ Sound protocol for medical emergencies
✔ Low staff-to-dog ratio
✔ Safe timeout areas to help deal with behavior problems
✔ Plenty of space, no crowding
✔ Fun activities, such as games and social opportunities
✔ Outdoor activities when weather is warm and dry
✔ Indoor activities during inclement weather
✔ Posted itinerary so you know what your dog will be doing each day
✔ Video access via Internet so you can see your dog at various times each day

socialization to feeding him and giving him opportunities to relieve himself, a daycare is a bit like a home away from home for your pet while you work. Like a daycare for children, a doggy daycare can be a fun place for a dog to spend time. Above all else, however, it should be a safe environment for your beloved pet when you can't attend to his needs yourself.

The best doggy daycares have certain criteria for the animals they accept into their programs. First, all dogs who attend daycare should be healthy, and you will likely be asked to provide a written health clearance from your vet before your dog is admitted. Likewise, most daycares require owners to show proof that their dogs are up to date on their immunizations. The exact shots that a particular business requires may vary, but any immunizations mandatory under the law, such as the rabies vaccine and initial shots for distemper and parvovirus, will be included. Other common immunization requirements for daycares include the kennel cough (*Bordetella*) vaccine and booster shots for distemper and parvo.

Although providing health clearances and proof of immunizations can be inconvenient, requirements like these are intended to keep everyone as safe as possible. Just one dog with a flea infestation can share the problem with every other dog at the daycare. A dog who has been accosted by ticks can likewise share these parasites with other dogs. As such, many daycares require all canine guests to be on monthly flea and tick preventative medications. Some facilities also require that dogs be spayed or neutered to participate in playtime with other dogs.

In addition to a daycare's health requirements, a responsible facility will also require all dogs to meet certain criteria relating to temperament. A temperament test can help the caregivers determine whether a dog will interact well with other animals at the facility. While aggressive behaviors will cause a dog to fail this evaluation, there may be varying degrees of passing among other pets. Most daycares offer playgroups and other social activities, in which only the best-tempered dogs should participate.

For the sake of safety, many daycares separate the dogs into groups of similar size for interaction with one another; even the friendliest Bullmastiff can inadvertently injure a Toy Fox Terrier. Some facilities may further group animals by their age or play styles. While they may be well matched in size, a rambunctious Weimaraner puppy is likely to annoy or injure a more timid senior Chow Chow. The more care and planning a daycare puts into its admission process and groupings, the more reassured you should feel about trusting the business with your dog.

A good doggy daycare would not put a Yorkshire Terrier and a German Shepherd together for playtime due to the big size difference.

If you have trouble finding a daycare that accepts your application, this does not mean that your pet is a bad dog. Some dogs are simply not cut out for a daycare setting. In this situation, a better option may be hiring someone, such as a dog walker or pet sitter, to care for your dog one on one. Most dogs do not require 'round-the-clock companionship but need short walks or exercise sessions while their owners are away each day.

Dog Sitter or Boarding Kennel?

At one time or another, most pet owners need to leave their pets behind while they travel. Perhaps a monthly business trip is part of your job, or maybe you enjoy vacationing in the Caribbean each winter. While you might consider taking your dog along on shorter trips, your pet may be better off staying either at home or at a boarding facility when your trip is not pet friendly.

Your dog can have a vacation of his own! Many boarding facilities offer amenities for their four-legged guests' enjoyment and comfort.

Like dog walkers, pet sitters make a living caring for animals when their owners are away. In the pet sitter's case, however, a dog's owners are gone for longer than a typical work day. A pet sitter may come to your home a few times each day or stay in your home with your dog for the entirety of your trip. Although the latter scenario will be more expensive, it offers pets more company and vigilance while you are out of town. This type of arrangement is often ideal for dogs with health problems or animals who suffer from separation anxiety.

Just as you must trust a dog walker with both your pet and a key to your home, you similarly need to feel completely comfortable with anyone who pet-sits for you. Word-of-mouth recommendations can be invaluable, as are recommendations from your breeder, rescue group, veterinarian, or local humane society. Interview a potential pet sitter as carefully as you would a dog walker or daycare provider, and keep looking if you get a bad feeling about a particular person.

I once had a pet sitter cancel on me just days before a family vacation to Florida. My first reaction was to remind the person that she had signed a contract with me. When she responded by begrudgingly agreeing to sit for my dogs after all, I thought better of the situation. I ultimately opted to release her from the contract because I no longer felt comfortable with her. A family member was kind enough to take her place, and I felt much better knowing that my dogs were in the loving hands of someone I trusted.

A boarding kennel performs nearly all the same tasks that a pet sitter does, except a kennel keeps your dog on its own premises instead of at your home. I have to admit that I used to think that boarding a dog was like sending him to jail while his owners enjoyed a luxurious vacation, but a good friend who opened a boarding kennel a few years ago showed me just how wrong I was. Certainly, boarding businesses must be evaluated as carefully as any other business that cares for your pet, but I now realize that my friend's business is just one of many that treat dogs like royalty while their owners are away. I have often joked that I would rather stay at Karen's kennel myself than go on a lavish vacation.

Use similar criteria to evaluate a boarding kennel as you would for a doggy daycare. The biggest difference between these businesses is that a kennel will be keeping your dog overnight. This begs the question—will caregivers be with my dog overnight as well? This is another question with no single correct answer. In Karen's case, her kennel is situated adjacent to her home, making it easy as can be to check on her canine guests at any time. She also has a closed-circuit monitoring system so she can keep an eye on all the dogs even after she has tucked them in for the night.

Boarding kennels also require owners to provide health clearances to make sure that no dog places another at risk. Once again, these prerequisites are to keep all the dogs safe, so they are worth the extra time it may take for you to obtain copies of your dog's records from his veterinarian. Be sure to allow yourself plenty of time prior to your trip to gather the necessary paperwork. If you choose to go the boarding route, check on your chosen kennel's availability as soon as possible. These businesses are often booked solid months in advance of the summer season as well as peak travel holidays such as Thanksgiving and Christmas.

CHAPTER 10

TRAVELING WITH YOUR DOG

The only thing my dogs seem to enjoy more than meal times is accompanying me when I leave the house. Whether the journey is as simple as a leisurely walk around our neighborhood or as time-consuming as driving into the city in five o'clock traffic on an errand, they are always hopeful that it will be their turn to tag along. I have been fortunate in that all my dogs enjoy car rides. This certainly helps when the time comes for annual veterinary checkups, although their excitement usually wanes as soon as I pull into the vet's parking lot. True traveling, however, takes a bit more planning to make the trip safe and enjoyable for everyone involved.

Road Trip!

If your idea of the perfect vacation is spending a week at a lake house—or, as we Mainers like to call it, "going uptah camp"—taking your dog along for the trip may be one of the things

Your dog deserves a beach vacation, too!

you enjoy most. Many dogs relish activities like hiking, swimming, and relaxing around a glowing campfire. You may also be able to take your dog with you when visiting faraway family or friends. Whatever the destination, taking a dog on road trip is often the easiest way to travel with a pet.

Introduction to Car Travel

If you are concerned that your dog may not enjoy riding, there are several steps you can take to make the process less stressful for him. Both people and pets often fear things that are unfamiliar, so the first step is exposing your pet to car rides as early and often as possible. By taking your dog on short trips while he is still a puppy, you will help him overcome any anxiety he might have about riding. Soon, he will likely even come to look forward to joining you on short excursions.

Whenever you take your dog in the car, take along treats. Edible rewards for good behavior will help him form a positive association with riding in the car. Also, be sure to take along drinking water to make sure your dog stays hydrated. This is important regardless of the season because running your car's heater in February can be just as taxing on your dog as the noontime sun in the middle of July. Keep these introductory trips short, but if you are gone for a long time, also remember to stop for a potty break.

If your puppy appears to dislike riding, you may need to take things more slowly. In this situation, begin by simply sitting in the car with your pet when you have no plans for starting the engine. Again, offering treats can help your dog view spending time in the car as a positive thing. You may even consider feeding him a meal there.

If your dog tolerates sitting in the car well, next try turning the ignition key so he can get used to the sound of the engine. Switch on the radio, turn up the air conditioning, and even turn on your blinker or windshield wipers to help him adjust to the various sounds. Continue offering treats throughout this process, and he will likely begin to see the car as just another place where he spends time with his favorite people.

Canine Seat Belts and Crates

You would never allow a human family member or friend to ride in your car without wearing a seat belt, and you should never allow your dog to do it, either. In the event of an accident, an unsecured animal can be thrown across the interior of your vehicle or even out through a window or the windshield. Dogs can be flung into other passengers, injuring both themselves and the people in the process. Pets who are allowed to roam freely about a car can also cause

Secure in his crate is a safe way for your dog to travel by car.

accidents by distracting their drivers.

Canine seat belts, also called car harnesses, make traveling with dogs much safer. These devices attach to the vehicle's own seatbelts to limit the animal's mobility while inside the car. You can release your pet from his harness as quickly and easily as you take his leash off when you return home from a walk.

If you prefer to let your dog move around a bit more than a seat belt permits, you may opt to use your dog's crate for car travel instead. Simply secure this enclosure with your car's seat belt to hold it in place before embarking on your journey. The safest crate models for car travel are those with rigid exteriors, such as those made of hard plastic or fiberglass. Wire crates, while perfectly safe for home use, simply aren't strong enough to protect your pet in an accident.

Dealing with Motion Sickness

Some dogs jump at the chance to go for a ride but end up feeling nauseous as soon as the car starts moving. If your dog suffers from motion sickness, it can put a damper on your travel plans faster than you can say "stain remover." Fortunately, you can take some simple steps to prevent your dog from experiencing such unpleasant reactions to riding.

Take breaks to let your dog relieve himself and get a drink of water.

Begin by making your dog's space in the car as comfortable and pleasant for him as possible; having him face forward can help tremendously. In addition to making the ride safer for your pet, a canine seatbelt can help keep him facing the front of your vehicle. Opening windows just an inch or two to let in fresh air while riding and stopping for occasional breaks can also perk up a weary traveler.

You can often prevent canine motion sickness by giving your dog ginger before a ride. If you keep fresh ginger on hand for cooking or baking, give your dog a small slice about a half an hour before travel. Many owners find it easier to offer their pets one or two gingersnap cookies instead. If your ride will be a long one, bring along more cookies to give to your dog as needed.

What To Bring

Prior to traveling with your dog, make a list of all the things he will need during the trip. Check each item off as you pack it. You may even want to use a special bag to keep all of his provisions together. Here is a sample list to get you started:

- ✔ Canine seatbelt
- ✔ Crate and liner
- ✔ Leash and collar and/or harness affixed with identification tags
- ✔ Food
- ✔ Water for the ride
- ✔ Set of travel dishes
- ✔ Favorite toys and treats
- ✔ Cleanup bags for potty trips
- ✔ Flashlight for nighttime potty trips
- ✔ Coat or sweater, if weather is cold
- ✔ Brush
- ✔ Pet wipes and/or towel
- ✔ Medications, if needed
- ✔ First-aid kit
- ✔ Name and number of veterinarian in the area of your destination
- ✔ Your pet's health records (including proof of mandatory vaccinations)

You can also purchase ginger in supplement form. If you go this route, ask your veterinarian about the proper dosage for your pet.

In general, it is best to avoid feeding your pet large amounts of food directly prior to going on a car ride. The less your dog has in his stomach, the less nauseous he may feel. Do offer him a small amount of water before leaving, however, and give him a chance to drink more whenever you stop for a potty break.

Many dogs eventually outgrow motion sickness. You may be able to help your pet adjust to car travel by taking him for shorter rides regularly. If he continues to experience stomach upset when riding, however, it may be best to avoid taking him on nonessential trips in the car. Your veterinarian may be able to prescribe an anti-nausea medication for unavoidable or especially long car trips. Owners give these drugs, which induce mild sedation, to their pets shortly before travel.

Flights

If you will be traveling a long distance from home, you may prefer flying to your destination instead of driving. Many airlines allow dogs on their flights, although certain restrictions apply. It also may not be advisable to fly with your pet depending on his age, breed, or health. Check with your veterinarian before booking your trip to make sure that your dog is well suited to air travel.

Only very small dogs with very small crates are allowed in the passenger cabin.

Pet-Friendly Hotels

With more than half of all US households now including dogs, it makes sense that pet travel has become a big industry. Although it may be necessary to leave our pets behind when we go on certain business trips or vacations, it can be fun to take our dogs along when circumstances make it possible to include our four-legged family members. Just like you, your dog enjoys a change of scenery or week of warmth in the midst of an otherwise bone-chilling winter. In order to make this happen, though, we must have pet-friendly accommodations.

Hotels that allow canine guests were few and far between just a few decades ago, but today more and more businesses are welcoming people with dogs. Even some of the biggest names in the hospitality industry now have pet policies that make it possible to travel with a dog in comfort and style. In addition to conventional resorts, you may also find bed-and-breakfasts, cottages, or timeshares that allow pets to stay with their owners.

Several websites offer searchable lists of pet-friendly lodging from one-night stays to long-term vacation rentals. Some also list nearby pet-related businesses, and some even allow travelers to input their routes to find accommodations at every point along their way.

Pet Friendly Hotels: www.pet-friendly-hotels.net

Bring Fido: www.bringfido.com

Pets Welcome: www.petswelcome.com

Go Pet Friendly: www.gopetfriendly.com

Official Pet Hotels: www.officialpethotels.com

As with airlines that allow canine passengers, hotels will charge an additional fee for dogs. You will also be required to follow each establishment's rules during your stay. For example, many hotels stipulate that pets must remain on leashes whenever they enter public areas. A hotel may also have a one- or two-dog limit per room.

Whenever possible, choose a hotel room on the ground floor when staying with your dog. This location will make it more convenient for taking your pet outdoors for potty trips. Always bring along cleanup bags with you, just as you would when walking your pet elsewhere. And make a point of letting the hotel staff know when you leave the premises each day so they can schedule housekeeping accordingly.

Smaller dogs—those whose crates can fit under the seats in front of their owners—are often allowed to ride in the plane's cabin with the human passengers. Medium or large dogs are often relegated to the cargo hold of the plane, where the passengers' baggage is kept during the flight. This area is neither heated during cold weather nor cooled during hotter weather, so it is a less-than-ideal location for pets. It can also be loud and scary for any dog.

Brachycephalic Breeds and Flying

Brachycephalic (short-nosed) breeds may experience respiratory distress riding in the cargo hold, so cargo flights are not recommended for them. Many airlines have even banned breeds such as the Shih Tzu or French Bulldog from flying in the cargo areas of their planes due to unfortunate veterinary emergencies that have occurred on flights with these breeds in the past. Some airlines impose breed-specific bans only during the hottest or coldest months of the year, but even if a company allows your brachycephalic dog to ride in the cargo space, most vets advise against it. If your dog is small enough to ride with you in the cabin, that is the best option for his health. If you own a larger brachycephalic breed, such as a Mastiff or Chinese Shar-Pei, it is safer to book a pets-only flight or drive to your destination.

Recognizing the need for a safer alternative, a few companies have come to the rescue of dogs whose owners prefer not to check their pets like luggage when traveling. These airlines specialize in transporting pets, monitoring them, and attending to their needs throughout their flights. The one downside of booking a flight with one of these carriers is that you won't be able to accompany your pet for the ride, but he will never be unsupervised or in an unsafe area of the plane.

Basic Protocols for Flying with Your Pet

Even if your dog is small enough to fly in your plane's cabin, you must make arrangements for him to accompany you in advance. Not all flights allow canine passengers, and some airlines limit the number of pets they allow on each flight. Expect to pay a small additional fee, and make sure you know all of the airline's conditions ahead of time as well. Most companies only allow pets to travel in rigid crates, for instance. You may also be required to provide a copy of your dog's vaccination records as well as a recent letter from his veterinarian stating that your dog is healthy enough for air travel.

Your dog must remain inside his carrier at all times during your flight. Be sure to offer your pet a chance to relieve himself before entering the airport. If the flight will be a long one, you may want to line his crate with scented indoor housetraining pads and pack a few extras inside your carry-on bag. If your pet does eliminate during the flight, take him—in his crate—to the restroom to swap out the soiled liner for a fresh one.

If your dog will be traveling in the cargo compartment of the plane, secure his crate door with a bungee cord to prevent it from opening accidentally. Although you may be tempted to add a lock to the door, bear in mind that this will prevent airline employees from being able to reach your pet in the event of a crisis. Give your dog a drink of water and a chance to eliminate prior to the flight, and be sure to follow the airline's protocol for picking him up after the plane lands.

International Travel

If you will be traveling outside the country with your dog, you may need to provide additional paperwork before your pet is allowed on or off the plane. The exact requirements vary, depending on the location to which you are heading. Begin by contacting the consulate or embassy of the country where you will be staying to ask about their regulations for pet travel. Some countries require import permits for pets, for example. Others require that all paperwork be filed a certain number of days or weeks in advance. Be aware that some nations require that dogs remain in quarantine for a certain period of time upon arrival.

Next, contact your veterinarian to make sure that your dog meets all the standards set forth by the destination country. If your pet needs any new shots or boosters, make an appointment to have them administered as soon as possible. If you will need a health certificate or vaccination certificate, arrange to obtain them from the veterinarian's office, and double-check in advance that you have all required paperwork. The worst time to realize that you don't have an important document is right before you board your flight, when you find out that your pet is not permitted to travel.

Small pets can be toted in soft-sided carriers but are safer in rigid crates for travel.

CHAPTER 11

CARING FOR THE SENIOR DOG

Watching your dog grow from a puppy into an adult can be bittersweet. Although you might miss some things, like sweet puppy breath, you may not miss others, like housetraining accidents. Still, it's comforting to know that your beloved adult dog has many years ahead of him. When you realize that your precious pet is entering his senior years, though, it may start to feel more bitter than sweet, but rest assured that this part of your dog's life can be every bit as enjoyable and rewarding for both of you as the rest of the years you have spent together.

As dogs move through adulthood, they go through numerous phases when their behavior or needs change. The senior years are no different in this way. Caring for a senior dog isn't difficult, but it does require a certain amount of knowledge and patience. Knowing what to expect can make it easier for you to be the best senior dog owner you can be.

Signs of Aging

Your pet's breed, activity level, and overall health may cause him to age more quickly or slowly, but you will probably first notice signs of aging in your dog sometime between five and ten years of age. Some dogs don't show signs of their age until they are well into their senior years. My eleven-year-old Cocker Spaniel Damon still races around the house like he did when he was two. His brown and white coat also still looks much the same as when he entered adulthood. His half-sister Molly, who is only eighteen months older,

Graying of the coat, especially around the face and ears, is a telltale sign of a dog's aging.

began taking the stairs more slowly when she was about eight, however, and her black ears started turning gray around the same time.

Moving more slowly, especially when getting up from a lying position, is common among older dogs. Taking a bit longer to ascend staircases or hills is likewise perfectly normal for an older dog. If your dog appears lame, however, a trip to the veterinarian is in order. Your dog's vet can tell you if your pet is suffering from an injury or arthritis, a common affliction among aging pets.

Graying fur is another common sign of canine aging. It is seen most around a dog's eyes and muzzle, although you may not even notice this change if your dog's coat is a lighter color. In addition to graying, you may notice that your pet's coat becomes thinner or duller as he gets older. If your dog has bald patches, though, ask your vet to examine him. These symptoms could also be signs of a health problem, such as hypothyroidism. Your vet may also be able to suggest ways to improve the look of your healthy senior dog's coat. Essential fatty acid supplements are often helpful for restoring shine, and they can also reduce joint stiffness.

Many seniors enjoy their usual activities, just at a slower pace.

Losing Teeth

Dental problems are common in aging dogs, especially dogs who have not had their teeth brushed regularly through adulthood. If your dog is suffering from periodontal disease, he may have loose or broken teeth. Even if your pet doesn't act like his mouth hurts, it is important to have your senior dog's mouth examined if you notice tooth problems or discoloration. Plaque and tartar coat teeth in dangerous bacteria, which are transported throughout your dog's body every time he swallows. All of these germs actually increase your pet's risks for numerous health problems, including heart, liver, and kidney disease.

To remedy this situation, schedule a professional dental cleaning with your dog's vet. She will perform a full examination on your pet prior to the procedure. Although a canine dental cleaning requires anesthesia, the rewards far outweigh the risks for most dogs, even those who have entered their senior years. In fact, having the cleaning performed can even extend your dog's life. Your vet may need to remove any diseased or broken teeth during the cleaning, but your pet will feel much better with a healthy, clean mouth.

Your senior dog looks to you for the same love, care, and consistency that he's always known.

When you pick your dog up from the vet following a dental cleaning, your pet will be tired and possibly a bit groggy. Take him home, allow him to rest as the remainder of anesthesia wears off, and follow your vet's directions closely. Most pets can start eating again the next morning and are completely back to normal in just a couple of days.

Even if your dog has had multiple extractions, he may still be able to return to eating regular kibble, although some owners swap to wet food anyway. What matters most is that you start brushing your pet's teeth as often as possible so that the plaque and tartar don't return. Think of brushing your senior dog's teeth as a way to protect his whole body from disease.

Eyesight

You may notice that your aging dog's eyesight isn't as sharp as it used to be. He may have an especially hard time seeing in the dark, bumping into things in rooms that he used to navigate easily with or without the lights on. Eye problems are common in older dogs, but the exact cause can vary. Small changes in vision are normal for seniors, but if your dog experiences a significant vision loss, this, too, is a reason to schedule a veterinary exam.

Cataracts are especially common in older dogs. Many breeds, such as the Smooth Fox Terrier and the Bichon Frise, are prone to this condition, which causes the lens of your dog's eye to become progressively cloudy. Eventually, the lens becomes completely opaque, leaving the dog blind. In many cases, owners can see cataracts, although veterinarians often notice them earlier. The good news is that this condition can be reversed; a simple surgery to replace the problem lens with a synthetic one has a success rate of between 90 and 95 percent, even if the dog has had the cataract for a long time.

Other canine vision problems aren't as simple to solve, and glaucoma is one such condition. This disease, which causes increased pressure within the eyeball, is sometimes treatable with a series of eye drops. Because glaucoma is painful, however, surgery becomes necessary if these medications do not relieve the intraocular pressure relatively quickly. In many cases, the best outcomes are achieved by surgically removing the affected eye. Unfortunately, a dog who has suffered from glaucoma in one eye is more likely to experience the same problem in his other eye.

A friend of mine is currently dealing with this very issue in one of her own Cocker Spaniels, who had his second eye removed recently. Although my friend had hoped to save her dog's vision, she is now resigned to helping him—and herself—deal with this loss. I often tell people in this situation about a conversation I once had with a canine ophthalmologist. She told me that if dogs could describe their days to us, they wouldn't bother telling us about what they saw or even what they heard; they would tell us about the things they smelled. In her opinion, this is the sense that dogs value the most.

Two other eye diseases that usually afflict older dogs are progressive retinal atrophy (PRA) and progressive retinal degeneration (PRD). Both PRA and PRD are inherited conditions that cause gradual but unavoidable loss of eyesight. Some breeds, like the Samoyed and the Tibetan Spaniel, are more prone to these diseases than other dogs, but any breed or mixed breed can suffer from them.

A cataract is evident by cloudiness in the eye.

The Samoyed is among the breeds prone to degenerative eye disease.

While owners cannot prevent their pets' vision loss, they can help their pets deal with the loss. Keeping furniture in the same places and using extra caution around stairs are especially helpful. Most owners are amazed by how quickly and easily their dogs adjust to losing their sight, however. The canine species is far more resilient than many of us often realize.

Hearing

You may notice that your older dog's hearing isn't quite as acute as it once was. Hearing loss is extremely common in aging pets, but it is also one of the easiest conditions to work with in dogs. At first, your dog's hearing loss may be minimal. He may come to you when you call him, but he might not hear the parcel delivery truck as it rounds the corner at the top of your street any longer. Later, your pet might not even hear when the driver comes to your door for a signature.

One of the best ways to minimize the effects of age-related deafness in dogs is to use visual cues when you teach him commands. You can add a cue at any time, but if you do it whenever you teach your dog a new command, you will already have a way of communicating with him if he ever loses his hearing. You can still teach your dog words such as "sit" and "stay," but by simply moving your hand in a specific way unique to each command, you effectively offer your pet two ways of understanding what you are telling him.

It is especially important that you never allow a dog with a hearing impairment off his leash in public or even outside your home in an unfenced area. In order to follow your commands, a deaf dog must be looking at you at all times. If he ever gets away, he won't hear you or anyone else calling him. My dog Molly has been completely deaf for over a year now, and she does wonderfully responding to my hand signals. Although I miss seeing her ears perk up at the sound of my husband or son coming through the door, she still gets as excited as ever once she sees them walk into the room.

Appetite

As dogs age, they sometimes begin to value food a bit less than when they were younger. An older dog who once raced over to his dish at feeding time and licked the bowl clean within just minutes might no longer get excited over his dinner. He may even leave a few pieces of kibble in the dish. If this happens to your dog, try not to worry. Simply keep an eye on him to make sure that he is eating enough. A lighter appetite isn't the same thing as a loss of appetite. If your dog starts eating significantly less food than normal for him, contact your vet to have him checked out. Loss of appetite is among the symptoms of numerous health conditions.

If it turns out that your dog is simply uninterested in eating, there are a few things you can do to whet his appetite again. It could be that your dog has become bored with eating the same thing every day. To make his kibble more appealing, try adding a small amount of water and heating the food up a bit before presenting it to him. This twofold strategy adds a gravy-like coating to the food, which softens the kibble and also releases more of the food's scent. Since dogs rely so heavily on their sense of smell, this simple change is often enough to win over a suddenly picky eater.

If your dog still doesn't seem interested in his food, it may be time for a change. Sometimes just swapping to a new brand or formula does the trick, but if you want a surefire way to bring back your dog's excitement over eating, try feeding him canned or home-cooked food with—or instead of— dry fare. You can either add the wet food as a supplement to his existing diet or transition him over to a completely new regimen. Just be sure that you adjust the amounts to keep his daily calorie intake the same.

Diet Modifications

If you haven't already switched your dog to a senior food formula, you should consider doing so when your dog starts showing signs of aging. Senior diets typically contain fewer calories, less protein, and more fiber than adult foods. While nutritionists continue to debate how much

Some senior dogs maintain a hearty appetite but may need food and treats that are easier to chew and digest.

protein and fiber older dogs need, you should base your decisions about diet modifications on your individual pet.

My dog Molly was two years old when she was diagnosed with idiopathic epilepsy. After about a year of trying different medications to manage this common illness, her

veterinarian and I finally arrived at the combination and dosages of these drugs that worked best for her. She takes a very low dose of phenobarbital, along with gabapentin and potassium bromide, both of which have far fewer side effects than the pheno does. Still, because this anticonvulsant can lead to liver and kidney issues after prolonged use, I have opted to feed her a food that is lower in protein now that she is a senior.

If your dog has remained especially energetic into his senior years, you may choose to keep his protein intake the same. Dogs who are active, healthy, and not overweight can even continue eating their regular adult food. Talk to your veterinarian to determine which choices are best for your dog.

Weight Loss or Gain

For most dogs, the senior years come with a slowing metabolism. The same treats you used to feed your beloved pet with no problems may now start manifesting as added weight around your dog's midsection. While this is to be expected, it doesn't mean that the extra pounds are acceptable. Added weight will place your senior pet at increased risk for a variety of health problems, including arthritis, diabetes, and heart disease. Being overweight even increases a dog's tendency to suffer from constipation and flatulence.

Just as you may make modifications to your senior dog's meal regimen, changing the way you offer treats is also important if he becomes overweight. The best treats for pets who need to lose weight are verbal praise and extra playtime. If you worry that your dog will miss his edible goodies too much, switch to "light" treats or give your pet Brussels sprouts or broccoli florets instead. Just remember that even fresh, healthy vegetables contain calories, so feeding too many of them can keep him from losing his extra weight.

I have found that a great practice with an overweight dog is to hand-feed him his meals each day. This simple practice can also help your pet eat more slowly, which can aid in preventing conditions like gas. You can even divide your dog's meals into several smaller portions to help him feel fuller throughout the day when you must reduce his overall caloric intake.

While many dogs gain weight as they get older, some pets may lose some fat or muscle with age. If your dog falls into this category, switching to a food formula containing more carbohydrates, fat, and protein might be a better idea than switching to a senior food. If your dog has lost a significant amount of weight—10 percent or more of his total body weight—schedule a vet visit to see if a health issue could be the cause.

Activity and Exercise Needs

If your dog is thriving, there is no reason to make any changes to his exercise regimen or play schedule simply because he is entering his senior years. Many dogs can go for long walks, hikes in the woods, and even reasonable jogs as they get older. If your pet competes in an athletic pastime, such as agility or rally obedience, he can keep participating as long as you both enjoy it. It may be necessary to limit jumping activities if your dog begins to show signs of joint problems, however.

Remaining as active as possible is one of the most important factors in a senior dog's good health. It is easy to assume that an older dog won't enjoy tagging along on a hike, but be careful about making such sweeping judgements. Unless an activity is particularly arduous or long, allow your pet to give it a try, especially if he has participated in it before with good results.

Obesity can compromise a dog's quality of life, especially in his senior years.

Canine Cognitive Dysfunction

Just as older people can suffer from dementia, dogs can experience memory loss as they move through their senior years. The technical term for this condition is canine cognitive dysfunction (CCD). A dog suffering from this problem may become disoriented in familiar places, searching for a door that he has walked through many times each day for years. He may also stare at walls or other inanimate objects, experience housetraining regression, or stop responding to his own name.

The best thing you can do for your pet is show him kindness and patience in these moments. Repeating or yelling his name will not help him remember it, but one of the best things about dogs is that most members of this species will respond to virtually anything as long as you say it nicely. Admonishing your pet for housetraining accidents also won't remedy the situation. Doggy diapers can help, though.

There is no cure for CCD. As your dog's owner, you must adjust your expectations of him to match his diminishing abilities. You may not be able to help your pet remember yesterday, but you can fill today with as much love as possible.

This doesn't mean that your senior pet needs to walk as far or as fast as possible each day. You should never push any pet to exercise beyond his limits, but even older dogs should have the opportunity to move around and play each day. Use extra caution when the weather is especially warm, always provide access to fresh drinking water, and be on the lookout for any signs that an activity is too much for your pet. Watch out for excessive panting or reluctance to keep going, for example, but know that most dogs will stop and rest when they become tired.

If your dog has any health problems that limit his physical activity, talk to your veterinarian about the best type and amount of exercise for him. And remember that daily activities such as walking up and down stairs numerous times each day count as exercise. When Molly started slowing down on the stairs, I was tempted to start carrying her instead of letting her walk. A good friend of mine, who also happens to be Molly's breeder, discouraged me from doing so, however. She pointed out that this regular exercise was probably doing Molly's body good, even when she moved more slowly. I do carry her if she is having an especially difficult day, but whenever she seems up to it, I allow her to go up and down the stairs herself. Some days, she even gives her brother a run for his money.

Adjusting Your Daily Routine

As your dog enters his senior years, you might need to adjust your daily routine in small ways that will make his life easier or more enjoyable. Older dogs tend to sleep more than younger animals, so don't be surprised if your dog is ready for bed a bit earlier in the evening or wants to sleep a bit longer in the morning.

If your dog used to join you for a daily run, he may need to cut back to just one or two shorter jogs each week instead as he gets older. If he suffers from an orthopedic problem—a common ailment of many aging pets, you may even have to start running without him and using a more leisurely walk with your pet as a cool-down when you return. Just remember that adjusting your schedule doesn't mean leaving your pet out of your daily routine. Just as you may miss your dog's company for a run, your pet will likely miss the activity, too. It is important that he still has fun and interesting things to do as he gets older.

Some dogs stop playing with toys in their senior years, but this doesn't mean that play has to become a thing of the past. If you used to play fetch with your dog each day, but he no longer seems interested in the game, come up with new games to keep him active. If your dog is food-motivated, use this trait to your advantage by playing food-finding games with him. Take a handful of treats out to your backyard and play a game of chase, offering one of the goodies whenever your dog catches you. You can also hide treats around your yard for your dog to seek out. An older dog may even enjoy replacing his daily game of fetch with lying by your side as you garden or read a book outside. What matters most is that you make time for your pet and continue to offer him opportunities to do things with you.

Regular activity helps a senior dog stay fit and healthy.

PART III

TRAINING
AND BEHAVIOR

CHAPTER 12

HOUSETRAINING YOUR DOG

The first type of training most dog owners undertake is housetraining. While their primary goal may be to teach their new pets where—and where not—to eliminate, they are doing much more than saving their homes from messy accidents when they embark on this journey: they are also starting an important dialogue with their dogs. When you begin training your dog in any way, you show him how to learn, how you will respond when he behaves in different ways, and what rewards he will receive for his compliance with your requests.

Crate Training

You may have purchased a crate for your dog to give him a quiet place to sleep or eat his meals away from the commotion of the rest of your home, but this enclosure can also serve as a valuable housetraining tool. Dogs possess a natural aversion toward soiling the area in which they sleep, and owners can tap into this instinct to help their pets create good potty habits.

Until your dog is reliably housetrained, place him in his crate whenever you can't supervise him.

Always offer your pet a chance to relieve himself before moving him to his crate, as well as when you let him out. Never leave him inside the crate too long, but do continue to return him to the crate if

Your puppy's crate is not just his special area; it also serves as a housetraining aid.

he is long overdue for eliminating. While he is still a young puppy, you may try taking him to his potty spot every twenty minutes until he finally goes.

In the beginning, a puppy may fuss when you place him in his crate and shut the door. You mustn't allow your new pet to manipulate you with these pitiful protests. Remain strong and continue his training, allowing him to come out only after he stops crying. He needn't be silent for several minutes, just long enough that he doesn't link his pleas to your opening the door.

Be careful never to make the crate seem like a punishment. Although you may use the crate as a place to keep your pet while you clean up his housetraining mistakes, never admonish him as you put him in his crate. The point of the crate is to contain your pet, not punish him. If he forms a negative association with his crate, he may develop a strong dislike of it.

Establishing a Potty Routine

As soon as your dog arrives, establish a potty-training routine. The number of times you head to your dog's potty spot each day will depend on his age and current level of housetraining. Some puppies begin housetraining while they are still with their breeders. A rescued dog may already be fully housetrained—but not always—when you adopt him. Puppies will need to eliminate more often than older animals, but even adult dogs may need frequent trips in the beginning in order to catch on to the routine. Keeping the schedule consistent is the best way to make sure that any dog masters housetraining.

Another step that improves a dog's chances of success with housetraining is keeping track of when he eats and drinks, when he eliminates where he is supposed to, and when and where he has accidents. In just a few days, you may start to see a trend in terms of when he is making the most mistakes and what circumstances may be leading up to them. For example, your puppy may do well throughout the day but falter at night. Consider what else might be happening to cause this problem. Are family members becoming so immersed in homework or watching television that they forget to take the pup out following his evening meal? Is your dog drinking from his water bowl after his last trip to his potty spot at night? Whatever the problem may be, identifying it is half the work of solving it.

To start, lead your puppy to the proper potty spot on leash.

Positive Reinforcement and Rewards

As soon as your dog eliminates in the proper spot, praise him and return inside with him. Some owners offer their pets treats when they eliminate where they are supposed to, but this can sometimes distract the animal from the task at hand. The last thing you want is to interrupt your pet while he's eliminating. Most dogs do just fine with a verbal reward alone.

If your pet doesn't go—or if he goes where he is not supposed to—do not reprimand him. He will likely infer that you are displeased with him, but chances are good that he will not understand why. When you must clean up a housetraining mess, place your dog in his crate in another room or ask someone else to take him out of the room and watch him while you clean the floor or carpet. If your dog sees you cleaning the area, it could give him the impression that his job is to make messes and that your job is to clean them up. True or not, this is not what you want to teach your pet.

Avoid giving your dog a verbal potty cue until he has learned the words you have chosen for these acts. Hearing you repeat the phrase "go pee-pee," for example, will mean nothing to your pup. In fact, it may even keep him from learning what these words mean. Instead, wait until your dog begins eliminating and then say the words in an upbeat tone as he goes. Starting off with good timing is crucial if you want to teach your dog to eliminate on command in the future.

Set Him Up for Success

Although housetraining is about teaching your dog, his success is strongly linked to your commitment to this important task. While life can certainly get busy, sometimes making it difficult for us to keep up with our many commitments, training and caring for your new pet must remain at the top of your list. If you make housetraining a top priority, your dog is sure to learn the proper place for elimination. Some dogs catch on faster than others, but you will accomplish housetraining more quickly if you go about it in a patient, persistent, and positive way.

To further set your pet up for housetraining success, use accidents to help him understand where he should eliminate. For instance, when your pet has an accident, move solid waste or a urine-soaked paper towel to your dog's potty spot temporarily to show him the right place for this activity. Many dogs learn more quickly when their owners provide them with this overt clue.

You can also help your dog succeed by remaining cheerful, even on a day with numerous accidents. Cleaning up after your dog will never be fun, but you won't have to do it for long. As soon as he starts associating going in the proper spot with your enthusiasm and praise, he will want you to repeat that reaction again and again. For this reason, keep lavishing him with praise each time he eliminates in his potty spot even after he's reliably housetrained.

Housetraining Problems

If your dog seems to be having accidents in a particular spot, it could mean that you are not cleaning up after him thoroughly. Simply absorbing urine with a paper towel or rag isn't enough to get the area clean. If you don't clean the floor or carpet with an odor-absorbing product, you risk a return to the scene of the crime. Remember, dogs have remarkable noses. They can smell even the tiniest amount of urine left behind, and when they smell it, the scent will encourage them to eliminate in that area again.

Enzymatic cleaners, available from pet-supply retailers, work best for cleaning up

Housetrain an adult dog the same way you would a puppy: with praise and rewards.

In a suburban or urban area, the fire hydrant becomes the most popular spot on the block.

housetraining messes. Remember, though, never to use a product that contains ammonia to clean up after your pet. Urine contains ammonia, so any trace of it can trigger an accident.

It is especially important to be mindful of your dog's behavior during housetraining. Few things are as discouraging as finding a housetraining accident that you didn't realize had occurred—or as frustrating as stepping in it. Limit your dog's access to a small part of your home until you are confident that he is making true strides with housetraining.

Leashes, Walks, and Elimination

Whether you live in the city, suburbs, or the country, I recommend using a leash to take your dog to his potty spot until he has a firm grasp of where he should be eliminating. Even if your yard is securely fenced, you don't want your dog using your vegetable garden as a potty spot. Dog urine can also kill grass and plants, as well as leave strong odors behind, so it is preferable to designate one area for elimination. Once your dog is going where he should consistently, you can then try letting him head to his potty spot on his own.

If you live in an urban area or your yard is not securely fenced, you will need to continue using your pet's leash for potty trips. Ideally, you should take your dog to the same spot each time while housetraining. Remember, your dog will be much more likely to go in a spot where he has eliminated before. When walking your dog on potty breaks, take along cleanup bags every time. In addition to being an act of common courtesy, cleaning up after your pet is required by law in most municipalities. Failing to do so could leave you with a hefty fine.

If you have a securely fenced yard, your dog will eventually be able to go to his potty spot on his own.

Sample Schedule

Use the following daily timetable as a guide for establishing your housetraining routine for your dog, adjusting as necessary to account for your family members' schedules. If you aren't home at certain times of the day, arrange for a friend's or dog walker's help. If your dog is older, you may increase the times between potty trips accordingly. I recommend hanging a chart on your refrigerator so everyone in your household will be aware of your pet's housetraining schedule and progress.

6:00 a.m.	Head outside for your dog's first potty trip of the day.
7:40 a.m.	Feed your dog breakfast.
8:00 a.m.	Head outside again with your pet about twenty minutes after his breakfast.
10:00 a.m.	Following your dog's morning nap, take him to his potty spot.
12:00 p.m.	Crate your dog whenever you can't watch him. Take him out for a chance to eliminate before you put him in the crate.
2:00 p.m.	Remove your dog from the crate and take him out to potty. Offer him his midday meal and then take him out again about twenty minutes later.
4:00 p.m.	Older kids returning from school can offer the dog a potty break or take him on a short walk. Be sure that they keep your pet leashed at all times.
5:40 p.m.	Feed your dog his evening meal.
6:00 p.m.	Take your dog out for a potty trip shortly after his evening meal.
8:00 p.m.	Don't forget a mid-evening potty break; this is often a prime time for accidents.
10:00 p.m.	Remove your dog's water bowl and take him outside for his final potty break of the day.

Don't forget to record each trip, success, and mishap on a chart to help you identify any weak spots in your training routine.

CHAPTER 13

COMMUNICATING WITH YOUR DOG

Learning to communicate with a dog can be one of the most rewarding experiences of pet ownership. The language barrier between humans and canines can sometimes cause great frustration, however. When my dogs are ill, I wish more than anything that they could use words to tell me what is wrong. While training your dog, you might feel discouraged when he just doesn't seem to understand what you want him to do. With a little work on our behalf, though, communication between our species and our dogs can become heartwarming and productive.

The most important thing you can do to help your dog understand that you are his leader is to establish clear boundaries. The exact rules of your home may differ somewhat from mine, but what matters most is that you enforce the rules you create for your pet. If you do not, he will become confused about what type of behavior you expect from him. Some owners think that allowing dogs on the furniture sends the wrong message; others are comfortable sharing their beds with their dogs. Wherever your opinions fall regarding these and other matters, you simply must be clear and consistent.

A good bond starts with clear communication.

Common ways to instill good manners in your dog include teaching your dog to wait for your permission before eating, walking through doorways, and so on. Good manners and basic commands not only guide your dog in behaving the way you want him to but also help keep him safe.

When I started training my dog Jemma, I would give her the Sit cue to before offering her bowl at mealtimes. I would then tell her to "Leave it" as I placed the bowl in front of her. Through this process, she learned to wait until I pointed to her food and said "OK" before she ate. An overexcited dog might jump up for the food or try to reach the bowl as soon as possible; by teaching Jemma to wait for permission, however, I made the feeding process a calmer one for everyone involved.

I also taught Jemma that I make the decisions about food. Because I have two other dogs in my household, this lesson is an especially important one. If I accidentally drop a piece of food while cooking, Jemma remains wherever she was when she saw the item hit the floor. This can protect her from eating something that could hurt her, like chocolate. Just as importantly, it also prevents fights between Jemma and my other dogs.

Whenever heading outside with your dog, teach him to sit and wait as you open the door and walk through it first yourself. If your dog is a larger breed, this simple protocol will prevent him from knocking you down as you leave for a walk or a trip to his potty spot. It will also prevent

Your dog is the world's best secret-keeper.

your pet from rushing out the door and into the street or another dangerous situation. You can also teach your pet to heel—that is, to walk calmly beside you on his leash and stop whenever you stop. This more complicated training task can take a bit of time, but it will certainly make your walks more enjoyable.

Canine Body Language and How to Read It

People spend a great deal of time reading other people's body language. You may find a person with crossed arms less approachable than someone who stands with her arms behind her back—even if you do not consciously focus on either body position. Dogs also display and interpret feelings and intentions through mannerisms, but there are significant differences between human and canine body language. You may have been taught to a look a person in the eye to show your respect and goodwill. A dog, however, may interpret this gesture as a sign of aggression.

Dogs express themselves through numerous actions and poses. Some are more straightforward than others. A play bow, for example, is an obvious invitation to have some fun. In this position, the dog lowers his front paws to the ground while keeping his hind end up, usually with his tail wagging enthusiastically. An angry dog may stand with his ears forward and his tail raised and still as he bares his teeth.

Other feelings might be a bit more difficult for some owners to deduce from body language. Many people know that a scared dog may tuck his tail between his legs, but did you know that he might also raise a front paw or lick at the air? You might know that a curious dog might tilt his head, but he may also lean forward, standing tall on his toes. The meanings of many gestures are universal among the canine species, but as you get to know your dog, you will likely see at least a few displays of body language that are unique to him. Learning to interpret these behaviors correctly can be invaluable for training and living with your pet.

These dogs' body language is unmistakable: it's time to play!

Be a Kind Leader

Some dog owners mistakenly assume that they need to establish themselves as the alpha with their dogs, but but nothing could be further from the truth. Establish rules that make your household a more pleasant place for everyone who lives there, not rules that simply allow you to throw your weight around.

When your dog behaves badly, you must intervene, but your goal should always be to stop the unpleasant behavior and show your pet how to behave properly. Reprimands, such as yelling at or striking your pet, will not result in good behavior; they will only frighten your dog and make it harder for him to learn the right way of doing things. Praise your pet when he does well and forgive him swiftly when he makes a mistake. Your job is to make it easier for him to succeed.

When your dog misbehaves, use a firm tone of voice to redirect him. You may need an impromptu remedial training session with your dog at these times, but keep the training brief and your attitude positive. When he complies with whatever command you are trying to re-instill, offer effusive praise. Most dogs want nothing more than to please their owners. A heartfelt "good boy!" or scratch behind the ears will encourage your dog to work even harder to win your approval next time.

Canine Vocalizations

If your dogs are anything like mine, they probably "talk" to you every day. Depending on your pet's breed or individual habits, he may bark, growl, bay, whine, or whimper. Each of these vocalizations has its own variety of meanings, depending on how and when the sounds are expressed. Knowing how to translate them can help you understand your dog better and make everything from training to everyday life more pleasant for both of you.

Barking is probably the broadest category of sounds that dogs make. A bark can indicate alarm, boredom, demand, fear, or even a desire to play. As you get to know your pet, you will likely notice a range of tones in his various barks. I can usually tell when my dogs are barking to alert me that someone is coming to my door even before they start running toward it. I can even tell whether I know the person or not just as quickly. While Jemma has the friendliest disposition of my three canines, she sounds simply ferocious when she sees the need to announce a visitor she does not know.

Growling often indicates an aggressive feeling, although it can also be part of innocent play. It is paramount that you know the difference, however, for the sake of safety. On one hand, an aggressive growl can be a precursor to a bite, so many owners discourage their pets from this particular vocalization, ending a play session immediately if their dogs "go there." On the other hand, my husband allows our dogs to growl during playtime with him as long as their tails are wagging.

Baying, whining, and whimpering are often seen as annoying sounds, but it is important to pay attention to these vocalizations. They can indicate that your dog is

in trouble. A hound dog may bay if he discoverers an intruder in your home. Other dogs may whimper if they are hurt or upset over something. Giving in to manipulative vocalizations—such as a plea to be released from the crate—can have unwanted consequences, but you should always first try to make sure that your dog isn't trying to tell you something important before discounting these sounds.

With ears forward and teeth bared, this dog sends a warning not to come any closer.

How to Use Words and Body Language

When people apologize for saying my last name wrong, I often joke that, much like a dog, I will answer to almost anything as long as it is said nicely. The proper pronunciation of Gagne is *GAHN-yay*, but it rarely bothers me when people say *GAG-nee*, as many do. Dogs are indeed the same way when people do or say something that isn't quite right, as long as their intentions are good. Dogs are incredibly perceptive judges of character. I am definitely not joking when I say that if my animals take a strong disliking to a particular person, chances are good that I will trust their assessment.

Even though we don't rely exclusively on words to communicate with our dogs, learning how to communicate with our pets through certain words and gestures is undeniably helpful in numerous situations. The average dog understands about 165 words. It is no coincidence that your dog gets excited when he hears you say the word "walk." It also isn't a coincidence if your dog slowly backs away when you utter a resounding "oh, no!" after he has raided the trash. Sometimes it is your tone that your dog recognizes, but many times he also connects a word to its meaning, regardless of the circumstances or sound of your voice.

Teaching words is a bit different from training him to follow commands in that you aren't trying to elicit a specific behavior. For this reason, it can be simple to expand your dog's vocabulary with just a little effort. When you feed your pet his dinner, say the word "food." When you fill his water bowl, say the word "drink." Using this approach repeatedly will instill these words in your dog's brain so that he remembers them in the future.

Hand signals can be just as effective as verbal cues in training your dog.

When I say the word "crate," my dogs instantly start heading to their kennels, partly because they know they that will get a treat for their trouble—but the fact that they know where to go means that they have learned this word. This type of understanding comes in handy when one of my dogs is trying to tell me something. When I ask, "Do you want a drink?" and the dog in question responds excitedly, I inevitably find the water bowl empty.

Whether through words, body language, or both, you want your dog to come to you reliably.

You can also communicate with your pet through body language. A fun exercise to try with your pet is yawning in his presence. Studies have shown that the stronger your bond with your dog is, the more likely he will be to yawn after he sees you do it. While there may be no practical result for playing instigator in this way, you can use this test as a springboard for discerning how much attention your dog pays to your behavior and gestures.

Many dogs are more likely to come when called when people squat down and open their arms while issuing the Come command. This simple body language actually saved my dog Jemma from running away on the day she joined my household. After slipping out of her collar, Jem darted out of my yard and across the street into a neighbor's driveway. As I followed her, she continued on her way, clearly the faster runner of the two of us. Just for a moment, she stopped and looked back at me. In the blink of an eye, I had to choose between approaching her and trying to get her to come to me. My instincts told me to go with the latter. I dropped down to my knees on the asphalt and opened my arms in a welcoming gesture. I hadn't even said her name yet when she came running to me. I have since adjusted her collar and practiced this recall technique repeatedly.

The Canine Senses

You may have heard that dogs cannot see colors. Although this is not true, your dog does not see the world in the way that you do. A dog's eyes have only two sets of cones, compared to the three that a person's eyes have. This means they can only see shades of yellow, gray, and blue. Of all a dog's senses, sight is one he relies on the least.

The other is taste. While your dog might like food

A dog's hearing is much more acute than a human's.

even more than you do, his tongue contains only about one-sixth the number of taste buds as yours. This deficit simply means that he enjoys his meals without the wide range of seasonings many people need to make their food appealing.

A dog's hearing, however, puts a person's ears to shame. A young or healthy adult dog can hear many sounds a person cannot. Most humans hear sounds up to a level of 20,000 hertz, whereas dogs usually hear up to 60,000. The canine species also has twenty-four muscles in their ears, which allow dogs to move these body parts more than people can with the six ear muscles we have. Breeds with pricked ears, such as the German Shepherd Dog and Pomeranian, typically hear better than dogs with hanging ears.

The only sense that rivals a dog's hearing is his scenting ability. A dog's nose is forty times more sensitive than a person's. Your pet relies on his sense of smell for recognizing friends and other animals and for learning about new people, places, and things. Some dogs even use their sense of smell for helping others, as search-and-rescue animals and drug-sniffing police dogs do.

While a dog's sense of touch is often overlooked, its importance should never be undervalued. Many dogs enjoy ear scratches and body massages as much as people do. Your touch can serve as a reassuring gesture to your pet when he is anxious or frightened. It is important to understand that not all dogs like being hugged or held, though, so if your dog pulls away from you, let him go. Chances are good that he will come back to you later for some attention on his own terms.

Why Do Dogs Do That?

Even people who consider themselves the kindred spirits of dogs often find some canine behaviors downright confusing. One of my dogs, who shall remain nameless here, has a terrible habit of eating feces if I miss a pile when cleaning up the yard each morning. Even though I know the reasons for this common behavior, I can't help but feel appalled by what I see as a disgusting habit. Other owners who have dealt with this or similarly unpleasant behaviors have asked me, "Why do dogs do that?"

Coprophagia—yes, there is actually a technical term for poop eating—is something that dogs learn from their mothers. Part of a dam's job is to clean up after her pups when they defecate. Some dogs find comfort in imitating this behavior as a way to clean their own environment. The best way to avoid coprophagia is by cleaning up after your pet promptly each time he defecates.

Grass eating, while less repulsive, can cause a dog to vomit. Old wives tales tell us that this is in fact the animal's objective, that a dog who is feeling ill eats grass to induce regurgitation. The truth is that grass eaters only vomit about a quarter of the time. Most vets think that dogs graze on their owners' lawns to fulfill a nutritional deficiency, such as too little fiber, in their diet.

Eating grass is a puzzling pastime of some dogs.

A high-five for understanding each other.

Another canine habit that many people find distasteful is a dog's tendency to sniff at people's private parts. It's hard to say whether this behavior is more embarrassing for the dog's owner or the owner's guests. Most of us simply try to turn away or otherwise avoid this rather rude inspection whenever it happens, but you may wonder why dogs do this in the first place. When a dog encounters new people, he sniffs at them to gather information. A person's pheromones, which are most concentrated in the more private parts of our bodies, can tell a dog about a person's sex, general age, and health. They can even tell a dog about the person's current mood.

Distracting a dog from this behavior is indeed the best way to deal with it, although you should understand that he has no idea that he is being rude. He is simply trying to be social.

Mounting behavior is a different matter. This, too, can be an annoying situation for both pet owners and the people who end up on the receiving end of this common canine gesture. Although it may seem as if the dog is either acting out sexually or trying to express dominance over another dog or even a person, most trainers today feel that a dog mounts when he (or she) is feeling overstimulated or overexcited. Yes, even females engage in this activity! As with most unwanted behaviors, diverting the dog's attention is usually the best course of action.

CHAPTER 14

TRAINING
YOUR DOG

"**D**og training" is a simple term, but it encompasses a wide range of exercises and techniques that owners can use to help their pets learn and become well-behaved companions. Polite dogs are welcome in far more places than unruly ones. From teaching the basic commands to showing your pet how to perform fun tricks, training can be useful, gratifying, and a whole lot of fun.

What Is Positive Training?

Although dog owners have been training their pets to perform various tasks for centuries, formal obedience training has been around only since the late 1930s. Before this time, and for a while afterward, so-called dog training had been a jumble of techniques—some well-intended yet misguided, others downright cruel. Most strategies were based on intimidating a dog into acting a certain way and punishing him, often severely, when he did not comply.

Positive training focuses on rewards, not punishments.

Russian psychologist Ivan Pavlov taught the world a great deal about learning through associations with his work in classical conditioning. You have undoubtedly heard of "Pavlov's dog," who predictably salivated every time he heard a bell ring. The work of American psychologist and behaviorist B. F. Skinner offered additional insight into learning through his work with operant conditioning, or learning based on consequences. Several decades later, trainers such as Karen Pryor and Dr. Ian Dunbar were among the first people to adapt positive learning approaches to successful training programs for pet dogs. Dunbar, a veterinarian, even went on to found the Association of Pet Dog Trainers (APDT) in 1993.

Even today, there are no licenses or regulations for working as a dog trainer. Put simply, anyone can assume this title and teach dog owners how to train their pets.

Clicker Training

Clicker training has become one of the most popular forms of positive dog training. An owner utilizing this technique holds a small plastic device called a clicker as he or she teaches the dog specific commands. As soon as the dog performs the desired action, the owner presses the clicker and then immediately offers him an edible reward. As the owner repeats this exercise, the dog begins to associate the sound of the clicker with not only the forthcoming reward but also the correct behavior.

This training technique isn't difficult, but it does require precise timing. If an owner clicks too early or too late, the animal may link the sound to a different action. Most owners learn how to time the clicks with a little practice, however.

As the dog masters a particular command, the owner then stops using the clicker and starts decreasing the frequency of the food rewards. The purpose of the clicker and treats is to teach and reinforce new commands, not to make the dog reliant on them indefinitely.

One of the biggest advantages of the clicker is that it works well with dogs of all ages. Some breeders introduce puppies to a clicker before they head home with their new families. You can even use the premise of clicker training if your dog is hearing impaired—using a flash of light instead of the noisemaker. Many owners use a simple penlight for this purpose, blinking it whenever they would otherwise make the clicking sound.

When selecting food rewards to use with clicker training, make sure that the treats you choose are your dog's favorites. Many trainers recommend using high-value food items for training because dogs will work for them. My dogs love most treats, but they are definitely most motivated when a piece of meat is on the line. Whatever treat you offer, be sure to cut it into bite-sized pieces that your pet can chew and swallow quickly to limit distractions.

If your dog isn't food motivated, you can certainly substitute another type of reward in place of an edible one. A dog who lives for playing ball, for example, will work hard for a chance to chase and fetch his toy. Each time your dog complies with a command, click your clicker and toss his tennis ball. When he returns, wanting you to throw it again, issue the command and continue the game when he performs the desired behavior.

For this reason, it is of the utmost importance to use discretion when selecting a dog trainer or training technique to use with your pet.

The most successful training methods for helping a dog become a well-mannered pet are also the most humane. Positive reinforcement focuses on rewarding dogs for what they do right instead of punishing them for what they do wrong. While there are many different styles of positive training, no positive method will ever employ such techniques as yelling or striking a dog, using prong collars or shock devices, or disciplining your dog harshly in any other way.

Teaching Basic Commands

Most owners begin training by teaching several basic commands. These are the actions you will turn to again and again throughout your dog's life to help him behave properly in virtually any situation. They are also the commands upon which more complex training is based. For instance, you may be content teaching your dog to stay for a minute, or you might decide to teach him how to hold this position for several minutes. Before he can learn the more difficult task, however, he must first master its most basic form.

Watch Me

Before I teach any other commands, I like to give a dog a lesson in learning, so to speak. The Watch Me command helps ensure that you can hold your pet's attention when you need it most. Long after your dog has learned all the basics, this simple command can divert his attention away from anything that threatens his focus or safety.

Holding a treat up by your forehead or temple, say the words "watch me" in an upbeat tone. As soon as your dog looks up at you, offer him the reward in return for his attention. I find that

Watch Me is a good foundation for the rest of your training.

most dogs catch on to this command quickly due to its ease, so it is a great confidence builder for early training, but you should keep practicing it even once you move on to more challenging training tasks. I begin and end each training session with Watch Me in an effort to start and finish on positive notes.

Sit

If a dog-training command could win an award for having the most followers, the Sit command would surely take the blue ribbon. Most owners start training by teaching their dogs to sit, and for good reason. This, too, is an easy task for most dogs. Even the youngest puppies can often master it in no time. Sitting is also a starting point for many other commands and tricks.

To teach your dog to sit, hold a treat up in the air and slowly move it back and over his head. Most dogs react to this maneuver by moving into the Sit position as they look up to follow the treat. If yours does not, be patient and keep trying. As soon as you see those knees bend and your pet's bottom hit the floor, say the word "sit" and offer the treat. You can eventually phase out the food treats and give your dog an enthusiastic "good sit" once he is in position. To teach an accompanying hand signal, raise one arm with your elbow bent as you use the other hand to provide the treat.

Down

Once your dog has mastered sitting on command, you can move on to teaching him to lie down. Whenever possible, train your dog with single-syllable commands. Instead of saying "lie down," simply use the word "down." This shorter term will be easier for your dog to learn. The Down command is useful in numerous situations, such as when you want your pet to act more calmly. Putting your dog in the Down position before you open the door to greet company, for example, can prevent him from jumping on your guests out of excitement.

As your dog looks up, his rear end goes down into a sit position.

With your dog in the Sit position, hold a treat in front of him and slowly lower it to the floor. Most dogs respond to this movement by lowering their bodies in hopes of reaching the reward. As soon as your dog's elbows touch the ground, say "down" as you release the treat to him. To teach the hand signal for the Down cue, simply straighten your elbow from the Sit cue as you lower your arm in a downward motion.

Sit-Stay and Down-Stay

To teach your dog to hold the Sit and Down positions longer, use the Stay command. This training tool can be especially useful in multiple-pet households; for example, I frequently use this command to dissuade my dog Jemma from chasing my cat. It is also useful for preventing my dogs from running to the window to bark when they hear people walking past our house.

With your dog in either the Sit or Down position, say the word "stay" as you back away from your pet. To add a hand signal, hold your hand in front of you like a stop sign as you move away. You must move slowly in the beginning, or your dog may get up to follow you. If he does, simply put him back in a Sit or Down position and try again.

Keep this exercise short in the beginning; back up only a foot or two at first before moving back to your dog and rewarding him. When he's reliable for short times and at close distances, gradually extend both time and distance. Reward your dog when he stays in position until

Always greet your dog happily when he comes to you.

you return to him, and don't move on to longer Stays until he's reliable with shorter Stays. Eventually, you'll be able to walk in a circle around your dog and even leave the room with your dog holding the Stay position.

Come

If you teach your dog only one command in his lifetime, let it be this one. Training your dog to come to you when called can save his life if he ever gets away from you. This command is also useful for calling your dog to a meal or to go for a walk.

One of the easiest ways to teach the Come command is by catching your dog in the act. Whenever your pet is moving toward you, bend your knees and open your arms to welcome him as you say the word "come." Always reward your dog for complying with this command, whether you do it with praise alone or with a treat as well. Following this strategy will help ensure that your dog comes to you each and every time you say the word because coming to you means good things for him. You never want your pet to fear or be anxious about coming to you.

You can also teach the Come command by placing your dog on a leash and using it to pull him gently toward you. This approach will work well as you transition to practicing commands outdoors or in unfamiliar places, which is a great way to solidify your dog's training once he masters the basics. A dog who complies with commands despite the distractions of strangers, noises, and countless new scents is well on his way to becoming a reliably trained animal.

Leave It and Drop It

When walking your dog outdoors, you will inevitably encounter items that you do not want your dog to touch. Since dogs react to new objects much like small children do—everything tends to go straight into their mouths—the Leave It and Drop It commands are often among the most useful and treasured commands for pet owners. Discarded chewing gum, cigarette butts, and small dead animals are just a few of the unsavory items you'd probably prefer that your pet not pick up.

Leave It and Drop It are essential commands for the safety of your dog and your belongings.

To teach your dog to leave an item, use a treat or one of his favorite toys. As you place this item in front of your pet, step between him and the object as soon as he moves toward it. When he either stops or backs away, say the words "leave it" and offer him an alternate reward. Praise him when he accepts the replacement item.

To practice the Drop It command, allow your dog to pick up a favorite toy, perhaps after you throw it. While he is holding it, extend your hand with your palm facing up and say "drop it." If he complies by releasing the item into your hand, offer him an edible reward as a replacement as you say, "good drop it!" If he does not comply, gently pull the item from his mouth and issue the command again when he begins releasing the object. As soon as he does, offer rewards—just not the item you have taken away.

Wait

The Wait command can be one of the most versatile commands that you teach your dog. Use it whenever you want your pet to stop whatever he is doing for a short period of time. I often use this command for car rides. When we arrive at our destination, my dogs always want to jump into the front seat and exit the vehicle with me. I, however, want to make sure that I have their leashes securely in hand before I even touch the door handle. Commanding my dogs to wait stops them from moving toward me just long enough for me to gain the control I need to keep them safe.

To teach the Wait command, hold a treat in front of your dog with your hand open. If he moves toward it, close your hand and move it farther away. Continue to prevent your dog from taking the treat, but as soon as he stops moving toward it, say the word "wait." Once he grasps

Say it Only Once

When you want nothing more than for your dog to sit, it is tempting to say the word "sit" over and over, but using any command too much before your dog has an understanding of its meaning can be counterproductive to the training process. If you say "sit" while your dog is still standing, he may associate the word "sit" with the behavior of standing instead of with the behavior you want him to perform.

Even after your dog has learned a command, avoid repeating the word as you issue the instruction. Your dog must learn to comply the first time you say the word. Saying it three times may give him the false impression that he only has to sit when you say the word continually or more emphatically. He also might begin to associate the action with the sound of "Sit-sit-sit" instead of with the intended single-syllable command. You, of course, realize that this is a single word repeated three times, but your dog may misinterpret it as an entirely different word.

If your pet does not comply the first time you issue a command, neither reward him nor beg him. Simply return to an earlier phase of his training, where you show him what you want from him and wait for him to comply before saying the word you want him to associate with the action. Dogs are intelligent creatures who are always learning. It is up to us as their owners to make sure that they are learning the correct things.

this first step, try placing the treat on the floor in front of him—similar to the way you practiced the Leave It command. Instead of rewarding him as he waits, however, use the word "OK" to tell him when he can stop waiting and take the reward.

Once your dog has mastered the Wait command with a treat, adapt it to other situations, such as waiting to enter or leave the house through various doorways. Perhaps you keep a towel in your home's entryway for wiping off dirty paws after walks. Teaching the Wait command can help keep those muddy paws off your clean floors or carpets.

Heel

You might assume that heeling is reserved for dogs who will be competing in obedience trials or other organized activities, such as dog shows. Indeed, animals participating in these and other canine sports must learn to heel, but this command can also be a practical tool for anyone who enjoys walking a dog on a leash. Put simply, heeling is walking politely on a leash. A dog who knows how to heel will walk when his owner walks and stop when his owner stops.

Heeling is perhaps the most challenging of all the basic commands. Training a dog to heel isn't difficult per se, but it can be time-consuming. Because this command encompasses several

Without good on-leash behavior, walks are no fun for the dog or the owner.

steps, the best way to teach it is by breaking it up into smaller, more manageable tasks. Start by simply walking with your dog. After he seems to understand that he is supposed to walk with you, begin stopping periodically and placing him in the Sit position, rewarding him for his compliance. After a moment or two, begin walking again, repeating this exercise several times. Eventually, your dog will automatically stop and sit when you stop walking.

If you wish to compete in obedience with your pet, I strongly recommend working with an experienced trainer for the Heel command. A trainer can offer you valuable insight and tips for setting your dog up for success in the ring, such as starting off on a specific foot when you want your dog to move with you. If you simply want a pleasant walking companion, however, keep practicing heeling on your own. Just as there are many different training techniques, there are also many different owners who approach training with their own subtle nuances that often work perfectly for their pets.

Training Classes for Different Ages and Levels

If you wish to participate in a dog training class, you can safely do so as soon as your puppy has had all of his shots, typically around the age of four months. The first class that most trainers offer is puppy kindergarten. Like kindergarten for children, this introductory course helps prepare young dogs for the more difficult work they will take on in future classes. One of puppy kindergarten's main purposes is, in fact, simply socializing young animals to the class setting. Pups must be able to tolerate other animals and their owners before they can move on to a novice training class. Kindergarten will also introduce your dog to the most basic commands, such as Sit and Come.

You may sign up for a novice class, also called a beginner class, directly following puppy kindergarten. You may also take a novice class with an older dog who is new to training. While some beginner classes have age limits, many welcome all dogs and owners who want to start learning. A novice class will teach basic commands and offer some socialization as well. More complicated training tasks, such as heelwork, probably won't be part of this course.

What to Look For in a Trainer

It may surprise you that the role of a dog trainer is not to train your dog, but rather to teach you how to train your dog. Although some trainers will, in fact, work one-on-one with your pet, it is important even in these situations that you practice the exercises with your dog as well. You want your dog to respect your authority just as much, if not more so, than anyone else's.

When searching for a trainer, ask for recommendations from people you trust. Other dog owners, your breeder or veterinarian, or your local humane society should be able to point you toward the best trainers in your area. If you find a trainer online or through an ad on the bulletin board of a pet-supply store, ask the person to provide references and be sure to follow up on them. Another way to learn more about a particular trainer before signing up for a course is by asking to sit in on a class.

A good trainer uses positive methods only. He or she should also be patient and possess an obvious love of animals. Take your dog with you to meet the trainer, and watch his reactions closely. If he seems uncomfortable with the person, keep looking. A bad reaction doesn't necessarily mean that the trainer is a bad person—or even a bad trainer—but it does indicate that he or she won't have the best rapport with your animal. Although it can certainly be challenging at times, dog training should be fun for both you and your dog.

Advanced training classes may entail heelwork, staying for extended periods, and off-leash work. Even if your dog already knows basic commands, he may have to graduate from a novice course before being admitted to an advanced course. This prerequisite helps ensure that all canine students in the advanced class are ready for the more difficult training exercises, thus increasing their chances of success.

Advanced classes may take place in indoors, outdoors, or even at a busy public location. Working with dogs in a more hectic setting can help instill compliance with commands even among a wealth of tempting distractions. Training your dog to sit and stay in your backyard is an entirely different task from teaching him to do so at a crowded park or on a city street.

Why Punishment Doesn't Work

I like positive training because of its humaneness. Even if they were effective, approaches such as yelling or striking an animal under the guise of teaching him are, in my opinion, cruel and unnecessary. At its core, dog training is about learning how to communicate with the canine species. In this way, domineering techniques that incite fear are simply one-way communications that convey a do-it-or-else message. I don't want my dogs to fear me; I want them to learn how to behave properly in a variety of situations so that they can live their best lives. But the fact is that punishment doesn't work anyway.

Numerous studies have shown that the only thing heavy-handed training techniques teach dogs is to be fearful and aggressive, particularly toward the person imposing the punishment. Many times, animals don't even link a punishment to whatever they did wrong. In fact, punishments can even cause a dog to associate being punished with the wrong action.

Consider a dog who recently had a housetraining accident. His owner might not notice the puddle for several minutes—say, until she steps in it. Now suppose she reacts by yelling and scolding the dog. Since the dog is no longer urinating on the floor, he doesn't realize that it was the urinating behavior that upset his owner so much. Even if the owner catches the dog in the act of eliminating—and scolds him precisely at that moment—he still likely won't realize that his owner is angry because of where he urinated. He may link her outrage to the act of eliminating itself, thinking that there must be something wrong with urinating. This type of misunderstanding can lead to a dog's postponing elimination to the point of causing a health problem, such as a urinary-tract infection. And, as you may have guessed, it also does nothing to help him with the task of housetraining.

Working with other dogs in an outdoor setting gives you the chance to practice among distractions.

Maintaining Consistency in Training

Busy schedules can make it difficult to fit dog training into your daily routine, but practicing commands with your pet on a daily basis is the best way to help your dog remember what he has learned. You will almost certainly see better results if you train for fifteen minutes each morning and evening instead of dedicating an entire Saturday afternoon to working on training each week.

Think of dog training like learning your multiplication tables in school. The reason you instantly recall that 6 times 8 equals 48 is that you practiced this math problem over and over in elementary school. Similarly, your dog needs to practice the Sit command many times before it becomes second nature for him. No matter how well your dog performs during a single day of training, he must continually revisit the commands you teach him to master them.

Another important part of providing your pet with consistency is using the same words and hand signals each time you work with your dog. If a fellow household member or friend helps with training your pet, this person should also stick to the vocabulary and visual cues you establish. When teaching Jemma to heel, I began using the phrase "let's go" for when I wanted her to start walking with me again. Occasionally, my seventeen-year-old son takes Jemma for walks. On a recent trip around the block with both of them, I realized that he had been using the phrase "come on" for this part of heeling. I also noticed that Jemma didn't respond as well to this phrase, likely because I taught her something different. Her hesitance to keep going when he said "come on" was not her fault. It also wasn't his; rather, it was mine for not thinking to give him this important information.

CHAPTER 15

BEHAVIOR PROBLEMS AND SOLUTIONS

What do you picture when you hear the words "behavior problem" in relation to a pet dog? An unruly animal whose irreversible issues have led him to a shelter? Behavior problems are indeed among the top reasons that 3 million animals are surrendered to shelters each year. What this information tells us is that solving behavior issues is a major key to reducing the unwanted animal population.

Behavior problems rarely start out as big issues, but rather as small ones that owners either tolerate or fail to deal with properly. Ignoring the problem is never the answer. Positive training can prevent many of these problems, but nipping an issue in the bud can also make a considerable difference in how much a behavior problem disrupts both your life and your dog's.

Aggression

Growling and biting are two of the most overt signs of an impending aggression problem. Neither behavior means that a dog has reached a point of no return, however. To better understand why a dog is acting out in these ways, it is important to consider the circumstances surrounding the behavior.

A dog might growl at a child who tries to pick him up. This dog may even bite if the child doesn't heed his universal canine warning. Although biting is never acceptable, it is vital to understand that the dog has no other way of expressing himself in this situation. To a toddler, giving a dog is hug is display of love, but if the dog feels too restricted, the situation can become dangerous quickly. An animal who feels cornered or trapped is more likely to act aggressively, which is why it is paramount not to leave a dog unsupervised with a young child—ever.

Some dogs never act aggressively with people but growl or lunge as soon as they see another dog. Although an owner may consider this form of aggression less dangerous,

Most dogs growl or bark in warning before real aggressive behavior occurs.

it, too, can turn into a big problem. A dog who acts aggressively toward other animals can injure them or himself in the process. He can even place people at risk if a physical altercation ensues.

Behaviorists often suggest desensitization to solve dog-to-dog aggression, but this approach requires the utmost vigilance and patience. An owner might walk the dog where they can see other dogs from a distance and use positive reinforcement to reward peaceful behavior; for example, offering treats when the dog is nonreactive: no barking, growling, or lunging. As the dog becomes comfortable at a distance, the owner may decrease the distance between his dog and other dogs, but this kind of progress can take several months. The dog should also remain on his leash at all times in public.

As much as an owner may hope to overcome this problem completely, the reactive dog may never reach the point of safely interacting with other animals. In these situations, the best thing an owner can do is not take the dog to places that other dogs frequent, such as dog parks or pet-supply stores. A dog like this needs to be the only pet in the household, and it is his owners' responsibility to keep a safe distance between him and other animals.

Some dogs act aggressively without warning or apparent reason. This is one of the most difficult situations, one that requires the help of a professional. If your dog is acting aggressively and you are unsure why, schedule an appointment with your veterinarian. In some cases, an underlying health issue can be at the root of the problem. If your vet rules out a physical cause, seek the assistance of a professional trainer or behaviorist right away. Don't wait for the problem to escalate.

Resource Guarding

If your dog growls at others (animals or people) when they get too close to his food or toys, he is resource guarding. Resource guarding can lead to aggressive behavior, such as biting, if owners do not address it promptly. A dog may guard his belongings out of fear that another pet may take them, or he might act out when people approach them. Either situation can lead to a dangerous physical altercation.

You may have heard that the best strategy for preventing resource guarding is placing your hand in your puppy's dish while he eats. This advice has been passed down from generation to generation for decades, and while it might discourage resource guarding in some dogs, it can cause others to feel even more strongly that their food is being threatened. Placing your hand in your pet's bowl can even cause your puppy to bite your fingers unintentionally. Instead, I recommend hand-feeding a dog who resource-guards. This exercise shows the dog that you control the food, and it also allows him to practice gentle behavior around this vital resource.

Even dogs who usually possess the sweetest temperaments can act aggressively around food or bones. For this reason, is it essential to use caution whenever feeding your pet or when retrieving empty bowls.

Remember also that bags or bins of dog food can also trigger resource guarding. I once purchased a large box of dog biscuits at the pet-supply store. Because I wanted to wash the empty bin I used for treats before refilling it, I left the box sitting in my kitchen that evening. When bedtime rolled around, I couldn't find Molly in any of her usual spots. I eventually found her fast asleep next to the box. When Damon moved too close, Molly immediately awoke and snapped at him. Luckily, she missed, but I quickly realized that leaving a box of treats sitting around was not a safe option.

If the object of your dog's resource guarding is a toy or other nonfood item, I recommend taking it away. Sometimes only certain toys, such as those with

Dogs can act protective over "high-value" treats and toys.

food flavors or scents, stimulate guarding. At other times, an object as seemingly insignificant as a favorite ball triggers possessive behavior. The rule in my home is that if a dog guards an object, he loses it—at least for the time being. Items that I suspect will incite guarding, such as cow ears, are reserved for when my dogs are in their crates with the doors closed. Prevention is always the preferred approach with any behavior problem.

Nuisance Barking

One of the most annoying canine behavior problems is nuisance barking. This issue can arise under different circumstances. Perhaps your dog starts barking as soon as you place him in his crate, or maybe your pet barks and howls whenever you leave him at home alone. My dogs' favorite time to bark incessantly is when someone walks by our property, especially if that person is walking a dog. Whatever circumstances prompt your dog to bark excessively, it can lead to a number of problems—from angry neighbors to fines or even eviction notices.

The best way to deal with nuisance barking is to provide your dog with plenty of other things to occupy his time. Toys, particularly the chewable variety, can help a dog pass time either in his crate or when he must spend time alone in another part of your home. If passersby tempt your pet to bark, make a note of the common times of day when the problem most commonly occurs, such as when a school bus drops neighborhood kids off nearby. Switching on a television or radio at this time can distract a dog from focusing on the noises and people outdoors.

If your dog barks when you are home, consider teaching him the Enough command. When your dog starts barking, grab a treat and wait for him to stop. All you need is just a moment of

Does your dog love the sound of his own voice?

silence to reward the behavior. As soon as he is quiet, calmly say the word "enough" as you offer him the edible reward.

Be careful not to deal with barking by raising your voice. Many owners deal with barking by yelling at their dogs to stop, but many dogs interpret yelling as "human barking" and simply think that their owners are joining them in this fun activity.

Inappropriate Chewing

Chewing is a natural pastime for dogs, especially for young ones who are still teething. However, plenty of older dogs enjoy chewing, too, so it is important to keep providing your pet with plenty of opportunities to indulge safely. When a dog begins chewing inappropriate items, such as his owners' shoes or furniture, this normal canine activity becomes a problem behavior.

If your dog has a variety of chew toys, you have already taken the first step to resolving inappropriate chewing. If he has become bored with any of his playthings, the next thing you need to do is change things up a bit. Put away the older items and replace them with a few new options. Don't toss any toys in good condition because your dog may welcome them into the mix later on.

Rotating chew toys is one of the easiest ways to maintain a dog's interest level.

When your dog destroys one of your possessions by chewing it, resist the urge to give the item to him as a toy. While you may have no need for a single cross-trainer, allowing your dog to chew it like he did the other one sends the wrong message to your pet. He must understand that the only items he is allowed to chew are the toys that belong to him. You can help ensure his success by removing as many objects

Don't underestimate the damage that a chewer can do.

from his reach as possible. If you catch your dog chewing an inappropriate item, take it away swiftly and offer him a chew toy in its place, praising him if he accepts it.

For items that you can't remove from your pet's grasp—some dogs have a penchant for gnawing on woodwork—avoid leaving your dog alone near these objects. A dog prone to inappropriate chewing should be crated when you leave home. You can also use materials such as large pieces of cardboard to block your dog's access to immovable items.

Chasing

Many dog owners are perplexed by their pets' chasing behavior. Some dogs, particularly sighthounds like Greyhounds and Whippets, deeply enjoy chasing everything from cats to cars. Even the dog may not fully understand why he enjoys chasing, but it likely has to do with the exhilaration that a chase provides. It may also be linked to a strong prey instinct, as is the case with many terriers, such as Norwich Terriers and West Highland White Terriers. Allowing this behavior, however, can be dangerous for both the dog and any other animal involved.

If your dog chases your cat, it is vital that you take precautions to protect your feline pet. By doing so, you will

Greyhounds are among the sighthounds with deep-rooted chase instincts.

also protect your dog from the possibility of nasty scratches and bites—the only ways that a cat can defend herself if she becomes cornered by a dog. Create a space where your cat can go but your dog cannot, such as a gated room of your home. Although it won't stop your dog from chasing, it will keep everyone safe.

Teaching obedience commands such as Stay and Leave It can discourage chasing. You can prevent your dog from chasing moving objects, such as cars or bicycles, by never allowing your dog off his leash in public. If you have a fenced yard, pay close attention to your pet whenever he is outdoors, and never assume that he cannot climb over or dig under the fence to reach the object of his excitement. You may never teach your dog to stop chasing, but you can control this undesirable behavior.

Escaping

Just as some dogs have a strong instinct to chase after animals or moving objects, others possess a strong drive to escape. Whether these dogs scale fences, dig underneath them, or slip out open doors whenever an opportunity arises, they place their lives at risk with this dangerous

Be very cautious with a determined escape artist.

behavior. Owners must remain one step ahead of "escape artists" at all times. Installing fences at an appropriate height for your particular dog and extending the panels into the ground can help, but not even these tactics are foolproof. Certain breeds, such as the Australian Terrier and Beagle, can easily escape some types of fences, so even with a safeguard such as this, it is important to supervise a canine escape artist at all times. The most effective way to prevent a dog from escaping is keeping him on his leash whenever you head outdoors with him.

Food-Related Problems

Many canine behavior problems are focused on food, although not all of them involve aggressive actions. Some are stealthier.

Stealing

A brazen dog may build enough confidence over time to steal food from his owner. Although I hate to admit it, when life gets busy, my family is more likely to indulge in a takeout meal in front of the television. Rather

A food thief will help himself whenever the opportunity arises.

secure in her position of top dog in the household, Molly began a short-lived career as a food thief about a year ago. While I was engrossed in finding out which character wouldn't make it to the end of the season finale of my favorite series, Molly helped herself to the vegetables that had fallen off my Italian sandwich and onto the edge of my plate. I was amazed that my formerly well-mannered dog had taken to this rude behavior at the age of twelve.

If your dog steals food from your plate, I recommend doing the same thing that I did with Molly. I promptly removed her from the room until we finished eating. When Molly gets too close to my plate now, I use our hand signal for No, which is a slow back-and-forth motion of my index finger. As soon as I do this, she backs away, but I still have to keep an eye on her.

Counter Surfing

Taller dogs often indulge in a different kind of food crime—counter surfing. When my son makes a sandwich on our kitchen island with Jemma watching close by, he often tells her before returning ingredients to the refrigerator, "Just because you can, doesn't mean you should." I always smile at this, but then add a firm "Leave it" just to be sure she understands. While counter surfing can be an annoying behavior, it can also be a dangerous one. Eating food that is toxic to dogs or even too much of any item can make your pet sick.

To prevent counter surfing, place food items in the fridge, in cabinets, or on high shelves that your dog cannot reach. You cannot expect even the most obedient dog to resist the urge to eat food that you leave within his grasp, especially when you are no longer present. Counter surfing

Mealtime Tips

If your dog attempts to steal food or begs during meals, the best thing to do is remove him from the room while you are eating. Your dog's crate is an ideal tool for dealing with these problems; put your dog in his crate with a treat or favorite chew toy until you've finished your meal. Another option is to train your dog to sit or lie down quietly in a particular spot, such as on his dog bed, a reasonable distance away whenever you eat.

is one behavior problem that owners can solve by themselves in a matter of minutes by simply eliminating the temptation.

Begging

Begging may seem like a victimless crime, but, for some people, this common canine habit can cause a lot of unnecessary anxiety. I have a family member who allows her dog to sit in front of her and bark every time she eats. Unfortunately, she responds by giving the dog a piece of whatever she is eating to silence her. As you can imagine, this dog has learned that barking gets her what she wants, so the problem has only worsened over time.

It is vital that you do not give in to begging. I also discourage owners from sharing food directly from their plates, even with dogs who don't beg for it, because this can often cause a dog to become a beggar down the road. Bear in mind that the dog's sitting too close or staring while you eat is as much a part of begging as fussing or barking.

Despite the "puppy-dog" eyes, dogs must learn that the kitchen table is off limits.

Terriers were literally born to dig.

Digging

Some dogs dig to escape or chase, while others dig purely for the enjoyment of the activity. It is easy to discern the pets who dig just for fun because they will dig almost anywhere at any time. Much to their owners' chagrin, however, many dogs seem to favor digging in flower beds or vegetable gardens. Whether you spend entire weekends planting and pruning or your idea of landscaping is simply mowing the grass, chances are good that you don't want large holes all over your property.

Digging can be one of the most difficult behaviors to stop. For this reason, I recommend allowing it—within reason, of course. Set aside a small area in your yard, away from any fences, where your dog can have some earth and dig it, too. If he starts digging elsewhere, lead him back to the designated location and encourage him to dig there instead. As silly as it might sound, you might encourage him by digging a little yourself. If your pet resumes digging in the proper spot, praise him, but if he returns to an unacceptable location, keep redirecting him. It may be necessary to bring him indoors for a short time to thwart his stubbornness, but eventually your dog should learn that he can dig, but only in this one spot.

Jumping Up

Many dogs jump up out of excitement. Although you may not be bothered by this behavior with a smaller dog, a larger animal can knock over a child or small person. Jemma was already a jumper when we adopted her, and I knew that I could not allow her to keep jumping up because she could inadvertently hurt someone with her boisterous greetings.

Anxiety Aids

Several companies offer special jackets made of heavy material meant to make a dog feel more secure during storms. For example, the Thundershirt, which is said to help with numerous types of dog anxiety, provides gentle pressure to calm the dog, compared to the effects of swaddling a human baby. The Storm Defender is made specifically to help dogs with fear of storms; its special metallic lining is designed to shield the dog from the static charge buildup that occurs when a storm is approaching. Dog owners have reported success with these garments, and while success will vary depending on the individual dogs, they can be worth a try.

If your dog jumps up for attention, turn around at once. Do not speak to or engage your pet in any way because attention is what he is seeking. Instead, move out of the way so that jumping up on you isn't an option. As soon as your dog's feet hit the floor, you may turn back and greet him calmly—*calmly* is the key here because an overly excited greeting can cause the dog to resume jumping. Some owners also find it helpful to squat down or kneel to greet their dogs, thus making jumping unnecessary.

To discourage jumping up while instilling polite behavior, place your dog in the Sit or Down position upon greeting him. Reward him with attention and petting only after he has responded to your Sit or Down cue. Do the same when guests come to your home or you meet people while out and about. You want your dog to learn that sitting calmly will get him attention, while jumping up will not.

Separation Anxiety

If your dog tries to slip out the door with you whenever you go out, or he barks or howls relentlessly whenever you leave him behind, he may suffer from separation anxiety. In addition to being unpleasant for anyone within earshot, this behavior problem can incite anxious feelings in both dog and owner. Knowing that the dog is upset often makes the owner feel guilty about having to leave him behind, even when it is necessary to do so. As much as it may seem to help in the short term, taking your dog with you whenever you go out isn't a practical long-term solution.

This is another situation for which I recommend seeking the guidance of a professional trainer or behaviorist who has the experience to assess your dog's situation and offer you individualized advice. In milder cases, resources such as doggy daycare can be helpful by providing your pet with company and activity while you're at work, but even this solution isn't a complete fix—you won't be able to bring your dog to daycare each and every time you must leave your home. Working with a trainer will help you learn techniques to ease your dog's discomfort when he must be home alone.

Fear of Thunder

Many dogs are fearful of loud noises, such as thunder. Although Molly is rather stoic in every other way, I could always tell that storms frightened her when she was younger. This dog, who never wanted to cuddle at other times, would suddenly appear in my lap whenever the skies turned dark. Back then, she could hear the thunder long before I could. I suppose the deafness that has come with her senior years is a blessing in this way. Or maybe she has simply moved past her fear. Even when I can feel the thunder, she is now indifferent when a storm hits.

The best thing you can do for your pet if he is scared of thunder is to be there for him as I was for Molly—and as I continue to be for Jemma, who also dislikes thunder. Don't coddle your dog, because this is rewarding the fearful behavior, but spend time with him and try to distract him from the storm with something he enjoys, such as an indoor game of fetch or playtime with his favorite toy. If he doesn't want to play, make sure that he has access to an area where he feels secure, such as his crate or a particular room, with freedom to come and go as he pleases; confinement can increase his anxiety.

Some trainers recommend desensitization, in which you regularly play recordings of thunder sounds while rewarding the dog for calm behavior or doing something that he enjoys, such as playing a game. You want him to learn to associate the sound of thunder with positive things. And while an actual storm has other components that a dog can sense, such as changes in barometric pressure, noise desensitization may be helpful. (*Note*: You can try desensitization for other noises that incite fear, such as the sound of the vacuum cleaner.)

Some dogs suddenly become lap dogs during a thunderstorm.

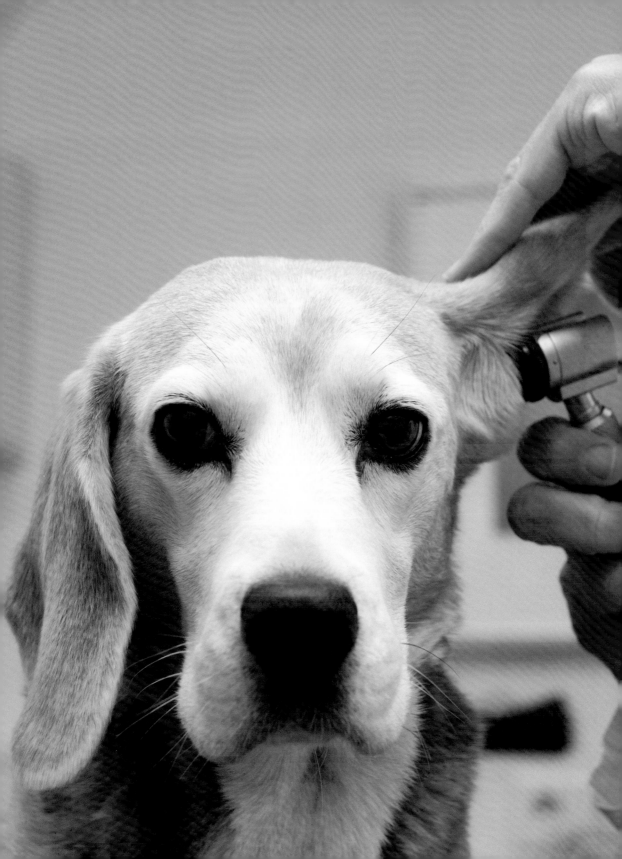

PART IV

HEALTHCARE

CHAPTER 16

VISITING
THE VET

Your veterinarian is your biggest ally in keeping your dog happy and healthy. Your dog will need a vet for preventive care and for care related to injuries and illnesses as they arise throughout your pet's lifetime. Although some dogs become nervous when visiting the vet, many learn to see these trips as fun (or at least tolerable) excursions away from home. The friendlier the vet and the rest of the veterinary staff, the more likely your dog will be to accept going to the vet as just another part of his routine.

General Well Visits

The best way to stay on top of your dog's health is to schedule regular wellness exams for him. Although routine care might seem unnecessary if your pet is obviously healthy, it is important to understand how adept the canine species can be at hiding illness—yet another trait that domestic dogs inherited from their wild ancestors, and one that has remained strong despite generations of living with human caregivers. Many times, owners do not realize that

Choose a vet who makes your puppy feel comfortable.

a dog is sick until the disease has progressed to a serious point. Veterinarians, however, are trained to identify the symptoms of illness as early as possible, increasing the dog's chances of recovery substantially.

Puppies

As soon as you know when you will be bringing your new puppy home, schedule his first vet visit. Calling ahead can help you get him in for an appointment soon after his homecoming even if your veterinarian is scheduled several weeks in advance. Ask if you should bring anything with you, such as a stool sample, and start making a list of any questions you have for the vet. In addition to health matters, veterinarians can also advise clients on feeding, training, or virtually any other issue that pertains to pet care.

Your puppy's actual checkup shouldn't take long, but it is an important step in making sure that he is healthy. In addition to examining your dog's body, the vet will probably ask you several questions about his history and how he has been acting since you brought him home. Once the vet has finished, be sure to ask your questions and listen carefully to the answers.

Although most vets keep treats on hand, make a point of bringing a few with you so the staff can offer them to your new pet. This simple exercise will help your pup form a positive association with going to the veterinary clinic. Treats can also serve as a pleasant distraction if your pet is nervous.

Adult Dogs

Adult dogs should visit the veterinarian annually for checkups. These wellness exams will be much like your dog's first exam, with the vet weighing your dog, going over his whole body, and asking about his behavior. If you are concerned about anything regarding your pet's health—no matter how small it may seem—mention it to the vet.

In addition to performing a wellness exam, your vet may also be willing to perform simple grooming tasks, such as clipping your dog's nails or cleaning his ears. If you are unsure of how to handle these tasks yourself, ask the vet to show you. Since these tasks are part of your dog's routine care at home, it is important for you to become comfortable with them.

Senior Dogs

Since health problems can strike older dogs more quickly than younger animals, many veterinarians recommend scheduling two wellness exams each year once your dog enters his senior years. One of the biggest factors in the successful treatment of many illnesses is early

Vital Signs

Knowing how to perform simple tasks, such as taking your dog's temperature, can help you monitor his physical condition should he become ill, but you must have a frame of reference for your dog's vital signs in order to interpret the information you collect. You also need to know how to take your dog's temperature and pulse.

It is a myth that a warm nose is always a sign of a fever in the canine species. Warm ears, on the other hand, often indicate an abnormally high body temperature. You will need a rectal thermometer for taking your dog's temperature; coat it in petroleum jelly to make inserting it into your dog's rectum more comfortable for your pet and easier for you. A healthy dog's body temperature should fall between 100.5 and 102.5 degrees Fahrenheit (38 and 39.1 degrees Celsius).

Take your dog's pulse by placing a finger on the femoral artery on the inside of his thigh. A puppy may have a slightly slower heart rate than an adult dog: a pup's normal range is between 70 and 120 beats per minutes, whereas an adult's may fall between 70 and 180. Toy breeds, such as the Brussels Griffon and the English Toy Spaniel, often have the highest heart rates—up to 220 beats per minute.

If you are concerned that your dog may not be breathing properly, place a small mirror directly in front of his nostrils. Healthy puppies and adult toy breeds should take 15 to 40 breaths per minute, and all other healthy adults should take 10 to 30 breaths per minute. A panting dog may take as many as 200, however.

Measure your dog's heart rate or respiration when you know that he is healthy and calm. A quick way to measure is to count the number of beats or breaths for 15 seconds and then multiply that number by 4 to determine the beats/breaths per minute.

detection. Your older dog may also need to visit the vet more often if he suffers from arthritis or other chronic conditions.

Your vet can help you and your dog navigate the issues that often arise with age. He or she can provide insight into dietary changes, let you know if your dog needs to lose weight or take it easier on the exercise front, and tell you what to look out for as his risks for certain conditions increase.

Vaccinations

Vaccinations have come under a lot of fire in recent years in both human and veterinary medicine, but these inoculations play an important role in keeping dogs healthy. At one time, it was common for diseases such as parvovirus to wipe out entire kennels. Without vaccinations, many dogs would still die from this and other dreadful diseases. The rabies vaccine is required by law, and several other shots, including distemper, hepatitis, and parvovirus, are considered core vaccines.

At one time, most vaccines required annual booster shots, but extensive research has shown that the immunity provided by many shots lasts much longer than originally thought. The rabies vaccine, which was once required every year, is now only mandatory every three years in most states. If you are concerned about overvaccinating your dog, ask your vet to perform a titer. This blood test will show which antibodies have remained strong enough in your dog's body to make booster shots unnecessary.

Vaccinations have greatly limited the spread of certain deadly canine diseases.

Optional Vaccinations

Your dog's need for certain vaccines depends on both his lifestyle and your geographic location. Most doggy daycares and boarding kennels require the kennel cough vaccine. More formally known as Bordetella, this illness is remarkably similar to the common cold in humans. While it doesn't pose much risk to otherwise healthy pets, kennel cough is highly contagious and can become serious in rare cases when it doesn't resolve on its own.

Most dogs living in warmer areas or wooded regions should receive the Lyme disease vaccine to protect them against the disease of the same name. Spread by a tiny arachnid called the deer tick, Lyme disease has been diagnosed in all fifty American states. Opinions vary on how much the Lyme vaccine protects dogs who have already been exposed to this illness, however. Talk to your vet about your pet's risk factors to decide whether he should get this shot.

Another vaccine that your dog may or may not need is the shot for leptospirosis. More commonly known as "lepto," this disease is spread through the urine of infected animals. Dogs living in rural or suburban areas face the highest risk for lepto because their yards are more likely to be frequented by the wild animals that most often spread this disease. Unfortunately, the possible side effects of the lepto vaccine can rival the actual illness in their intensity, so usually only dogs with a legitimate risk are advised to receive this shot.

CHAPTER 17

PARASITES

Just the sound of the word "parasite" can make some dog owners start itching or squirming instantly. By definition, a parasite is an organism that lives off another living thing—in this case, a dog. Although most of us prefer not to think about parasites, a little knowledge and planning can prevent these canine pests and the health conditions they cause from accosting our precious pets.

External Parasites

External parasites are organisms that latch on to the outside of your dog's body. Fleas, ticks, and mites fall into this category.

Fleas

Fleas are tiny insects that feed on the blood of dogs and cats. Because they can jump distances of several inches, fleas can move easily from one animal to another. Flea infestations are among the most common parasitic problems that dogs face.

The base of the tail is a popular place for fleas to congregate.

The best way to prevent a flea infestation is by applying a monthly flea and tick preventive medication to your pet. Sold under various brand names, the most common type is a topical solution that is applied to the back of a dog's neck; it then gradually spreads over the rest of his skin in about 48 hours. Most medications of this kind protect pets for about a month, after which they must be reapplied.

If your dog becomes infested with fleas, you will notice him scratching incessantly. You should examine his body carefully in search of fleas or "flea dirt," a common term for the digested blood that fleas leave behind on their host animals. If your dog has a short or light coat, it may be easier to spot fleas, while dark or thick fur can make it much more challenging. Using a flea comb can help. After moving the comb through your dog's hair, wipe the comb with a damp paper towel. If you see dark-colored specks, chances are good that they are flea dirt.

Consult your veterinarian before you treat your dog for fleas. Many over-the-counter treatments contain dangerous chemicals, so your vet can point you toward the safest choices. Because fleas can live without a host for several months, you will also need to treat your home with a spray or fogger. Follow the product's directions carefully. If you do not rid both your pet and your home of fleas and their eggs, a reinfestation will surely occur.

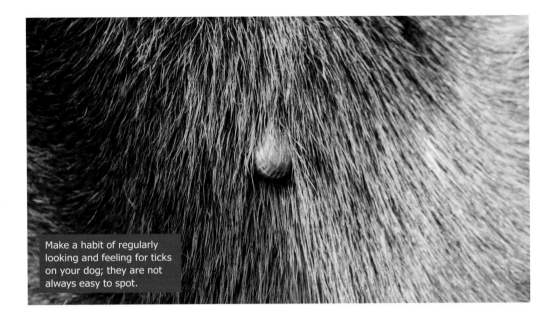

Make a habit of regularly looking and feeling for ticks on your dog; they are not always easy to spot.

Ticks

Ticks are even more insidious than fleas. These arachnids cause no itching or other reactions when grabbing hold of their hosts because their saliva contains a natural anesthetic that prevents people and pets from feeling them latch on. Once a tick attaches itself to your dog, it begins gorging on blood and increasing in size. Because most ticks are so small, many owners do not even notice a tick until it has become fully engorged. By this time, the tick may have already transmitted dangerous illnesses, such as Lyme disease or Rocky Mountain spotted fever, to your pet.

Many monthly flea preventives also work for ticks. Before your vet will prescribe a prophylactic medication, however, he or she will likely want to perform a blood test for tick-related illnesses. If your dog tests positive for any of them, he will need prompt treatment. A dog may show no symptoms of a recent infection, but more advanced cases can include signs such as fever, lameness, and lethargy. Whether your dog is showing symptoms or not, your vet will prescribe antibiotics if your dog tests positive for a tick-borne disease.

If you find a tick on your pet, don a pair of plastic gloves and use a pair of tweezers to remove it gently. After grabbing hold of the parasite, pull it straight out without applying too much pressure. If you hold it too tightly or twist it at all, you could sever the tick's body from its head, leaving the latter part embedded in your dog's skin, and any part of the tick left behind can cause an infection. If this happens, visit your vet for help in removing it safely. After you remove a tick, place it in a small amount of rubbing alcohol to kill it before disposing of it. You should also clean the area of the bite with some fresh rubbing alcohol to reduce the chance of infection.

Mites

Relations of ticks, mites also attach to a dog's skin. These tiny creatures actually burrow into the skin and lay eggs, causing the dog intense itching and irritation. Mites are much smaller than ticks, so spotting them with a naked eye can be nearly impossible. Your vet can confirm the presence of this parasite by examining your dog with a scope.

Dogs catch mites from other dogs who have become infected with these parasites, so a large part of prevention hinges on keeping your dog away from affected animals. Unfortunately, this can be easier said than done, as any area frequented by dogs can become a possible site for mite transmission. Boarding kennels, doggy daycares, grooming businesses, and even veterinary hospitals are common places for dogs to pick up mites. Ivermectin, the effective ingredient in some heartworm preventives, has also been shown to prevent mites in a wide range of animals, but your vet will have to determine if this preventive is safe and effective for your pet.

A dog with mites will scratch intensely. He may also have crusty sores or a skin rash, though the latter can be difficult to see at first on a heavily coated breed. Over time, many dogs fighting mite infestation will suffer from hair loss as well, exposing the rash.

Even the dog park can pose a risk for mite transmission.

Your vet will prescribe a special shampoo for treating mites. Like flea treatments, this product will likely contain some harsh chemicals. Since mites are so difficult to eradicate, though, these ingredients are an important part of the treatment process. In order to stop a mite infestation, you must kill all of the mites as well as their eggs, which can take time and repeated doses.

Internal Parasites

As difficult as it can be to spot tiny ticks or mites on your pet, internal parasites can be even stealthier in the way they attack a dog—from the inside of his body.

Heartworm

Heartworm disease occurs when a mosquito carrying this internal parasite bites a dog. The parasite is introduced directly into the dog's bloodstream, where it begins to grow and make its way to the animal's heart—a life-threatening situation. Dogs face the greatest risk of becoming infected with this parasite during the warmer months, but it is important to realize that mosquitoes can breed when the air is as cool as 57 degrees Fahrenheit (14 degrees Celsius), making it possible for your dog to be bitten by a carrier at virtually any time of the year in many parts of the United States.

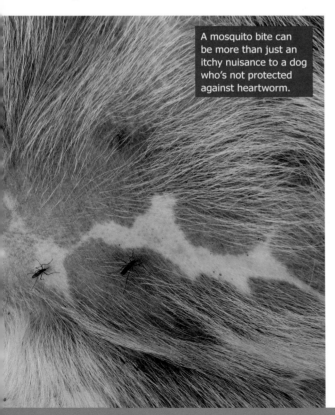

A mosquito bite can be more than just an itchy nuisance to a dog who's not protected against heartworm.

You can prevent heartworm disease from striking your pet by giving him a monthly preventive medication. You may opt to discontinue this medication during the coldest winter months, or you may keep your dog on it year-round, the latter being the safer option. When administered correctly, heartworm preventive is nearly 100-percent effective at preventing the disease.

Symptoms of heartworm disease include coughing, fatigue, resistance to exercise, and weight loss. By the time these signs appear, however, the illness has usually advanced to a dangerous stage. Treatment for heartworms consists of a series of injections, which may be administered over a twenty-four-hour period or during two separate veterinary visits, about a month apart. The dog must be hospitalized during treatment and monitored carefully afterward because shock and other adverse reactions are common. Preventing heartworm is easier, less expensive, and much safer than treating it.

Hookworms

As their name implies, hookworms are hook-shaped parasites that set up residence in a dog's small intestines. Causing anemia and inflammation, these worms can become a life-

If everyone picked up dog waste every time, the risk of parasite infestation would be greatly reduced.

threatening problem if they are left undiagnosed too long. Like other types of intestinal worms, hookworms can be prevented by dog owners who keep their pets and their potty spots clean. These worms are spread through infected fecal matter, so being selective about where you walk your pet can also be helpful. Any areas where people do not clean up after their pets pose a particularly high risk.

Symptoms of hookworms include dark or tarry stools, diarrhea, and even constipation. The worms themselves cannot be seen without the help of a microscope, so taking stool

samples with you to the vet for routine exams are the best way to diagnose this problem before more serious signs of illness occur. Your vet will treat your dog with a deworming medication, which typically works for this and other types of intestinal worms. Additionally, the heartworm preventive that you give your dog monthly may serve to protect your dog from hookworm infestation.

Roundworms

Since adult roundworms are a few inches long, you may notice these internal parasites in your dog's droppings or vomit. Some owners say these light-colored worms resemble cooked spaghetti. You can prevent roundworms the same ways you do other intestinal parasites. To keep your pet's feet as clean as possible, you may want to establish a habit of cleaning your dog's paws with wet wipes after walks or trips to dog parks; dogs ingest intestinal worms when self-grooming.

A dog suffering from roundworms may have a swollen and/or painful belly. He may also experience diarrhea, vomiting, and weight loss. Deworming should eradicate the worms and relieve the dog's symptoms, but a follow-up dose of the medication may be necessary.

Tapeworms

Tapeworms are named for their flat, tape-like appearance. As they grow, the worms break off into smaller pieces that may or may not be visible to the naked eye. When owners see these worms in their dogs' droppings, the light-colored segments resemble sesame seeds. Many dogs

Oral deworming medications are usually successful in eradicating internal parasites.

react to tapeworms by scratching or licking their hind ends, particularly around the anus, where worm segments are also often seen.

The same protocols of keeping your dog and his environment clean and free of fecal matter can help prevent him from ingesting tapeworms. Another way to prevent this internal parasite is to treat flea infestations promptly and thoroughly because external parasites can actually infect dogs with tapeworms.

Many vets treat tapeworms with oral medications, which are often the most effective at removing these internal parasites from a dog's body. It is essential that owners administer the full course of medication, however, even if the symptoms disappear quickly.

Whipworms

Whipworms are another intestinal parasite named for their shape. Thick at one end and narrowing toward the other, these worms can cause serious illness when they appear in large numbers within a dog's body. A dog in the early stages of a whipworm infestation may show no signs of illness, but eventually the parasites cause bloody diarrhea, dehydration, and weight loss.

The same preventive methods and treatments used for hookworms and roundworms will work for whipworms. And just like the others, prevention is ideal.

CHAPTER 18

ILLNESSES
AND INJURIES

Even the healthiest dogs can suffer from an illness or injury at one time or another. Some dogs also end up facing chronic yet manageable diseases. In many cases, you will need to seek veterinary care for your pet, but knowing how to deal with smaller problems on your own can be enormously helpful. Many times, you can even improve your pet's outcome in a more serious situation by knowing what to do before taking him to the vet.

Minor Problems and How to Deal with Them

You can sometimes treat and monitor small problems at home. Should your dog's condition worsen, or you are unsure of what to do next, never hesitate to contact your dog's veterinarian. The staff can help you determine whether your dog needs to be seen and can often provide you with advice for simple treatments if a veterinary visit is not needed.

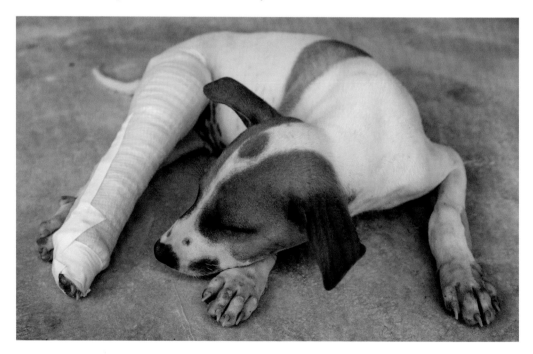

Bee Stings

If your dog spends time outdoors regularly, chances are good that he will suffer a bee sting at some point. Some dogs even chase after stinging insects like bees, unaware of the consequences until the painful moment of no return. The most common areas for stings are a dog's face, paws, or the inside of the mouth—yes, some dogs actually try to eat flying insects. In rare cases, a dog may even open a wasp's nest and suffer multiple stings at one time.

The most universal reaction to a bee sting is swelling, but, in more serious cases, a dog may have difficulty breathing or collapse. Even if your dog is only displaying minor signs of a sting—a small amount of swelling, for instance—it is important to seek veterinary treatment as soon as possible in case a more severe reaction is to follow.

When you call the veterinary clinic, the receptionist may instruct you to apply an ice pack to the sting to reduce swelling while you wait to see the vet. The vet will then likely give your dog an antihistamine to counteract his body's response to the sting. Depending on the severity of his reaction, he may also require IV fluids or an overnight stay to monitor his condition. Most importantly, you will learn how your dog responds to stings. This knowledge can help you and your vet form a crisis plan in case he is ever stung again.

Cuts and Scrapes

You can treat minor cuts and scrapes at home with styptic powder, antibiotic spray, and bandages; you can even tear a clean white T-shirt into strips to serve as a bandage in a pinch. Once you tie a strip around the cut, use your hand to apply pressure over it. If you cannot stop the bleeding from a cut, or if the bleeding is profuse, cover the wound and head to the nearest veterinary hospital at once.

If the wound is a minor one, clean it with plain saline solution or hydrogen peroxide once you have stopped the bleeding. Next, apply an antibiotic spray to the area and use gauze to cover the wound before wrapping it with a self-adhering bandage, which can be found in pet-supply stores or pharmacies. Conventional bandages made for people do not work well for dogs

Did You Know?

It is always helpful to have a second set of hands when you must take your dog to the vet. While the other person focuses on driving, you should call ahead to let the staff know you are on your way. The receptionist or a veterinary technician may offer you advice for making your dog more comfortable during the ride.

First-Aid Tips

When it comes to canine first-aid, the old scouts' adage about always being prepared applies. Here are a few tips that will make any veterinary emergency easier:

1. Keep a well-stocked first-aid kit in a convenient location at home. Most of the same items you keep on hand for human medical emergencies will also be helpful if your pet becomes ill or injured. Additionally, stash the following items in your pet's kit:
    - ✔ a small flashlight
    - ✔ your pet's rectal thermometer
    - ✔ a small mirror for checking respiration
    - ✔ styptic powder
    - ✔ tweezers

2. Keep a backup kit in your vehicle in case an emergency occurs away from home with your pet. If you take your pet hiking, transfer this mobile kit to one of your packs.

3. Post phone numbers for your dog's regular veterinarian, emergency vet, and poison control in a convenient location in your home (I post mine on the inside of a kitchen cupboard door), and enter this information into your cell phone. The worst time to go searching for this kind of info is in the middle of an emergency.

4. Learn canine CPR. Do you know what to do if your dog starts choking? Do you know the proper way to handle him if he is seriously injured? Your local humane society or pet-supply store may offer a course to teach pet owners these important lifesaving skills.

5. Place a decal on your primary exterior door or nearby window stating that your home includes a dog. Many pet-supply stores now sell these stickers. If you have more than one dog or other animals, write this information on the sticker with a permanent marker. In the event that your home ever catches fire, this will tell emergency workers that your pets are trapped inside.

because of their fur. Self-adhering bandages, however, stick only to themselves when wrapped. Some canine brands are even made with a bitter-tasting deterrent for discouraging dogs from licking or chewing at the wrap. They are also reusable, making them cost effective as well.

Natural Preventive Methods

Natural approaches for the prevention and treatment of illness are sometimes the safest options. Yogurt can help prevent yeast infections in dogs taking antibiotics, for instance. Other times, though, natural remedies can actually do more harm than good. Some dog owners swear by using garlic as a natural flea remedy, insisting that adding fresh garlic to a dog's food will make his blood less appealing to fleas. Unfortunately, certain natural methods, including this one, also have their share of critics. Many people counter that garlic is far less effective at preventing fleas than conventional preventive medications. Also, as many vets will tell you, garlic contains the same ingredient that makes onions unsafe for dogs: a derivative of sulfur, called thiosulphate, that causes anemia in members of the canine species.

Other popular natural remedies commonly used in dogs include echinacea, kelp, and St. John's wort, but each one of these can lead to or exacerbate health problems. Echinacea can be problematic for dogs suffering from immune disorders, kelp poses risks for dogs with autoimmune thyroid disease, and St. John's wort can increase the effects of certain drugs, including anesthesia. Before you try any natural approach, discuss it with your dog's vet.

Mild Diarrhea or Vomiting

All dogs suffer from diarrhea or vomiting periodically. A new treat or too much of a familiar one can sometimes lead to tummy trouble. The good news is that both conditions are usually temporary, resolving on their own given a little time and a sensible approach. For diarrhea, add a little canned pumpkin—pure pumpkin, not the sugary pie filling—to your dog's next meal. Interestingly, this same treatment can help with canine constipation as well. Also, be sure that your dog has plenty of fresh water, as diarrhea can lead to dehydration.

If your dog has vomited, continue to make fresh water available to him, but skip his next meal. Most dogs just need a little time for their stomachs to settle after throwing up. Don't be surprised if your dog experiences more than one incident of diarrhea or vomiting, but if either problem persists for more than 24 hours—or if it is accompanied by other symptoms, such as lethargy—it's time to take him to the vet. Diarrhea and vomiting are symptoms of numerous illnesses, so it is important to make sure your pet isn't suffering from one of them.

Natural Treatment Options

Like certain natural preventives, some natural approaches to treatment work remarkably well. If your dog suffers from itching due to food intolerance, give him a bath in Epsom salt to relieve this annoying symptom.

Other natural treatments do not work as well or as quickly as conventional medications, though. In less serious situations, owners may be willing to take a little extra time to avoid using drugs that may have damaging side effects; other times, however, treating a medical condition quickly is a deciding factor in an animal's prognosis. The final say of how to treat your dog will always be yours, but discussing the situation with your veterinarian is the best way to make sure you have the most thorough information before making your decision.

Common Canine Illnesses that Require Veterinary Attention

Some illnesses are more common in dogs than others. The following conditions require veterinary care, but, with a little help, owners can learn to manage them in between visits.

Autoimmune Diseases

Autoimmune diseases, such as lupus, are chronic illnesses that cause a dog's immune system to attack its own body. A wide range of symptoms—including fever, lethargy, loss of appetite, painful joints, and skin lesions—can appear with this type of disease. Veterinarians do not fully understand what causes autoimmune disorders, but a diagnosis is typically made with a series of blood tests.

Hydration is important for a dog experiencing any kind of stomach upset.

Treating an autoimmune disease is tricky business. Following a dog's diagnosis, he may need to be hospitalized for his first treatment, especially if he is in a state of hemolytic crisis, which is the technical term for the rapid destruction of a large number of red blood cells. You may be able to treat less severe incidences at home once you and your vet determine the best medications and dosages for your pet. A special diet can also play a therapeutic role in the treatment of this type of illness.

Deep-chested dogs are at a greater risk for the potentially deadly bloat.

Bloat

Bloat occurs when a dog's stomach twists and becomes overfilled with gas, leaving no way for the gas to escape. Also called gastric torsion, this potentially deadly condition can happen to any dog, but it is most common in large, deep-chested breeds such as the Great Dane or Standard Poodle. Signs of bloat include abdominal pain, drooling, general discomfort, and unproductive vomiting (dry heaving). Some dogs even collapse. Bloat is a true medical emergency that needs immediate veterinary attention and often requires surgery. If your dog appears to be suffering from bloat, get him to the nearest veterinary hospital right away.

Although the exact cause of bloat is unknown, veterinarians have identified certain circumstances that often precede a bloat attack, such as consuming large amounts of food or water in a short period of time, waiting too long to empty the bowels, and engaging in too much physical activity directly following a meal. For many years, vets thought that using raised feeding dishes also increased a dog's chance of suffering from bloat. Other studies, however, suggest that eating from elevated bowls may actually decrease the risk. While more research will be needed for a definitive answer about raised dishes, we do know that the risk of bloat increases with a dog's age.

Eye Injuries

Because dogs investigate so many situations with their noses, their faces can be injured remarkably easily. Running through vegetation, getting into a fight with another animal, and

Reading the Signs

You can tell a lot about a dog just by looking at him and petting him. The most obvious sign of good health is an alert demeanor. A dog who moves slowly or seems uninterested in what is going on around him may be feeling under the weather. Of course, sometimes it just takes a little motivation to get a dog going. If one of my dogs is acting sluggish, the first thing I do is head to the treat jar. All three members of my canine crew are highly food motivated. If I can open the cover without all three waiting in line for a treat, I know something isn't right.

Other signs of good health include bright eyes, pink ear skin, and a lustrous coat. Excessive discharge, redness, or tearing can signal an eye problem. Dark discoloration on the inside of the ear, excessive wax, or a foul odor can indicate an ear infection. A "shiny" coat is a relative term; not all breeds have glossy coats, but what matters is that your dog's coat looks normal for him. A dull coat or the appearance of dry, flaky skin can be a symptom of several health problems.

To judge a dog's health, also pay attention to his routine behaviors. Is your dog slow to get up in the morning? Is he drinking an abnormal amount of water? Has his appetite for food waned? A yes to any of these questions is a warning sign. It may not mean that your dog is sick, but it definitely means that you should pay attention to see if he is displaying any other symptoms.

Be sure to keep an eye on your dog's elimination habits as well. Is his urine a clear yellow with no signs of blood? Are his stools firm with no mucous or signs of worms? Is he eliminating easily without straining? A yes to each of these questions indicates good health, but if you notice other symptoms, a problem could still be present.

Remember, you know your dog best. If you feel that something is wrong with your pet, listen to your instincts and schedule an appointment with your veterinarian. Even if you can't quite put your finger on what is wrong, having your dog examined will accomplish two things—getting him help if he needs it and putting your mind at ease.

even just playing too rambunctiously can lead to injuries. A dog's eyes often bear the brunt of these mishaps.

You might not see your dog get hurt, but you will notice quickly that something is awry if one or both of his eyes are injured. If your dog is pawing at his eye or rubbing it against your furniture or carpet, gently take his head into your hands to get a better look. Redness, tearing, and swelling are all signs of an eye injury. You might also see a mass of tissue or blood protruding from the eye. Remain calm, but get your dog to his veterinarian promptly if you suspect your dog has sustained an eye injury.

Breed-Specific Diseases

Some health problems appear much more frequently in certain dog breeds. While not every member of a particular breed will suffer from these illnesses, the risk is heightened for these dogs. The following chart shows some of the most common breed-specific diseases.

DISEASE	BREEDS MOST COMMONLY AFFECTED
Cardiomyopathy (heart disease)	Bernese Mountain Dog, Boxer, Cavalier King Charles Spaniel, Doberman Pinscher, German Shepherd, Rottweiler, Saint Bernard
Cataracts	Australian Shepherd, Bichon Frise, Cocker Spaniel, Labrador Retriever, Miniature Poodle, Standard Poodle, West Highland White Terrier
Cushing's disease	Boston Terrier, Boxer, Dachshund, Dandie Dinmont Terrier, Labrador Retriever, Maltese, Yorkshire Terrier
Diabetes	Australian Terrier, Cairn Terrier, Dachshund, Keeshond, Miniature Schnauzer, Samoyed, Standard Schnauzer
Epilepsy	Beagle, Belgian Tervuren, Golden Retriever, Labrador Retriever, Keeshond, Shetland Sheepdog, Vizsla
Hip dysplasia	Alaskan Malamute, American Staffordshire Terrier, Bulldog, French Bulldog, Golden Retriever, Laborador Retriever, Mastiff, Pug, Rottweiler, Saint Bernard
Hypothyroidism	Boxer, Cocker Spaniel, Dachshund, Golden Retriever, Great Dane, Greyhound, Labrador Retriever

How to Give Medications

Giving a dog medication ranks as one of the least fun parts of pet ownership—just slightly above cleaning up housetraining mistakes for many people. Some medications are certainly easier to administer than others; for example, the chewy treat-like doses of monthly heartworm medication always go over better than pills or liquid medicines with most pets. Many vets recommend placing a pill toward the back of your dog's tongue and then holding his mouth closed as you rub his throat to stimulate swallowing. I've given my dog a pill every day for more than a decade, and I can tell you that a dog never comes to enjoy it. When I used this approach for several days in a row, Molly took to hiding when she saw me grab her pill bottle.

I have found that the easier way to medicate a dog is by hiding the pill inside a treat. Pet-supply stores now sell special pocket-style treats made for this purpose, but I have always had a more creative style myself. My favorite delivery method is what I call the peanut butter cookie—a tiny biscuit smeared with a small amount of peanut butter which holds the pill neatly in place on top. I have also discovered that a tiny pill can be pushed into the flesh of an apple slice with the dog being none the wiser. For liquid medications, a needleless syringe can be helpful. You can either squirt the medication directly into your dog's mouth or release it onto a small piece of bread or other absorbent food.

Even with all of the experience I have racked up with this particular task, my dog still occasionally thwarts me. She will somehow chew and swallow the whole dog biscuit but manage to spit out a pristine white pill without a speck of peanut butter on it. Because of situations like this one, it is essential that you watch your dog carefully whenever medicating him to be certain that the medicine makes it all the way down the hatch.

The first thing the vet will do is examine your dog's eye, looking for any foreign matter. As you likely know from your own experiences, even a small speck can feel significantly bigger when it gets trapped in the eye. If a visual check yields no information, the vet will then assess your dog's reflexes, such as blinking and reacting to bright light.

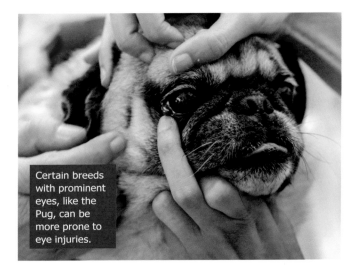

Certain breeds with prominent eyes, like the Pug, can be more prone to eye injuries.

The most common treatments for an eye injury include antibiotic drops or ointment and an Elizabethan collar. The latter item will keep your pet from continuing to paw at the eye, which can injure it further. Your vet may also prescribe an anti-inflammatory medication as well as an analgesic to reduce pain as your dog recovers. If the eye continues to bother him, the vet may need to re-examine your pet to see if deeper parts of his eye were affected by the injury.

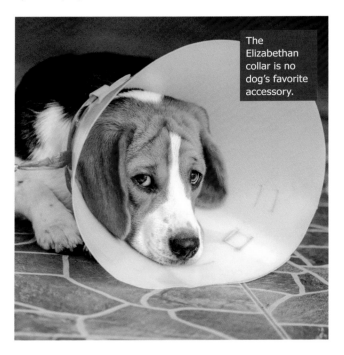

The Elizabethan collar is no dog's favorite accessory.

Heart Problems

For some dogs, heart problems come with old age; for others, cardiac illness is a secondary condition caused by long-term obesity. Sometimes, though, heart problems are genetic. The most important factor in the successful treatment of a heart condition is early diagnosis, making it vital for owners to know the symptoms and be vigilant about taking their pets for routine wellness exams.

Two of the most pronounced signs of heart disease include coughing and labored or rapid breathing. A dog with a heart issue may also suffer from edema, the technical term for an increase in water weight, manifesting as swelling and often seen in the dog's abdomen or legs. Heart problems cause some pets to act withdrawn or lose interest in activities they formerly enjoyed, such as exercise or play.

Surgery can sometimes correct heart defects in young dogs. For older animals with acquired heart disease, medications are often the best treatment. Drugs cannot reverse the condition, but they can manage the symptoms to slow down the course of the illness. A dog with congestive heart failure will continue to worsen over time.

Orthopedic Problems

Orthopedic injuries are common in canine athletes who spend lots of time running and jumping. These problems are also seen frequently in overweight dogs whose excess pounds

Purebred Health Registries

While genetic conditions such as hip dysplasia or heart problems cannot always be prevented, you can increase your chances of avoiding these and many other health issues in your pup by making sure that his parents were screened for them. You have no way of telling whether a particular puppy will develop a health condition down the road, but he runs a higher risk if the most recent dogs in his line—his parents and grandparents—suffered from them. For this reason, the best dog breeders have their breeding animals checked for the most prevalent health problems in their breeds.

If a breeder tells you that the dam and sire of a specific litter have OFA clearances for hip dysplasia, this means that these adult dogs have been certified by the Orthopedic Foundation for Animals to have healthy hip joints. Similarly, a dog with a CERF clearance has been examined and certified as free of eye disease by the Canine Eye Registration Foundation.

Make sure that clearances are as up to date as possible. Most breeders certify a dog's hips only once, but breeds with eye issues should be checked more often, ideally within a year before breeding.

Certifications do not guarantee that a dog's puppies won't develop the conditions for which the parents have been cleared. Good test results do not even mean that the dam or sire won't develop these problems in the future. Both OFA and CERF clearances are simply precautions that responsible breeders take to help ensure that they are breeding the healthiest animals, which is the best way to produce healthy puppies.

Strenuous activity and genetics both play a part in orthopedic problems.

increase their chances of falling, even while performing simple tasks like walking on stairs. Depending on his breed, your pet may be predisposed to orthopedic issues—Mastiffs, for instance, are known to suffer from hip dysplasia.

Symptoms of orthopedic injuries come on more suddenly, whereas genetic conditions like hip dysplasia will present over time. If you notice your dog limping or hopping on three legs, it could be a symptom of an anterior cruciate ligament (ACL) injury. Dogs suffering from this common condition may require surgery to repair the problem. If the injury is less severe, a vet may recommend a forced rest period of six to twelve weeks. Owners can manage their dog's pain with anti-inflammatory medications during this time. The less invasive approach of extended rest is usually most successful with smaller dogs—those weighing less than 30 pounds (14 kg). If a dog does not show improvement, however, surgery may become the only option.

Arthritis may appear in areas of former orthopedic injuries; it is very common at the site of an ACL injury, for example. Arthritis can also develop over time in a dog who participates in regular high-impact exercise, even if the dog has never suffered an injury. Arthritis is also common in senior pets, even if they weren't particularly active younger adults. Although there is no cure for arthritis, its symptoms can be addressed with anti-inflammatory medications and analgesics to reduce pain. Owners can also provide dietary supplements, such as glucosamine, and creature comforts, such as memory-foam dog beds, to ease their pets' discomfort.

INDEX

Page numbers in **bold** typeface indicate a photograph.

A

AAFCO (Association of American Feed Control Officials), 89

accessories. *See* equipment, supplies, and accessories

ACL (anterior cruciate ligament) injury, 231

active-dog formulas, 83–84, **83**

activities. *See* breed-specific activities; sport activities

activity levels, 12–13, **13**, **155**, 161–162, **163**

acupuncture treatments, 48

adolescent stage, 67

adoption options
  adult dogs, **8**, 9
  health characteristics, 27–29, **29**
  locating your dog, 25–27
  pet characteristics, 27, **27**
  puppies, 8–9
  renaming dogs, 53
  senior dogs, 9

adult dogs
  adoptions, **8**, 9
  veterinarian visits, 209

advanced training classes, 192

aggression, 194–196, **194–195**

agility sport, 14, 114–116, **115**

aging signs, 154–155, **154**

Agriculture Department (USDA), 89

airplane travel, 150–153, **150**, **153**

AKC. *See* American Kennel Club

allergies
  food, 96–97
  people's, 19

"all-natural" food labels, 89

alpha dog, humans as, 175

American Kennel Club (AKC)
  National Agility Championship, 14
  recognized dog breed groups, 20
  registration names, 53

anaphylactic shock, 96

Animal Poison Control Center hotline, 133

anterior cruciate ligament (ACL) injury, 231

anxiety, 204

APDT (Association of Professional Dog Trainers), 117, 182

appetite changes, 158–159, **159**
  . *See also* dietary changes

applications for adoptions, 27

arthritis, 82, 231

ASPCA, Animal Poison Control Center, 133

Association for Pet Obesity Prevention, 94

Association of American Feed Control Officials (AAFCO), 89

Association of Professional Dog Trainers (APDT), 117, 182

autoimmune diseases, 224

B

baby in home, socializing dogs to, 71

BARF (bones and raw food) diet, 70

barking, 176, 197–198, **198**

basic commands
  Come, 186, 187, **187**
  Down, 185–186
  Down-Stay, 186–187
  Drop It, 188, **188**
  Heel, 189–190, **190**
  Leave It, 188, **188**
  practice sessions, **193**
  Sit, 185, **185**, 189
  Sit-Stay, 186–187
  Wait, 188–189
  Watch Me, 184–185, **184**

bathing, 99–101, **100–101**, 109

baying, 176

bee stings, 221

begging, 202, **202**

behavior problems
  aggression, 194–196, **194–195**
  barking, nuisance, 197–198, **198**
  chasing, 199–200, **199**
  chewing inappropriately, 198–199, **199**
  digging, 203, **203**
  escaping, 126–127, **127**, 200, **200**
  food-related problems, 200–202
  jumping up, 203–204
  resource guarding, 196–197, **196–197**
  separation anxiety, 204
  thunder fears, 205, **205**

behaviorist, 204

behaviors, natural, 180–181, **180–181**

bloat (gastric torsion), 225, **225**

boarding kennels, 143–145, **144**, 211

body language
  canine, 174–175, **175**, **177**
  human, 177–179, **177–178**

bonding, 5, 106

bones and raw food (BARF) diet, 70

boundaries, 60–62, 172

bowls, 38, **38**

brachycephalic breeds, 37, **136**, 152

breed groups, 20–21, **20**

breed rescue organizations, 24

breeders
  facilities, 25
  questions for, 22–23
  selection of, 22–23, **24–25**
  visiting expectations, 24–25

breed-specific activities

dock diving, 120–121
earthdog trials, 123–124, **124**
herding, 119, **119**
hunting, 121–123, **121–122**
lure coursing, 120, **120**
therapy certification, 123
breed-specific diseases, 227
brush types, 99, **99**
brushing
coat, 98–99, **98**
teeth, 107–108, **107–108**
by-products, in food, 90

C

canine bonding, 5, 106
canine cognitive dysfunction
(CCD), 162
Canine Eye Registration
Foundation (CERF), 230
canned dog food, 85–88, **87**
car travel, 143–150, **146**, **148**
cataracts, 156, **157–158**, 227
cats and dogs, 72–73, **73**
CCD (canine cognitive
dysfunction), 162
CERF (Canine Eye Registration
Foundation), 230
chasing, 199–200, **199**
checklists and questions
breeder questions, 22–23
crate sizing, 33
daycare, 142
dog walkers, 141
emergencies, 133
equipment, 43
foods to avoid, 92
groomer questions, 106
housetraining timetable, 171
plant cautions, 137
trainers, 191
travel packs, 149
chemical dangers, 134–135, **135**
chewing inappropriately, 133–
135, **134**, 198–199, **199**

children
aggression warnings, 194
dog adoption consideration,
19
food sharing issue, 70
introduction of new dog to,
55, 69–72
socializing dogs to, 69–70, **69**
. See also family
chocolate candy, 129–130, **129**
choke collars, 37
city breed dogs, 15
city dwellers, 62–64, **63**
cleaning supplies, 43–44, 169
clippers
coat care, 102
nails, **102**, 104
coat care, 15–17, 98–103, **98**
cold weather concerns, 135–136
collars and harnesses, 34–37,
36–37, 51, **229**
Come command, 186, 187, **187**
commercial dog foods, 80–84
common illnesses, 224–231
communication
behaviors, 180–181, **180–181**
canine body language, 174–
175, **175**, **177**
canine senses, 179–180, **179**
canine vocalizations, 176
human words and body
language, 177–179, **177–178**
overview, 172–174, **172–174**
coprophagia, 180
cords, household, 133–134, **134**
counter surfing, 201–202
country homes, 64, **64**
crates and crate training
air travel, **150**, **153**
car travel, 147–148, **148**
housetraining, 166–167, **166**
introductions to, 57, **57**
types of, **30–31**
uses for, 30–34
Cushing's disease, 227
cuts and scrapes, 221–222

D

daily schedules and routines,
18–19, 59, **59–60**, 138–139, **139**
dangers
chewing and mouthing,
133–135, **134**
holidays, 129–132, **129**
household, 126–129, **127–128**
weather, 135–137, **136**
deafness, 158
decorations during holidays,
130–131, **130**
dental care, 107–108, **107–108**
dental problems, 155–156
deskunking, 109
development stages, 65–67
deworming medications, **219**
diabetes, 227
diarrhea, 223, **224**
diet. *See* feeding
dietary changes, 35, 37, **84**,
159–160
. See also appetite changes
digging, 203, **203**
discipline, 175, 186, 192
. See also positive
reinforcement
distemper vaccine, 211
dock diving activity, 120–121
dog parks, 63, 75
dog sitters, 143–145
dog tags, 50, **50**, **53**
dog walkers, 140–141, **140**
doggy daycare, 141–143, **143**, 211
Down command, 185–186
Down-Stay command, 186–187
Drop It command, 188, **188**
drowning hazards, 127–128, **128**
dry dog food, 86, **86**
Dunbar, Ian, 182

E

ear cleaning, 105–107, **105**
earthdog trials, 123–124, **124**
eating hazards, 70, 92, 104,
128–129, **128**

elimination diets, 97
Elizabethan collars, 229, **229**
emergencies, 133
enzymatic cleaners, 43–44,
    169–170
epilepsy, 159–160, 227
equipment, supplies, and
    accessories
    bowls, 38, **38**
    checklist, 43
    collars and harnesses, 34–37,
        36–37, 51
    crates, 30–34, **30–31**
    food, 35–37
    gates, 41–42, **41**
    grooming, 38–39, **39**
    leashes, 32–34, **34–35**
    secure fencing, 42–43, **42**
    toys, 39–41, **40**
escaping, 126–127, **127**, 200, **200**
exercise, 110–113, **110–112**, 155,
    161–162, **163**
    . See also sport activities
exercise pens (ex-pens), 62
experiences, socializing to, **70**,
    73–74, 77, **77**
external parasites, 212–215, **212**,
    214–215
eye injuries,
eye problems, 156–158, **157–158**,
    225–226, 229, **229**, 230
eyesight, sense, 179

F
falls, dangers of, 126–127, **127**
family
    house rules, 47–48
    introductions to, 46, 55
    . See also children
family considerations, 18
feeding
    AAFCO guarantee, 89
    active-dog formulas, 83–84,
        83
    allergies, 96–97
    canned food, 85–86
    commercial foods, 80–84
    diet, changing, 35, 37, **84**

dry food, 86, **86**
food labels, 88–90
foods to avoid, 70, 92, 129–
    130, **129**
homemade diets, 90–91, **90**
intolerances, 96–97
moist food, 87–88, **87**
overview, 80, **81**, **85**, **88**
portion control, **93**, 94
prescription formulas, 84
puppy formulas, **80**, 81
raw food diets, 91–93, **91**
senior dogs, 82–83, **82**, 84,
    85, 87
supplements, 93–94
treats, 95, **95**
water, 96–97, **224**
female dogs, 10–11, **11**
fencing, 42–43, **42**
fireworks, 132, **132**
first day and night at home,
    57–58
first year development stages,
    65–67
first-aid
    kits, 133
    tips, 222
flat-faced breeds, 37, **136**, 152
fleas, 212–213, **212**
flyball, **114**, 117–118, **118**
food
    formulas, 82–83, **82**
    labels, 88–90
    manners, 173
food-related problems, 200–202
foods to avoid, 70, 92, 129–130,
    129

G
games, 111–113
gastric torsion (bloat), 225, **225**
gates, 41–42, **41**, 62
glaucoma, 157
go-to-ground events, 124
GPS trackers, 51, **51**
grass eating, 180
grinders, nail, **103**

groomers, **106**
grooming
    bathing, 99–101, **100–101**,
        109
    brushing, 98–99
    coat care, 15–17, 98–103, **98**
    ear cleaning, 105–107, **105**
    nail care, **102–103**, 103–105
    overview, 98
    teeth brushing, 107–108,
        107–108
    trimming, 101–103
grooming
    equipment and supplies,
        38–39, **39**
growling, 176
guests, behavior with, 76, **76**

H
harnesses, 35, 36, **36**
head halters, 36, **36**
health characteristics, 27–29, **29**
health issues
    anaphylactic shock, 96
    anterior cruciate ligament
        injury, 231
    arthritis, 82, 231
    autoimmune diseases, 224
    bee stings, 221
    bloat, 225, **225**
    breed-specific diseases, 227
    canine cognitive
        dysfunction, 162
    cataracts, 156, **157–158**, 227
    common illnesses, 224–231
    Cushing's disease, 227
    cuts and scrapes, 221–222
    dental problems, 155–156
    diabetes, 227
    diarrhea, 223, **224**
    Elizabethan collars, 229, **229**
    epilepsy, 159–160, 227
    eye injuries, 225–226, 229,
        229
    eye problems, 156–158,
        157–158, 230
    first-aid tips, 222

gastric torsion, 225, **225**
glaucoma, 157
health signs, 226
hearing problems, 158
heart problems, 227, 229–230
hip dysplasia, 227
hypothyroidism, 227
major problems, 220–223
medication, administering, 228
natural preventives, 223
natural treatment options, 223
orthopedic problems, 230–231, **231**
pet insurance, 48–49
plants and, 131–132, **131**, 137
progressive retinal atrophy, 157
progressive retinal degeneration, 157
purebred health registries, 230
sunburn, 104
teeth cleanings, 155
toxic foods, 70, 92, 129–130, **129**
toxic products, 104
vital signs, 210
vomiting, 223, **224**
. *See also* parasites; senior dogs
health signs, 226
hearing, sense of, 179
hearing problems, 158
heart problems, 227, 229–230
heartworms, 216–217, **216**
heat cycle, 11
Heel command, 189–190, **190**
help, from family and friends, 139–140
. *See also* professional help
hepatitis vaccine, 211
herding competition, 119, **119**
herding group breeds, 20–21, **20**
hip dysplasia, 227
hobby breeders, 23–24
holiday dangers

candy and chocolate, 129–130, **129**
decorations, 130–131, **130**
"holistic" food labels, 89
home, introductions to, 54–55, **54–55**
homecoming
boundary setting, 60–62
city dwellers, 62–64, **63**
country homes, 64, **64**
first day and night, 57–58
home safety, 45–50, 62
introductions, **46**, 54–57, **54–55**
naming pets, 52–54, **52**
restricted areas, 62
schedules, 59–60
stairs, **58**
suburban homes, 64–65, **65**
homemade diets, 90–91, **90**
hookworms, 217
hot weather concerns, 136–137, **136**
hound group breeds, 20
house rules, 47–48
household dangers
chemicals, 134–135, **135**
cords, 133–134, **134**
drowning hazards, 127–128, **128**
eating hazards, 70, 92, 104, 128–129, **128**
escapes and falls, 126–127, **127**, 200, **200**
fireworks, 132, **132**
plants, 131–132, **131**, 137
household introductions, 56–57, **56**
housetraining
cleaning up accidents, **47**, 169–170
crate training, 166–167, **166**
elimination, 170, **170**
leashes, 170
positive reinforcement, 168, **169**
potty routine, 60–61, 167, **168**
rewards, 168, **169**

sample schedule, 172
success tips, 169
walks, 170
. *See also* cleaning supplies
"human quality" food labels, 89
humane societies, 24
hunting activities, 121–123, **121–122**
hypoallergenic breeds, 19
hypoallergenic diets, 97
hypothyroidism, 227

I

identification options, 50–51
illnesses and injuries
autoimmune diseases, 224
bee stings, 221
bloat, 225, **225**
breed-specific diseases, 227
common illnesses, 224–231
cuts and scrapes, 221–222
diarrhea, 223, **224**
eye injuries, 225–226, 229, **229**
first-aid tips, 222
health signs, 226
heart problems, 227, 229–230
major problems, 220–223
medication, administering, 228
natural preventives, 223
natural treatment options, 223
orthopedic problems, 230–231, **231**
purebred health registries, 230
vomiting, 223, **224**
insurance, pet, 48–49
internal parasites, 216–219, **217–219**
international travel, 153
Internet
as resource for breeder selection, 22, 24
veterinarian research, 45
intolerances, food, 96–97
introductions

to crate, 57, **57**
to family, 55
to home, 54–55
to new baby, 71
to other pets, 56–57, **56**

J

jumping up, 203–204

K

kennel cough vaccine, 211
kennels. *See* crates and crate
  training
kennels, boarding, 143–145, **144**
kibble, 86, **86**
kindergarten class, 74, 190–191

L

large breed dogs, 13–15, **14**, 81
leashes, 32–34, **34–35**
Leave It command, 188, **188**
leptospirosis vaccine, 211
life expectancy, 82
lifestyle considerations, 13
locating your dog
  adoption options, 25–27
  breeder considerations,
    22–25, **24–25**
  purebred benefits, 19–22, **21**
lure coursing, 120, **120**
Lyme disease vaccine, 211

M

Maine Lab Rescue, 24
major problems, 220–223
male dogs, 10–11, **11**
manners, 173–174
martingale collars, 37
"meal" food labels, 83, 88, 90
mealtimes, 59, **59**
"meat meal" food label, 82
medication
  administering, 228
  deworming, **219**
microchipping, 51
mineral supplements, 93–94
mites, 215–216, **215**

moist dog food, 87–88, **87**
Molly, author's Cocker Spaniel,
  48
motion sickness, 148–150
mounting behavior, 181
mouthing dangers, 133–135, **134**

N

nail care, **102–103**, 103–105
nail clippers, 38
naming pets, 52–54, **52**
National Agility Championship
  (AKC), 14
national breed clubs, 24
natural preventives, 223
natural treatment options, 223
neutering, 10
"new and improved" food
  labels, 89
non-sporting group breeds, 20
novice training class, 191
nutrition. *See* feeding
nutritional supplements, 93–94

O

obedience trials, 116–117, **116**
on-leash behavior, **190**
"organic" food labels, 89
Orthopedic Foundation for
  Animals (OFA), 230
orthopedic problems, 230–231,
  231
other dogs
  in home, 70–72
  in public, 73–76
other pets
  introductions to, 56–57, **56**
  socializing to, 72–73, **72**, **73**

P

parasites
  deworming medications, **219**
  dog waste pickup and, **217**
  fleas, 212–213, **212–213**
  heartworms, 216–217, **216**
  hookworms, 217

mites, 215–216, **215**
  roundworms, 218
  tapeworms, 218–219
  ticks, 214, **214**
  whipworms, 219
parvovirus vaccine, 211
Pavlov, Ivan, 182
personalities, 11, **12–13**, 29
pet insurance, 48–49
pet stores, 28
pet-friendly hotels, 151
pets in household, introductions
  to, 56–57, **56**
pin brushes, 99, **99**
plants, health issues and, 131–
  132, **131**, 137
playdates, 70, 72
playing, 111–113, **112**
poop scoops, 44
portion control feeding, **93**, 94
positive reinforcement, 168, **169**,
  175, 182–184, **182**
PRA (progressive retinal
  atrophy), 157
practice sessions, **193**
PRD (progressive retinal
  degeneration), 157
prescription food formulas, 84
professional help
  behaviorist, 204
  boarding kennels, 143–145,
    144
  daycare, 141–143, **143**
  dog sitters, 143–145
  dog walkers, 140–141, **140**
  groomers, **106**
  trainers, 191
  . *See also* veterinarians
progressive retinal atrophy
  (PRA), 157
progressive retinal degeneration
  (PRD), 157
protein in diet, 82–83
"proven" food labels, 89
Pryor, Karen, 182
punishment, 175, 186, 192
  . *See also* positive
    reinforcement

puppies
  adoption benefits, 8–9
  development stages, 65–67
  dog food formulas, 81
  first night home, 58
  housetraining, 60–61
  kindergarten class, 74,
    190–191
  playdates, 70, 72
  selection of, 25, **25**
  teething, 66
  temperament, 12, 29
  veterinarian visits, 208–209
puppy food formulas, **80**
puppy mills, 28
puppy-proofing, 47–50
  . *See also* household dangers
pure breeds, 19–22, **21**
purebred health registries, 230
puzzle toys, 113

R

rabies vaccine, 210–211
rally obedience (rally-o), 117
ranking stage, 67
raw food diets, 91–93, **91**
rendered protein, 82
rescue adoptions, 25–27, **26**
resource guarding, **196–197**
retractable leashes, 33–34, **35**
road trips, 143–150, **146**, **148**
roundworms, 218
routines. *See* schedules and
  routines
rules, for home, 47–48, 126–127
rural settings, 64, **64**

S

safe places in home, 45–50, 62
safety gates, 41–42, **41**, 62
savings accounts, for pet's
  healthcare, 49
scenting ability, 179
schedule adjustments, 162–163
schedules and routines
  daily, 18–19, 59–60, **59–60**,
    138–139, **139**

housetraining, 167, **168**
veterinarian wellness visits,
  208–210, **209**
seatbelts, 147–148
selection considerations
  activity level, 12–13
  allergies, 19
  coat and grooming, 15–17
  daily schedules, 18–19
  family considerations, 18
  male or female, 10–11
  puppy or adult, 8–9
  purebred benefits, 19–22, **21**
  size, 13–15
  space considerations, 17
  spayed or neutered, 10
  temperament, 11, **12–13**, 29
senior dogs
  activity and exercise needs,
    155, 161–162, **163**
  adoption of, 9
  aging signs, 154–155, **154**
  appetite, 158–159, **159**
  arthritis, 82, 231
  canine cognitive
    dysfunction, 162
  care of, **156**
  diet modifications, 159–160
  eyesight, 156–158, **157–158**
  feeding, 82–83, **82**, 84, 85, 87
  hearing, 158
  schedule adjustments,
    162–163
  tooth loss, 155–156
  veterinarian visits, 209–210
  weight loss or gain, 160–161,
    161
senses, canine, 179–180, **179**
separation anxiety, 204
shampoos, 39, 101
shelter adoptions, 25–26
shorthaired breed coats, 16–17
Sit command, 185, **185**, 189
Sit-Stay command, 186–187
size
  crates, 32, 33
  dog breeds, 13–15, **14**
Skinner, B. F., 182

sleeping arrangements, 58, 61
slicker brushes, 99, **99**
"small bite" food label, 83
small breed dogs, 14–15, 81, 82
"small breed" food label, 83
sniffing people inappropriately,
  181
socialization stage, 66–67, **66**
socializing
  to adults, 68–69, **68**
  being an ideal guest, 76, **76**
  to children, 69–70, **69**
  dog parks, 75
  to new baby, 71
  to new experiences, **70**,
    73–74, 77, **77**
  other dogs at home, 70–72
  other dogs in public, 73–76
  other pets at home, 72–73,
    72, **73**
  overview, 68
  variety of people, 76
space considerations, 17
spaying, 10
sport activities
  agility, 114–116, **115**
  dock diving, 120–121
  earthdog trials, 123–124, **124**
  flyball, **114**, 117–118, **118**
  herding, 119, **119**
  hunting, 121–123, **121–122**
  lure coursing, 120, **120**
  obedience trials, 116–117, **116**
  rally, 117
sporting group breeds, 20
stairs, **58**
stealing food, 200–201, **201**
suburban homes, 64–65, **65**
sunburn, 104
supplements, 93–94
supplies. *See* equipment,
  supplies, and accessories

T

tapeworms, 218–219
taste, sense of, 179
TDI (Therapy Dogs

International), 123
teeth brushing, 107–108, **107–108**
teeth cleaning, by veterinarians, 155
teething, 66
temperament, 11, **12–13**, 29
terrier breeds, 20
therapy certification, 123
Therapy Dogs International (TDI), 123
therapy-dog work, 124–125, **125**
thunder fears, 205, **205**
ticks, 214, **214**
titer test, 211
tooth loss, 155–156
toothpaste, 39, 108
touch, sense of, 179–180
toxic foods, 70, 92, 129–130, **129**
toxic products, 104
toy breed dogs
    AKC category, 20
    characteristic, 21
    commercial food formulas, 81
    heart rate, 210
    life expectancy, 82
    medical conditions, 15
toys, 39–41, **40**, 113
trainers, 191
training
    basic commands, 184–190

classes, ages and levels, 190–192
clicker, 183
consistency, maintaining, 193
positive methods, 168, **169**, 175, 182–184, **182**
punishment, 175, 186, 192
traits, breed selection and, 16
transitional stage, 65–66, **67**
travel crates, 31, 147–148, **148**, **150**, **153**
travel packs, 149
traveling
    airplane flights, 150–153, **150**, **153**
    brachycephalic breeds, 152
    crates, 31, 147–148, **148**, **150**, **153**
    international travel, 153
    motion sickness, 148–150
    pet-friendly hotels, 151
    road trips, 143–150, **146**, **148**
    seatbelts, 147–148
treats, 95, **95**
trimming, 101–103, **102–103**

U

USDA (US Department of Agriculture), 89

V

vaccinations, 210–211, **211**
veterinarians
    choosing, 44–45, **44**, **208**
    other pet encounters, 74, 76
    teeth cleaning procedure, 155
    vaccinations, 210–211, **211**
    wellness visits, 208–210, **209**
vision problems, 156–158
vital signs, 210
vitamin supplements, 93–94
vocalizations, canine, 176
vomiting, 223, **224**

W

Wait command, 188–189
Watch Me command, 184–185, **184**
water requirements, 96–97, **224**
weather dangers, 135–137, **136**
weight loss or gain, 160–161, **161**
wellness visits, 208–210, **209**
wet dog food, 85–88, 180–181
whining and whimpering, 176
whipworms, 219
words and voice tones, 177–179, **177–178**, 193
working group breeds, **20**
worms, 216–219

Photo Credits

All photos courtesy of Shutterstock: Cover: Anna Hoychuk; Back cover: Minerva Studio
Title page: Ermolaev Alexander; Author photo: Scot Gagne

135pixels, 100; 3DMI, 30; absolutimages, 196; Africa Studio, 28, 128, 188; Crystal Alba, 156; Ermolaev Alexander, 89, 181; alexei_tm, 65, 176; Scisetti Alfio, 137 (top); SJ Allen, 53; Aree, 177 (top); Armadillo Stock, 129; aspen rock, 207; atiger, 170 (bottom); Artsplav, 39; Be Good, 175; bergamont, 92; Best dog photo, 122; Bianca L, 55; Mikkel Bigandt, 124; Bildagentur Zoonar GmbH, 24; Blend Images, 70; Javier Brosch, 144; Joy Brown, 36, 60, 75, 128; Nina Buday, 21; Canon Boy, 198 (top); MCarper, 165; Jaromir Chalabala, 88, 177 (bottom); Helga Chirk, 149; Nicole Ciscato, 146, 163; clearviewstock, 119; WilleeCole Photography, 57, 103, 101, 167, 218, 222; connel, 63; Cameron Cross, 153; Linn Currie, 121; S Curtis, 42; Josep Curto, 135; cynoclub, 114, 116, 142, 161, 195; Dancestrokes, 223; Daz Stock, 13; dezi, 6, 130; Marie Dolphin, 157; everydoghasastory, 36, 136; evp82, 35; Yuliya Evstratenko, 47; Sergey Fatin, 85; Henri Faure, 120; flywish, 105; Fotokostic, 72 (all); Fotyma, 202; Frenzel, 200; Blaj Gabriel, 228; Gajus, 172; gvictoria, 93; Ryan Haines Photography, 154; Mark Herreid, 115 (all); Jennay Hitesman, 31, 127; holbox, 174; horiyan, 134; Hurst Photo, 46; InBetweentheBlinks, 12, 225; irin-k, 221; Andrea Izzotti, 178 (top); Eric Isselee, 5, 73 (bottom), 178 (bottom), 194; Rosa Jay, 67; Jodie Johnson, 90; Jorgegrafias, 26; Josfor, 102; Aneta Jungerova, 29; Agnes Kantaruk, 201; KarvardakovA, 27; **Anant Kasetsinsombut, 216**; a katz, 37; Kichigin, 12; Peter Kirillov, 168; Aleksey Klints, 51; Rita Kochmarjova, 215; Patryk Kosmider, 164; kostudio, 199 (bottom); Irina Kozorog, 205; Michael Kraus, 52; Yuri Kravchenko, 173 (top); piya kunkayan, 214; Erik Lam, 152; Lapina, 54; Sergey Lavrentev, 150; Aksana Lebedz, 180; l i g h t p o e t, 182; logoboom, 71; Lunja, 19, 111229; Kamil Macniak, 231; anucha maneechote, ; Joyce Marrero, 76; Dorottya Mathe, 191; Maximilian100, 199 (top); Mega Pixel, 149; mekcar, 203; melis, 208; Melory, 143; Melounix, 34, 118, 160; MetAnna, 58; Aleksandar Mijatovic, 179; Antic Milos, 17; Minerva Studio, 187; MitchR, 217; Alex Mladek, 82; MNStudio, 69; Moncayofoto, 158; Monkey Business Images, 125; Monkey Focus, 137 (bottom); Kateryna Mostova, 110; Christian Mueller, 74; AleksandarMilutinovic, 139; Napat, 229; nattul, 84; KellyNelson, 112, 213; Vladimir Nenezic, 134; OlgaOvcharenko, 20; otsphoto, 66, 186, 198 (bottom); Constantine Pankin, 38; pedphoto36pm, 99 (both); Michael Pettigrew, 56; Photobac, 11; Photographee.eu, 41; photoshooter2015, 95; panotthorn phuhual, 212; StepanPopov, 86; David Porras, 25 (top); Victoria Rak, 185; Ashley Randall, 81; Ksenia Raykova, 16; Carsten Reisinger, 29; Riverstarwoman, 77; Fesus Robert, 80; Rocketclips, Inc., 8; Rohappy, 78; Yuriy Rudyy, 40; SasPartout, 98; Sbolotova, 95; Susan Schmitz, 227; schubbel, 159; Annette Shaff, 7, 166; Shevs, 132; MaxShutter, 197; SpeedKingz, 140, 183, 193; John Steel, 170 (top); Stone46, 45; StudioPortoSabbia, 25 (top), 155; sunstep, 220; Syda Productions, 68, 217; talitha_it, 224; Barna Tanko, 108; Gladskikh Tatiana, 59; thka, 138; Tiger Images, 92; tr3gin, 145; Tinxi, 209; TwilightArtPictures, 131; Maria Uspenskaya, 184; Alakin Maksim Valerevich, 102 (inset); Jim Vallee, 107; Jne Valokuvaus, 14, 148; Svetlana Valoueva, 190; Dmytro Vietrov, 79; Viktor1, 109; Makarova Viktoria, 83; Hong Vo, 92; Volga, 50; vvita, 73; Cameron Watson, 64; wavebreakmedia, 219; Ivonne Wierink, 44, 206, 211; Monika Wisniewska, 91, 148; Mariia Zhos, 169

About the Author

Tammy Gagne is a freelance writer who specializes in the health and behavior of companion animals. A three-time Dog Writers Association of America (DWAA) writing competition nominee, she has authored more than 150 books for both adults and children. She resides in northern New England with her husband, her son, and a myriad of feathered and furry creatures, including three dogs.